PERENNIALS

How to Select, Grow & Enjoy

HPBooks

Harper garden

McGourty garden

About the Authors

Pamela Harper is a well-known horticultural writer, photographer and lecturer. Among the many magazines in which her articles have been published are *American Horticulturist, The Avant Gardener, Flower and Garden, Garden Design, Horticulture,* and *Pacific Horticulture.* She has been a contributor to several Brooklyn Botanic Garden handbooks and guest-edited the one entitled *Flowering Shrubs.* Additional publications in which her photographs have appeared include *Encyclopedia Britannica, Ortho, Reader's Digest, The Smithsonian, Sunset* and *Time Life.* She has taken over 80,000 photographs of plants and gardens and is owner of the Harper Horticultural Slide Library.

Pamela gardened in England for many years, and her book, *The Story of a Garden,* was published there in 1972. Since 1968, she and her husband have lived in Connecticut, Maryland, and now in Tidewater, Virginia. Here, her garden-in-the-making consists of two flat, sandy acres on a sheltered creek off Chesapeake Bay. Many perennials are grown for evaluation in nursery beds of the kind described on page 26.

Fred McGourty is a landscape designer, lecturer, nurseryman, consultant and writer. For 15 years, Fred served as editor of *Plants & Gardens,* the *Brooklyn Botanic Garden Handbook* series. He wrote many articles for the BBG Handbooks, as well as the "Letter from the Garden" which appeared in each one. He is author of the Nursery Source Manual and American Gardens—A Traveler's Guide. Fred's garden articles have appeared in the *New York Times,* the *Royal Horticultural Society Journal, Esquire* and *Yankee.*

Along with his wife Mary Ann, Fred is an active gardener, especially with perennials, container plants and vegetables. Hillside, their showcase perennial garden in Norfolk, in the hills of northwestern Connecticut, has been the subject of feature articles in *American Horticulturist, The New York Times, Horticulture* and *Better Homes and Gardens.*

Six years ago, the McGourtys started Hillside Gardens Nursery, which specializes in uncommon perennials. Plants are sold only at the nursery, but as a sideline, Fred has developed an active landscape design division, creating perennial borders for clients in several states. He is a popular lecturer and also teaches short courses on perennials at the New York Botanical Garden and several other institutions. Fred is currently president of the Connecticut Horticultural Society.

Acknowledgments

Many friends have contributed indirectly to this book by way of garden visits, gifts of plants, and the day-to-day exchanges of experience—often lively—that go on between avid gardeners. We thank them all.

The following have helped directly by checking sections in which they have expertise: Michael Dodge (delphiniums), Roy Klehm (peonies), Sandra Ladendorf (seed raising), Warren Pollock (hostas), Brewster Rogerson (clematis), George Waters (irises), Dick Weaver (epimediums). Ken Beckett and Margaret Joyner read the entire manuscript and made many helpful suggestions.

Regional information was provided by Carl Amason, Ed Carman, Phil Chandler, Roy Davidson, Bob Haehle, Harland Hand, Faith Mackaness, James MacNair, Marshall Olbrich, Roger Vick of the University of Alberta, and Sue Van Walleghem of the Manitoba Department of Agriculture.

We also thank the many friends who let us photograph plants in their gardens, and in particular the following owners of gardens pictured in this book: Mr. & Mrs. Alan Bloom, Mr. & Mrs. Garland, Mr. Harland Hand, Mr. Peter and the Hon. Mrs. Healing, Mrs. Julian W. Hill, Mrs. Calvin Hosmer, Jr., Mrs. Alain Huyghe, Mr. Christopher Lloyd, Mr. & Mrs. F. Mackaness, Mrs. J.G. McBratney, Mrs. James Metcalfe, Mr. R.G. Meyer, Major & Mrs. W.F. Richardson, Sir John Thouron, Mr. John Treasure, Mr. & Mrs. A. Van Vlack, Mr. & Mrs. Andre Viette.

Published by HPBooks
A division of Price Stern Sloan, Inc.
360 North La Cienega Boulevard
Los Angeles, California 90048
ISBN: 0-89586-281-6
Library of Congress Catalog Card Number: 85-60116
© 1985 HPBooks, Inc.
Printed in U.S.A.
9 8 7

Technical Consultants for HPBooks:
Frank Shipe and Ruth Kvaalen

Photography:
Pamela Harper

Illustrations:
Doug Burton

Cover: Perennial border in the garden of co-author Frederick McGourty. Plants include *Chrysanthemem parthenium*, *Artemisia* 'Silver Mound', *Astilbe* 'Fire', *Heliopsis* 'Gold Greenheart', *Cimicifuga racemosa*, *Phlox* 'Sir John Falstaff', *Platycodon grandiflorum*, *Coreopsis verticillata*, *Stachys*, *Filipendula rubra*, *Lilium regale*, yellow lilies, and *Monarda*. Photo by Pam Harper.

Contents

Pleasures of Perennials

Apart from trees and shrubs, plants can be divided into three basic kinds—*annuals, biennials* and *perennials.* An annual grows from seed to flowering size and dies within 1 year. Annuals are invaluable for keeping borders colorful throughout the summer months, especially as edgings and for plugging gaps left by early-flowering bulbs. Biennials—foxgloves and hollyhocks, for example—usually take 2 years to complete their life cycle. Read more about annuals and biennials in HPBooks' *Annuals, How to Select, Grow & Enjoy,* by Derek Fell.

Most perennials, if not killed by disease, cold or unsatisfactory growing conditions, will live for many years. Some, called *short-lived perennials,* may last only 3 or 4 years, but their lives can often be extended by dividing them each year.

Other perennials, with—and sometimes without—division, may outlive the gardener who planted them.

Unlike trees and shrubs, which are also perennial plants, most perennials are *herbaceous.* Horticulturally, the term "herbaceous" refers to plants with fleshy, soft, non-woody stems. They differ from trees and shrubs in that the top growth of herbaceous perennials dies back in winter, but the root system remains alive and sends up new growth in spring. However, not all perennials always show this characteristic. Many perennials remain evergreen in some parts of the country. For instance, in Zone 4 of the climate map on page 42, the top growth of most perennials is dead by November, but in Zone 8 many of these still have their leaves in late December. In frost-free regions, some perennials not only keep their leaves, but flower all winter.

HARDINESS
The ability of a perennial to withstand cold is referred to as its *hardiness.* The terms *hardy perennial* and *tender perennial* were originally coined in England to identify plants that could or could not survive an English winter, which is approximately equivalent to that of the American Pacific Northwest. Most perennials survive much colder winters.

Hardy perennials are those that can survive low winter temperatures. Whether or not a hardy perennial can withstand high summer temperatures, drought or poor soil depends on the species. Not all hardy perennials are heat-tolerant.

Tender perennials are plants that cannot survive low temperatures. In colder climates, they are usually grown as annuals or houseplants, but these may be among the best perennials for warmer regions. Mealycup sage *(Salvia farinacea)* is one example.

The climate map on page 42 shows the various *hardiness zones* in the United States and most of Canada. The zone numbers indicate the average annual minimum temperature for each zone. Each of the plant entries in the encyclopedia section, starting on page 40, lists the *coldest zone* in which that plant usually survives.

THE ENGLISH INFLUENCE
Perennials have always been grown wherever there have been gardens, but it is with Britain that they are most closely associated. Perennial borders had their heyday there during the late 19th century and early 20th century, an age of large estate gardens main-

---

Above: Mixed chrysanthemums

tained by abundant cheap labor. Two famous English names of that era are William Robinson (1838-1935) and Gertrude Jekyll (1843-1932).

William Robinson abhorred the bedding out of plants in elaborate designs and campaigned for a more natural style of gardening. In his best known book, *The English Flower Garden,* he wrote that "true art is based on clear-eyed study of and love for nature." He developed beautiful gardens at his home, Gravetye Manor, East Grinstead, Sussex—now a luxury hotel. The gardens have been restored and may be visited.

Gertrude Jekyll was a talented artist and writer. All who saw the perennial borders at her home, Munstead Wood, agree that they were of an artistry never excelled before or since. Her book, *Color Schemes for the Flower Garden,* remains a classic.

Two influential Englishmen of our own time are Graham Thomas and Alan Bloom. Both have written many garden books. Gertrude Jekyll's gardens no longer exist, but plantsman and artist Graham Thomas knew and was influenced by her. In his role as Gardens Consultant to Britain's National Trust, he designed several borders of perennials grouped and graded to color in the Jekyll style. Two examples are those at Cliveden, Buckinghamshire and Powis Castle in Wales. Both can be visited. Opening times for these and other British gardens can be found in the annual publication, *Historic Houses, Castles & Gardens,* available from GHS Inc., Box 1224, Allwood, Clifton, NJ 07012.

After World War II, few people could afford to maintain extensive perennial borders, so perennials fell from favor. Their renewed popularity is due in large part to Alan Bloom, founder of Bressingham Gardens, Diss, Norfolk. They are England's largest commercial growers of perennials and a source of new plants for many American nurseries. Alan Bloom advocates the growing of perennials in island beds instead of in traditional borders. The extensive display gardens at Bressingham may be visited on certain open days—usually two afternoons each week from early May to late September.

In Alan Bloom's breeding programs, emphasis has been placed on compact, trouble-free plants suitable for today's smaller, owner-maintained gardens. A steady stream of good,

new plants from Bressingham crosses the Atlantic—two of the latest arrivals are the border phloxes *Phlox maculata* 'Alpha' and 'Omega', shown on page 133.

Many gardening books come from Britain, though this is not always apparent from the title. When reading them, bear in mind the different growing conditions. The English climate falls roughly into hardiness zone 8. Summers are short, not usually very sunny, and the temperature rarely reaches 80F (26C). Winter freezes are seldom prolonged, with 40F (5C) the average temperature December to February. Rainfall is probably less than you would expect. Average annual rainfall in London is 23 inches. Compare this to that of the following major U.S. cities: Los Angeles, 15 inches; San Francisco, 22 inches; Chicago, 33 inches; New York, 43 inches, and Miami, 59 inches. But in England, rain is distributed fairly evenly over the year and falls gently, so none is lost to runoff. And plants need less water under cloudy skies.

There is a wealth of British experience to draw on, but there is much we must do for ourselves. The United States leads the world in the hybridizing of bearded irises, daylilies and hostas, but much remains to be done, especially in bringing into cultivation neglected native plants, and in select-

ing finer forms of those already in cultivation. Butterfly weed is a good example. It is one of the best garden plants in those regions where it grows wild—New England to North Dakota, south to Florida, Arizona and New Mexico, but it is difficult to grow in Britain. Therefore it is *we* who must bring into cultivation the beautiful yellow and scarlet forms that are to be seen in the wild, but not yet commercially available.

OTHER PERENNIAL-TYPE PLANTS

The following groups of plants are generally perennial in habit, but are usually not called perennials.

Cacti and Succulents—These are perennials of a specialized kind. Most of them are evergreen and not very hardy, but they are important landscape plants in hot, dry climates, where they are often used in lieu of traditional perennials. They are also used to beautify gardens in many warm-winter regions. A detailed discussion of cacti and succulents is beyond the scope of this book, but two kinds, *Aloe* and *Opuntia,* are included on pages 48 and 127. For more on cacti and succulents, see HP-Books' *Plants for Dry Climates,* by Mary Rose Duffield and Warren D. Jones.

Mixed garden includes small trees, shrubs, vines, perennials, annuals and bulbs. Perennials in bloom are purple coneflower *(Echinacea purpurea)* and yellow rudbeckias.

Half-Hardy Foliage Perennials—In frost-free regions, many foliage plants usually considered houseplants become important perennials. These include coleus, asparagus fern (*Asparagus setaceus*), spider plant (*Chlorophytum*) and umbrella plant (*Cyperus alternifolius*). Aspidistra is marginally hardy in Zone 8, and Nippon lily (*Rohdea japonica*) in Zone 7. There are handsome variegated forms of these two plants. The New Zealand flaxes (*Phormium*) and the great gray-leaved cardoon (*Cynara cardunculus*) are hardy enough for some but not all Zone 8 gardens.

Ferns and Grasses—There are hundreds of perennial ferns and grasses that mix well with flowering perennials. Which are best for your garden depends on where you live, but the list below includes a few of the more outstanding ones. Most ferns need some shade. Most grasses need sun. Many ferns and a few grasses and sedges are evergreen.

Bulbs—These are perennials, but because of their distinctive structure they are usually treated separately. *Corms*, *tubers* and *rhizomes* are commonly included in this category, along with true bulbs. A list of summer-flowering kinds suitable for perennial borders appears on page 7. Descriptions of these are included in HP-Books' *Bulbs, How to Select, Grow and Enjoy*, by George Harmon Scott.

Spring-flowering bulbs are best kept out of perennial borders. They are likely to be disturbed when perennials are divided, and the leaves of many—especially daffodils—will be tawdry and semi-decayed when the border is otherwise at its best.

In cold-winter regions, tulips might be the exception, for they bring such welcome early color. Fosteriana tulips such as 'Red Emperor', 'Orange Emperor', 'Yellow Empress', and white 'Purissima' are among the most enduring. Try interspersing them with *Coreopsis verticillata*, which makes a ferny mat when the tulips are in bloom, then grows taller and hides the dying tulip leaves.

Shrubs—Some semishrubby plants can be treated as perennials and cut almost to the ground in spring, whether or not frost has killed the woody branches. These include butterfly bush (*Buddleia davidii*), bluebeard or blue-mist (*Caryopteris*), some plumbagos (*Ceratostigma*), honeybush (*Melianthus major*), Russian sage (*Perovskia*), fuchsias, cape fuchsia (*Phygelius capensis*), and California fuchsia (*Zauschneria*).

Many other shrubs mix well with perennials. If kept cut back to about 3 feet, the red-twig dogwood (*Cornus alba* 'Elegantissima') remains in proportion to other plants in the typical bed or border. The white-rimmed leaves have a cooling effect on brighter colors and the red stems have winter beauty, especially above a carpet of snow.

Other hardy shrubs that mix well

RECOMMENDED GRASSES

Over 200 kinds of ornamental grasses are commercially available. Of those we have grown, these are the most attractive. An asterisk (*) indicates our top choices. Hardy to at least Zone 5 except where indicated. Deciduous, best in sun except where indicated.

An excellent guide to the most popular of the grasses is *Ornamental Grasses for the Home and Garden* by Mary Hockenberry Meyer and Robert G. Mower, an inexpensive 16-page booklet. Write for bulletin No. 64 from the New York State College of Agriculture and Life Sciences, Cornell University, Ithaca, New York.

Arrhenatherum elatius bulbosum 'Variegatum' (Bulbous Oat Grass) 18 to 24 inches, light shade in hot regions.
Briza media (Perennial Quaking Grass) 1 to 2 feet.
Calamagrostis 'Karl Foerster' (Feather-Reed Grass) 4 to 6 feet.
*Carex morrowii 'Variegata' (Silver Variegated Japanese Sedge) 1 foot, evergreen, leaves green, narrowly edged with white. Sometimes sold as *C. conica* 'Variegata'. Light shade best.

Carex morrowii 'Aurea-variegata' or 'Old Gold' has creamy yellow leaves edged green—attractive but less hardy. Light shade.
Deschampsia caespitosa (Tufted Hair Grass) 2 to 3 feet.
Festuca (Blue Fescue) Many kinds under the names *F. caesia, F. cinerea, F. glauca, F. ovina*. Good edging plants. Need frequent division.
*Hakonechloa macra 'Aureola' 1 foot, light shade. Sold as H. albo-aurea variegata.
Helictotrichon sempervirens (Avena sempervirens) (Blue Oat Grass) 2 to 3 feet.
*Imperata cylindrica rubra (Japanese Blood Grass) 1 to 2 feet.
*Miscanthus sinensis (Eulalia Grass) 6 to 8 feet. The forms 'Gracillimus' (3 to 4 feet), 'Variegatus' and 'Zebrinus' are particularly recommended.
*Molinia caerulea 'Variegata' (Purple Moor Grass) 2 to 3 feet.
Pennisetum alopecuroides (Fountain Grass) 4 feet. *P. setaceum* is prettier but an annual in most zones, invasive in frost free ones.
Phalaris arundinacea 'Picta' (Ribbon Grass) 2 to 4 feet, attractive, useful but invasive.

RECOMMENDED FERNS

These are cold-hardy except where indicated. Some normally evergreen kinds may be deciduous at the limit of their hardiness. All do best in light shade.

Adiantum pedatum (Maidenhair Fern) 18 to 24 inches, deciduous.
Asplenium scolopendrium (Phyllitis scolopendrium) (Hart's-tongue Fern) 12 to 18 inches, evergreen.
Athyrium filix-femina (Lady Fern) 2 to 4 feet, sometimes more, deciduous.
Athyrium goeringianum 'Pictum' (Japanese painted Fern) 1 foot, deciduous.
Cyrtomium falcatum (Japanese Holly Fern) Zone 8, 2 feet, evergreen.
Dryopteris erythrosora (Japanese Shield Fern) 2 feet, evergreen.
Dryopteris ludoviciana (Florida Shield Fern) Zone 7, 2 feet, evergreen.
Matteucia struthiopteris (Ostrich Fern) 3 to 5 feet or more, deciduous, needs moist soil.
Osmunda cinnamomea (Cinnamon Fern) 3 to 4 feet, deciduous.
Osmunda claytoniana (Interrupted Fern) 3 to 4 feet, deciduous.
Osmunda regalis (Royal Fern) 4 feet or more, deciduous.
Polystichum acrostichoides (Christmas Fern) 2 to 3 feet, evergreen.
Polystichum munitum (Sword Fern) 2 to 3 feet, evergreen. The sword fern common in California gardens is the tender, *Nephrolepis cordifolia*.
Polystichum setiferum (Soft Shield Fern) Zone 8, 2 feet, evergreen.

with perennials include the evergreen or semievergreen abelias such as 'Sherwoodii' and 'Edward Goucher'. These are deciduous at their hardiness limit. Crimson pygmy barberry (*Berberis thunbergii* 'Atropurpurea Nana'), lavender, and the shrubby potentillas (*Potentilla fruticosa*) are other choices. So are *Hypericum frondosum* with its neat, blue-green evergreen leaves and small, bright yellow powderpuffs in summer, and the pink-flowered spireas of the *Spiraea japonica* and *S. × bumalda* groups, such as 'Anthony Waterer'.

Herbs—Some ornamental perennials have medicinal or culinary uses and are classified as herbs. A list of perennial herbs appears below. Detailed information on these and other herbs can be found in HPBooks' *Herbs, How to Select, Grow and Enjoy,* by Norma Jean Lathrop.

Ground Covers—A ground-cover plant is one of dense, low habit and vigorous growth. The perennial ones in the list below were selected because they're readily available, easy to grow and are able to hold their own in the front ranks of the perennial border without being unduly invasive or sprawling. These criteria eliminated the beloved lily-of-the-valley (*Convallaria*) which, where the soil and climate suit it, spreads so quickly that it should not be mixed with other perennials. The perennial ground covers in the list are described in HPBooks' *Lawns and Ground Covers, How to Select, Grow and Enjoy,* by Michael MacCaskey.

PLEASURES OF PERENNIALS

Perennials will please the impatient. Starting from scratch, you can create a pretty border within 2 years. Perennials can be planted close enough for quick effect because, unlike shrubs, most are easily moved if they start to crowd each other.

No group of plants is more versatile. There are numerous perennials for sunny sites, whether moist or dry, quite a few for boggy sites and many for moist, shady sites. No perennial *prefers* a dry, shady site, but a few will tolerate it.

Fragrance—Most flowers smell faintly sweet in quantity, or if held close to the nose. Few perennials are markedly fragrant, but the scent of lily-of-the-valley (*Convallaria*), ginger lilies (*Hedychium*), most dianthus, and many lilies—especially *L. regale, L. speciosum* and *L. auratum*—is sweetly pervasive.

Peonies, some border phlox and a few daylilies—especially lemon lily (*Hemerocallis lilioasphodelus*) and 'Hyperion'—have a pronounced though more subtle scent. So do primroses and such hostas as *Hosta*

BULBS AND BULB-TYPE PLANTS

This list includes true bulbs, corms, tubers and rhizomes. They are ones suitable for mixing with perennials.

Allium (some)
Agapanthus
Alstroemeria (can be mixed, but best in a bed of its own.)
Anthericum
Bletilla (extremely desirable where hardy.)
Canna
Chasmanthe
Clivia
Convallaria (invasive where it does well, best in a place of its own.)
Crinum
Crocosmia (excellent—'Lucifer' is one of the best named kinds.)
Dahlia
Eremurus (plant where roots will not be disturbed.)
Galtonia
Gladiolus byzantinus
Lilium
Lycoris
Nerine
Ornithogalum (but not *O. umbellatum,* which is invasive.)
Schizostylis coccinea (for Zone 8 south.)
Trillium (for woodland gardens.)
Tulbaghia
Tulipa sprengeri
Watsonia
Zantedeschia
Zephyranthes

HERBS

The following herbs are also ornamental perennials.

Achillea (Yarrow)
Acorus calamus (Sweet Flag) There is a variegated form.
Agastache (Anise-hyssop) Invasive, by seed.
Allium schoenoprasum (Chives)
Artemisia Some are invasive.
Chrysanthemum balsamita (Costmary)
Foeniculum vulgare (Fennel) Especially the bronze-leaved form.
Hyssopus officinalis (Hyssop)
Iris germanica florentina (Orris root)
Lavandula (Lavender)
Levisticum officinale (Lovage)
Melissa officinalis (Lemon-balm) Invasive.
Mentha (Mint) Invasive
Myrrhis odorata (Sweet Cicely) Excellent perennial.
Origanum (Oregano)
Pelargonium (Scented Geraniums)
Ruta (Rue) Desirable for its gray foliage.
Salvia (Sage) Purple and variegated forms of *S. officinalis.*
Satureja (Savory)
Symphytum officinale (Comfrey)
Tanacetum (Tansy) *T. vulgare crispum* has exceptionally pretty foliage. Slightly invasive, but controllable.
Teucrium (Germander)
Tulbaghia (Society Garlic)
Valeriana officinalis (Valerian) Excellent perennial.
Verbascum (Mullein)
Viola odorata (Sweet Violet). Desirable where hardy.

PERENNIALS FOR GROUND COVER

Many low, dense perennials can be used for ground cover. Some of the ones listed here are described in the plant encyclopedia.

Ajuga
Arabis
Arctotheca
Artemisia
Asarum
Aubrieta
Carprobrotus
Cerastium tomentosum
Coronilla varia
Gazania
Geranium species—several
Helianthemum
Iberis
Lamiastrum
Lamium
Lampranthus
Lantana
Lysimachia nummularia
Nepeta
Oenothera—several
Ophiopogon
Osteospermum
Pachysandra
Polygonum—several
Potentilla—several
Santolina
Sedum—many
Teucrium
Vancouveria
Verbena—some
Viola
Waldsteinia

Sedum 'Autumn Joy' is one of the best perennials for attracting bees and butterflies.

plantaginea, 'Royal Standard', and 'Honeybells'. A few perennials have an effluvia of flower or foliage that verges on the offensive.

Attracting Butterflies, Bees and Hummingbirds—Butterflies are so enchanting that most of us are willing to pay a toll for their presence in the garden by way of a few chewed leaves during the caterpillar stage. Butterfly weed *(Asclepias tuberosa)* and such sedums as *S. spectabile* and *S.* 'Autumn Joy' are supreme among perennials for attracting hoards of butterflies and bees.

Also popular with bees and butterflies are ornamental onions *(Allium),* yellow knapweed *(Centaurea macrocephala),* globe thistle *(Echinops),* mist flower *(Eupatorium coelestinum),* and, mostly with bees, bee balm *(Monarda).* Purple coneflower *(Echinacea)* attracts butterflies—and also the destructive Japanese beetle. Hummingbirds are drawn to flowers of tubular shape, especially red or scarlet ones.

Diversity—Perennials may be tall and stately, low and spreading, and just about every shape and size between. Individual flowers may be as large as dinner plates or, at the other extreme, so tiny that a magnifying lens is needed to examine them in detail. Shapes include cups, saucers, bells, bugles, trumpets, stars, daisies, crosses, hearts and many that defy description.

Flowers may face the sky or hang their heads modestly down. Some are single, some double and some in between. They may be borne one to a stalk or grouped in inflorescences (flower clusters) that differ as widely as the tall spikes of delphiniums and red-hot-pokers, the platelike heads of yarrow, the feathery plumes of astilbes, the globular clusters of globe thistle, or the white clouds of gypsophila. Colors span the rainbow and echo every mood—bright and gay, cool and calm, or occasionally somber.

Leaves—These are often beautiful in their own right, and infinitely varied—from the bold swordlike leaves of yuccas to the lacy ones of astilbes. The large leathery rounds of bergenia differ greatly from the slivers of liatris. Compare the quilted blue-gray leaves of *Hosta sieboldiana* to the curly variegated ones of *Hosta undulata,* or the silvery velvet ears of *Stachys byzantina* to the filigree of *Artemisia splendens.* Different shapes, colors and textures can be juxtaposed to create contrast in the border.

Flowering Season—Perennials can be chosen so the bed or border will have flowers for 7 months of the year, and in the mildest zones, the year around. By choosing plants that flower for several weeks, and at about the same time, you can achieve massed color for about 2 months. Or you can have scattered flowering throughout the growing season.

Flower Arranging—When you have your own flowers for cutting, you can create the massed arrangements that might be too expensive if you had to buy the flowers. Also, freshly picked flowers last longest.

Hybridizing—Many of our garden plants are man-made hybrids. Hybridizing has brought great pleasure to many generations of gardeners. Other hybrids occurred in the wild and were noticed among native stands as different in some respect—larger or more numerous flowers, double flowers, taller or shorter stems, or different colored leaves or flowers. Many more await discovery or introduction—the scarlet and yellow forms of butterfly weed *(Asclepias tuberosa)* are just two examples. Some of this work will be done by nurserymen and experiment stations, but much of it will be done, as it always has been, by gardeners like ourselves. For many, much of the challenge and satisfaction of gardening lies in hybridizing. We may have put men on the moon, but North American horticulture is still in its infancy—we can all be explorers.

Other Pleasures—For many gardeners, one of the biggest pleasures of perennials is in growing and caring for them. Wandering along a border on a sunny, summer day, dead-heading flowers, with pauses to look closely at a flower or watch a butterfly, is more a pleasure than a chore. Weeding occupies the hands while leaving the mind free. Not that the perennial garden is a lazy gardener's Eden. Blisters and backache are sometimes inseparable from the bliss. But for the most part, the required work is part of the pleasure.

Not least among the gardener's pleasures is that of sharing. Not that this is unique to gardeners, but they do have an advantage—a diamond ring cannot be divided to share with friends, nor can a chair be propagated to help furnish your neighbor's home. With perennials you can give away your cake and have it too when you divide a plant to share with a friend.

FOLIAGE PERENNIALS

Many perennials are grown for their beautiful foliage. The ones shown here are but a few of many. Hostas are perhaps the most popular and diversified of all the foliage perennials.

Salvia argentea

Marsh irises: *Iris pseudacorus* 'Variegata' (yellow stripes) and *Iris laevigata* 'Variegata'.

Hosta sieboldiana 'Elegans'

Hosta fortunei 'Albopicta' (background) and a variegated form of *Euonymus fortunei*.

BOTANICAL NAMES

When you buy a plant, should you ask for it by its common (popular) name or its botanical (scientific) name? You may have no choice because many perennials don't have common names. Just as often, the botanical name is also the common name, such as iris or chrysanthemum. Occasionally, the botanical name of a plant, *Hosta,* for instance, is more widely known than it's common name (Plantain Lily).

Only by means of botanical names can you find what you want in catalogs, understand most gardening books and lectures, and identify precisely which plant you're talking about. Poppy is a well-known common name, but *which* poppy are you describing? There are many. For instance, true poppies belong to the genus *Papaver.* Perhaps the poppy you're describing is not a true poppy at all, but a blue poppy or Welsh poppy (*Meconopsis*), a wood poppy (*Stylophorum*), a sea poppy (*Glaucium*), or a Matilija poppy (*Romneya*). As indicated by the botanical names in parentheses, each of these plants belongs to a different genus. Plants within each genus also have a species name. An oriental poppy is *Papaver orientale,* for instance.

Common names differ from one part of the country to another, and still more from one country to another. By contrast, the botanical name of a plant is unequivocally its own, shared by no other plant. The names of plants are more individual than those of people. There are many Jane Smiths but only one *Primula vulgaris.* Many plants bear the name *Primula,* and many the name *vulgaris,* but the two names in combination occur only once.

Don't let pronunciation be a stumbling block. Nobody is going to laugh if you get it wrong—we all do from time to time. Attempts to standardize pronunciation have been only partially successful and you'll hear names pronounced in different ways. What matters most is knowing which plant is meant.

How Botanical Names Are Used—In the encyclopedia beginning on page 40, major plant entries are listed by the botanical name of the genus. The family name and common name or names, are listed directly below the genus heading. For example on page 87, under the heading *Eryngium* (genus) appears the common name (Sea Holly) and the name of the family (Umbelliferae) to which Eryngiums, among other plants, belong. Under each main heading, selected species, hybrids, varieties and cultivars are discussed. These terms are described below.

Family—A family is a group of plants having certain common characteristics that may not be apparent, or of interest to most of us. Some families do have common characteristics of practical interest. For instance, many members of the borage family (Boraginaceae)—forget-me-nots, for one—have bright blue flowers. Plants of the daisy family (Compositae) are among the most likely to reseed themselves, and most of them need sun. Members of the pea family (Leguminosae) have nitrogen-fixing nodules on their roots which enable them to grow in poor soil.

Genus (plural, genera)—A family contains from one to many groups of related plants called *genera.* The genera *Anthemis, Aster, Chrysanthemum* and *Rudbeckia* belong, with many others, to the family *Compositae.* They differ from each other but they all have daisy-type flowers. The name of the genus appears in italics and begins with a capital letter. An exception to this is when the genus name is being used as the popular name, for example when discussing chrysanthemums or hostas.

Species—The term *species* is used for both the singular and plural form. Never use the term *specie.* Species (specific) names are written in italics but begin with a small letter, and are always used in conjunction with the genus name.

Occasionally, a genus may contain only one species—this is known as a *monotypic genus.* Most genera contain several, sometimes many, related species. The relationship is usually apparent. For example, the genus *Iris* contains species that differ in many ways, but most of them are readily recognized as irises.

Species are nature's plants, unimproved by man. Gardeners can sow seed of a species with reasonable assurance that the seedlings will look like their parent.

Generic names usually serve only to identify a plant, but many specific names tell us what a plant looks like or where it grows. For example, *alba* tells us that some part of the plant—usually the flower—is white, *rubra* that it is red, *azurea* that it is blue. *Alpinus* means that a plant grows in the mountains—it will probably be small compared to others of its kind. *Aquaticus* means that it grows in or near water, *maritima* by the sea, *pratensis* in meadows, *sylvatica* in woods. *Stolonifera* means that the plant spreads by stolons—it might be invasive. Plants called *mexicana* (from Mexico) probably aren't cold hardy; those called *sibirica* (from Siberia) are among the hardiest. Sometimes the meaning is obvious; sometimes it's no use guessing. If you want to know the meaning of the plant names, get *A Gardener's Dictionary of Plant Names* by A. W. Smith and William T. Stearn.

Variety—A plant can have only one specific (species) name. When it appears to have two, both written in italics with a small initial letter and without quotation marks, the second name is a *variety.* This is a term that confuses nearly everyone. We tend to talk about varieties of plants as we might talk about varieties of cheese, meaning merely that there are a lot of different kinds. A botanical variety, while similar to the species to which it belongs, differs in some constant way. *Amsonia tabernaemontana salicifolia* is similar to *Amsonia tabernaemontana* but has narrower leaves. Sometimes you will see it written *Amsonia tabernaemontana var. salicifolia,* but the "var." (short for variety) has been omitted in this book. Like species, a variety comes true from seed.

Cultivar—This stands for *cultivated variety.* Cultivar names are the fanciful ones that appear in single quotes and have an initial capital letter: 'Moonbeam' is a cultivar of *Coreopsis verticillata.* Many of our garden plants are cultivars. How do they come about?

Suppose you are walking through a field of buttercups when you spot one that is different from the others. Perhaps it is twice as tall, or half as tall, or perhaps the flowers are double, or a different color. You have a potential cultivar. Nature constantly throws up such variations, but unless they come true from seed, they soon die out. If you find such a plant in the wild, and think it has possibilities, it is up to you to take it home and divide it, or grow more plants from cuttings.

Most cultivars are not found in the

Above: Purple coneflower (*Echinacea purpurea*). Right: 'White Lustre' is a white-flowered cultivar of *Echinacea purpurea*. In background are *Echinacea purpurea* and gloriosa daisy.

NAMES THAT IDENTIFY PURPLE CONEFLOWER

Compositae: Family
Echinacea: Genus. One of many genera in the family *Compositae.*
Echinacea purpurea (Rudbeckia purpurea): One of the few species in the small genus *Echinacea*, formerly called *Rudbeckia*. The flowers are pink.
Purple coneflower: Common or popular name for *Echinacea purpurea.*
Echinacea purpurea 'White Lustre': A white-flowered cultivar.

wild but are hybrids created by crossing two or more species or existing cultivars. They do not usually come true from seed and some are sterile.

Hybrids—When an "×" appears before a species name, it means that the plant is a hybrid, or a group of hybrids, between two or more species—*Digitalis* × *mertonensis*, *Anemone* × *hybrida* and *Chrysanthemum* × *superbum*—for example. Such crosses between species, called *interspecific crosses,* are common.

When an "×" appears before the genus name—× *Solidaster,* for example—it means that the plant is a hybrid between two genera, in this case between an aster and a goldenrod. Hybrids between two genera are fairly rare.

Although the naming of plants is a science, it is not an exact one. Occasionally, a plant is deemed to have been put in the wrong genus and is moved to another. Not infrequently, it is then decided that it was in the right place after all and it is moved back where it began. Sometimes it doesn't quite fit anywhere and a new genus is created for it.

Species names change even more often. The correct specific name for a plant is the first one published, so although we may have known a plant for years by one name, when a researcher finds one published earlier, it has to be changed. Some-times another researcher then finds an earlier published name—or an even earlier publication of the original name—and it has to be changed yet again. Understandably, nurseries can't keep up with all of this, and some plants may be found in catalogs under two or three different names.

In the plant encyclopedia, we have usually used the name believed to be currently correct, with other names shown in parentheses. Occasionally, when a name change is very recent and little known, the more familiar name is listed first, with the newer name in parentheses. The main intent is to give the name that the plant is most commonly sold under by a majority of nurseries.

Ways of Using Perennials

In Northern climates, the terms *perennial* and *herbaceous border* go together as naturally as salt and pepper. Where summers are cool and winters long and cold, borders or island beds are often the most colorful and practical ways of growing perennials. Perennials bring peak color to Northern gardens just when the weather is at its most enjoyable—July and August. The gardening season lasts only half the year, after which the perennials go to rest—often tucked neatly under a blanket of snow. The gardener, also ready now for a rest, turns to other things.

In climates with mild winters, the gardening pace is more leisurely but longer sustained. Gardening often goes on all year long. If there is a color peak, it is more likely to be in spring,

and from shrubs, not perennials. In these regions, gardeners can grow camellias, azaleas, oleanders and the many other flowering evergreen shrubs. They may not wish to devote much space to perennial borders that would be bare or shabby for half the year, with no snow to conceal them.

This does not mean that there is no place for perennials in the warmer climates, but evergreen kinds become more important. In hot-summer regions, these include drought-tolerant cacti and succulents, and such architectural plants as New Zealand flax *(Phormium),* kangaroo-paws *(Anigozanthos)* and yuccas. These might be interspersed with small evergreen—or evergray—flowering shrubs, such as *Euryops* and *Gamolepis* with their similar yellow-daisy flowers, lavender, santolina, Jerusalem sage *(Phlomis fruticosa),* rock roses *(Cistus),* sun roses *(Helianthemum)* and rosemary.

ALTERNATIVES TO BEDS AND BORDERS

Although the main emphasis in this book is on perennials for beds and borders, this is not the only way of growing them, nor always the best way. This is especially true in milder climates.

Depending on climate, soil conditions and other natural features of your property, perennials can be used in a number of ways. A few of them are discussed here.

WOODLAND GARDENS

If you live on a wooded site, it would be a pity to destroy the trees to make way for a lawn and flower beds. With less effort and expense, perennials—including those called wildflowers—can be used with bulbs and ferns to create a woodland garden in character with the site.

Start by clearing out the underbrush and removing trees made spindly by crowding. It is usually an improvement to remove some of the lower

Above: Hedge-backed herbaceous border is traditional way of growing perennials. This one is in Pennsylvania. Hedge is hemlock. Since this photo was taken, the lawn has been replaced by paving so that plants can sprawl over border edge without being cut off by mower.

PERENNIALS FOR THE WOODLAND GARDEN

These need moisture and sun in spring but tolerate drier soil and shade in summer. Those best able to survive in dry shade are marked with an asterisk (*).

Adonis amurensis (summer dormant)
Anemone virginiana
Aquilegia canadensis
Aruncus dioicus
**Aster* (woodland species such as *A. cordifolius.*)
**Brunnera macrophylla*
**Chelidonium majus* (invasive)
Chrysogonum virginianum
Dentaria diphylla (summer dormant)
Dicentra eximia
Dicentra formosa
Disporum
**Epimedium*
**Eupatorium rugosum*
Galax urceolata (needs moist soil.)
Geranium maculatum
**Geranium endressii* (tolerates dry soil in cool regions.)
Gillenia trifoliata
Helleborus orientalis
Hepatica
Heuchera americana
**Hosta*
Liriope
Meconopsis cambrica
Mertensia virginica (soil must be moist in spring. Summer dormant.)
**Omphalodes cappadocica*
**Omphalodes verna*
Phlox divaricata
Phlox stolonifera
**Podophyllum peltatum*
Polemonium
**Polygonatum*
Primula vulgaris (needs moist soil in hot regions.)
Pulmonaria
Sanguinaria canadensis
Smilacina
Stylophorum diphyllum
**Symphytum grandiflorum*
Tiarella cordifolia
Trillium
Uvularia grandiflora
Vancouveria
Viola (many)

A woodland garden in Tennessee. Perennials include *Phlox divaricata*, celandine poppy (*Stylophorum diphyllum*), primroses and trilliums.

Feverfew (*Chrysanthemum parthenium*) blends well with shrubs, here with Japanese holly and pink hydrangea.

branches of remaining trees to let in more light. You'll need to provide a 6-inch-deep layer of surface duff (decayed plant material), if this does not already exist. In most wooded lots, the existing duff layer isn't this deep—falling leaves help, but supplementary mulching is usually needed. The duff will need to be replenished as tree roots make their way into the surface layer.

The woodland garden is not labor-free, but caring for it takes no more time than mowing a large lawn. Mulch paths look natural in such a setting. If a spade's depth of soil is dug out and a thick layer of newspapers laid down, topped with a mulch of shredded bark, weeds will neither root down from above the mulch nor spring up from below it. The dug-out soil, mixed with decayed organic matter such as peat moss, leaf mold, compost or sawdust, can be used to make beds alongside the path.

In the woodland garden, most of the bloom will come in spring, before the trees are in full leaf, after which emphasis will be on such foliage perennials as ferns and hostas. A list of plants suitable for woodland gardens appears above.

Yellow alyssum *(Aurinia saxatilis)*, candytuft *(Iberis sempervirens)* and moss pink *(Phlox subulata)* are showy, easy-to-grow perennials for a sunny rock garden or the front of a border.

SHRUB GARDENS

A shrub garden differs from a woodland or wildflower garden in having few, if any, forest-size trees; and therefore more light and sun and less root competition. A typical shrub garden will include small ornamental trees, especially those with attractive foliage or bark such as paperbark maple *(Acer griseum)* and probably a conifer or two, usually of columnar form, often with gray, blue or gold foliage.

The many shrubs will include both deciduous and evergreen kinds, and vines such as clematis may be allowed to ramble among some of them. Usually, the aim of a shrub garden is year-round interest, not short-season perfection. For this reason, bulbs are often included. The withering foliage of bulbs past their blooming stage is far less conspicuous in such a garden. Many perennials are also included, mostly of moderate height. These include such handsome foliage plants as hellebores and hostas, and those that carpet the ground, such as *Geranium endressii.* Flowers of simple form are esthetically more in keeping with such a setting. Plants with such flowers are usually the species—nature's plant—not the more exotic hybrids bred by man. Soft colors will predominate because most brilliantly colored perennials need full sun.

Peak color in the typical shrub garden will be in spring, when the majority of shrubs bloom. A simple shrub garden theme can be seen in many Southeastern gardens, where scattered pines are underplanted with massed azaleas, camellias and hollies, interplanted with bulbs and liriope. Such gardens are attractive all year and need little maintenance. Perennials suitable for woodland and shrub gardens are listed together in the list on page 13, but some may not succeed where there is intense root competition from large trees.

ROCK GARDENS AND SMALL GARDENS

A rock-garden plant is any type small enough to be in proportion to its rocky setting. This includes many perennials, some of them diminutive, rare or tricky to grow, others undemanding. Some small enough for rock gardens, yet big enough for the front of the border, are included in the plant encyclopedia, starting on page 40. The list at right includes other easily grown perennials for small gardens and rock gardens. Raised beds are another good way of bringing small plants nearer to eye level.

By means of rock gardens or raised

beds, a large collection of compact plants can be fitted into a small space without it seeming structureless.

BOG GARDENS

Quite a few perennials are adapted to marshy ground. The best of these are listed on the facing page, some of which are described in the plant encyclopedia, starting on page 40.

PERENNIALS FOR SUNNY ROCK GARDENS

Many of these could also be grown at the front of a border or raised bed. It was not possible to include in the nursery source list, page 156, the many small nurseries specializing in rock-garden plants. They are among the best sources for small perennials, and for some of the rarer tall ones. Many such nurseries advertise in the bulletins of the American Rock Garden Society. The society's address is on page 157.

Achillea tomentosa
Allium senescens glaucum
Alyssum montanum
Anemone pulsatilla
Antennaria dioica
Aquilegia (dwarf forms such as
  A. flabellata 'Nana')
Arabis
Arenaria montana
Armeria maritima
Aster alpinus
Aubrieta
Aurinia saxatilis
Campanula (many, especially
  *C. carpatica, C. garganica, C.
  portenschlagiana.*)
Dianthus Many are suitable.
  D. deltoides is particularly
  colorful and easy to grow.
Geranium dalmaticum
Geranium sanguineum lancastrense
Gypsophila repens (also the similar,
  more compact, *Tunica saxifraga
  (Petrorhagia).* Both are prettiest in
  their double pink forms.
Iberis sempervirens (there are
  several dwarf forms.)
Iris Many.
Oenothera missourensis
Phlox (many, including *P. subulata,
  P. bifida, P. nivalis.*)
Potentilla X tonguei
Potentilla verna 'Nana' (as listed in
  catalogs)
Saponaria ocymoides
Sedum (many)
Sempervivum (all)
Veronica prostrata (V. rupestris)
Veronica repens

A low-lying part of the garden that remains swampy can be beautified by growing perennials that thrive in such conditions. If such an area does not exist in your garden, it can be created by digging out soil to a depth of 2 feet and lining the hole with heavy duty plastic. Prick the plastic sheet in several places with a garden fork so excess water can slowly escape. Replace the soil, mixed half and half with peat moss or leaf mold. If the soil is poor, add some rotted cow manure. Most bog plants need or prefer acid soil, so *do not* add lime. On a smaller scale, a few bog-type perennials can be grown in a sunken plastic laundry tub sunk 1 foot or more deep, with a drainage hole punched in the bottom.

If a stream runs through the garden, the moist banks provide an ideal site for bog-loving plants,

This large bog garden includes candelabra primroses *(Primula helodoxa, Primula pulverulenta)*, *Iris pseudacorus* 'Variegata', *Sanguisorba canadensis* and *Polygonum bistorta* 'Superbum'.

Raised concrete edging is used to create a tiny bog garden for a single clump of double marsh marigold *(Caltha palustris* 'Flore Pleno') at lower left of photo.

PLANTS TOLERANT OF BOGGY SOIL

Most of these also do well in soil only moderately moist.

Astilbe
Caltha palustris
Chelone glabra
Eupatorium fistulosum
Eupatorium purpureum
Filipendula palmata
Filipendula ulmaria
Helenium autumnale
Hibiscus coccineus
Hibiscus moscheutos
Iris (many—see plant encyclopedia)
Ligularia
Lobelia cardinalis
Lysimachia clethroides
Lysimachia punctata
Lythrum salicaria
Primula (see plant encyclopedia)
Rodgersia
Sanguisorba canadensis
Tradescantia virginiana
Trollius
Zantedeschia aethiopica

Some wildflower nurseries sell native plants found in bogs and marshes, including the following:

Acorus
Arisaema triphyllum
Lysichiton
Orontium aquaticum
Peltiphyllum peltatum
Saururus cernuus
Sisyrinchium angustifolium
Symplocarpus foetidus
Veratrum
Vernonia

provided the water level remains constant. Many streams become dry ditches or raging torrents at some time of the year. These are not suitable places for plants unless a means can be found for controlling the water flow.

CUTTING GARDEN

Bouquets of cut flowers are a source of great pleasure to many gardeners—and to their friends. Others prefer to enjoy flowers in the garden. One such gardener, when asked "Don't you like flowers?," replied, "Yes, I like children too, but I don't cut off their heads and put them in vases." If one member of the household likes flowers in the garden, and another cut flowers, compromise by creating a separate area for growing flowers for cutting.

A cutting garden might be adjacent to, but usually not intermingled with, the vegetable garden. The reason for separating the two is that flowers used for arrangements may have to be sprayed with pesticides or chemicals not acceptable for use on vegetables. A few chewed flowers in the garden are not too noticeable, but when one looks you in the eye across the dinner table, blemishes are apparent.

A passing thought: There are times when many of us would prefer a bunch of garden flowers to the standard arrangements of hothouse-grown flowers offered by most florists. Few florists have access to a varied range

A cutting garden can include perennials suitable for dried arrangements. Here, dried plumes of *Astilbe* fill the basket, *Achillea* 'Coronation Gold' hangs below.

of garden flowers, and seasonal hobby income can be made by supplying these. Or, if you have the talent, you can supply and arrange garden flowers for weddings and parties.

The majority of perennials can be used for cutting and many are suitable for drying. Take a bucket of water into the garden when cutting flowers. Put the cut flowers up to their necks in water as soon as you cut them. Put the bucket in a cool place and let the flowers have a long drink, preferably overnight, before arranging them. Leaves below the water line should be removed, and woody stems should be crushed at the base.

Most flowers benefit from having the stems recut under water as they are arranged. Those exuding sap, such as *Platycodon* and poppies, or those with hollow stems, such as dahlias, should be held for 15 seconds in briskly boiling water before being plunged into cold water.

A plant needs its flowers only to set seed and cutting them will not weaken the plant—it may even make it stronger. Leaves are another matter because the plant needs these for its own survival. Cut sparingly, leaving at least two-thirds of the leaves on the plant.

MEADOW GARDENING

Many perennials can't compete with the grass of a meadow, but plenty can. Which will do best depends on where you live—observe what kinds grow in local fields. Daisy-type plants usually self-sow abundantly, which makes them well-suited to meadow gardening. A list of perennials suitable for meadow gardening appears at right. Don't expect all of those listed to do well for you. Successful gardening is, in part, a matter of finding out which plants do best under the conditions you can provide. There are bound to be some failures.

Seldom is a meadow garden achieved by broadcasting seed in a grassy field. Plowing the field before seeding may bring to the surface weed seeds that have long lain dormant and awaiting just this opportunity to germinate. You are more likely to succeed if you raise the plants in pots or nursery beds until plants are of substantial size. Then remove squares of sod, improve the soil and put the plants out. Those that take to the soil and climate will spread at the root, self-sow or do both.

Butterfly weed *(Asclepias tuberosa)* in a meadow garden on Martha's Vineyard.

PERENNIALS FOR THE MEADOW GARDEN

No one comprehensive list could serve all regions. The nursery source list on page 156 includes suppliers of mixtures formulated for eight different regions, including both annuals and perennials. The following are some of the most widely adapted perennials suitable for the meadow garden.

Achillea millefolium
Chrysanthemum leucanthemum
Cichorium intybus
Coreopsis lanceolata
Echinacea purpurea
Hemerocallis fulva
Liatris spicata (also good for wet meadows.)
Linum perenne
Lythrum salicaria (especially where wet)
Oenothera pilosella
Oenothera missourensis
Ratibida columnifera
Rudbeckia hirta (annual or short-lived perennial.)
Saponaria officinalis
Solidago

The time of year when meadows are mown, and how often, varies from region to region, and with what is grown, so get local advice. Obviously, if you mow off the flowers before they have time to set and scatter seeds, no self-sowing can occur.

CONTAINERS

There are many advantages to growing perennials in containers. Container culture allows more control over the plant's environment—soil and nutrient requirements—so gardeners can raise many plants that wouldn't ordinarily grow in their gardens. Containers offer a means of keeping in check perennials that might be too invasive for the bed or border. Almost any perennial can be grown in a container, but those of bushy or arching habit usually look better than those that grow upright. Agapanthus and chrysanthemums make good container plants.

For the most part, growing perennials in containers follows the same rules as growing them in the garden. But because the roots are confined, the plants are more dependent on you and it is even more important that the soil neither gets soggy nor dries out.

Soil—The ideal growing medium depends on what you want to grow, and on the kind of container. For instance, Japanese irises need a moist, acid soil, and gypsophila needs a lighter soil to which lime has been added. Baptisia does well in soil of low fertility, whereas peonies need a rich soil. Don't combine plants with such different needs in the same container. Soil in clay pots dries out quicker than in plastic pots, and in small pots quicker than in large ones.

A loam-based potting mix is preferable. If you have good garden soil, use in the potting mix a mixture of one part soil, one part peat moss, and one part coarse sand. Use more peat moss for plants needing rich, moisture-retentive soil, more sand for those that do best in a lean, sharply drained soil. If you need to buy a commercial potting mix, often referred to as *soilless* mixes, use one of the peat-based kinds, such as Pro-Gro, Jiffy-Mix or Pro-Mix. Bagged planting mixes sold as "top soil" are seldom of good quality and many contain no soil at all. They are often high in insufficiently decomposed organic matter and low in mineral content. Such mixes take up to several years to

Giant rose mallow (*Hibiscus moscheutos* hybrid) in container dominates a terrace. Containers can also be used to grow tender perennials that can be moved indoors or under shelter during the cold season.

break down enough to grow plants reasonably well. Most soilless mixes, including peat-based ones, dry out faster than those containing loam—in hot regions, plants in these mixes may need watering twice a day. Also, these mixes provide a less-firm roothold than loam, so tall plants have a tendency to topple when grown in it.

Fertilizer—The easiest way to fertilize perennials in containers is to stir a slow-release fertilizer, such as Osmocote 14-14-14 into the soil. In commercial potting mixes, use the quantity recommended on the fertilizer bag. In a mix containing fertile loam, or for plants that do best in soil of low to moderate fertility, use half the recommended quantity. This will feed the plants at a steady rate for 3 to 4 months. Where the growing season is long, add a sprinkling of 5-10-5 fertilizer in late summer. At the start of each ensuing growing season, apply slow-release fertilizer to the soil surface or lightly stir it in.

In cold climates, tender perennials such as agapanthus can be wintered indoors. Remember that soil in containers freezes before that in the bed or border, so plants that are marginally hardy in your area need winter protection if planted in containers.

Perennials don't necessarily have to be massed in large groupings—some also make excellent spot plantings. Here, purple loosestrife *(Lythrum)* and feverfew *(Chrysanthemum parthenium)* add a touch of color to a front entry.

Preparing the Soil

There are two approaches to gardening—grow only those plants that like, or tolerate, the sort of soil you have, or make the soil suitable for a wider range of plants. If your garden is large, you may want to do both—amending the soil in some beds, growing plants that favor existing conditions in others. No soil is perfect for every plant, but most perennials are adaptable. If you want freedom of choice, the soil must:
- Be free of weeds.
- Be well-drained.
- Contain adequate organic matter.
- Not be excessively acid or alkaline.
- Contain the elements needed for growth.

The four elements most likely to need supplementing are *nitrogen, phosphorus (phosphates), potassium (potash)* and *calcium.* These are discussed on the facing page. If the structure of the soil is good, the trace elements,

needed in tiny amounts, are usually present in adequate quantity. Soil acidity and alkalinity are discussed on page 21.

GETTING RID OF WEEDS
If the bed or border is being established on previously cultivated soil where there are only annual weeds, such as chickweed, these can be hand-pulled or dug under. If there are stoloniferous grasses, such as Bermuda grass, or such persistent perennial weeds as sorrel and dock, they must be dug out, roots and all. The easiest time to do this is in early spring, before there is much top growth. Choose a time when the soil is neither soggy nor baked hard. Chopping up perennial weeds and stoloniferous grasses with a rotary tiller merely spreads them around, and more will come up than there were before.

A less arduous way of killing persistent weeds is to cover the area with a thick layer of overlapped newspapers, topped with several inches of bark or sawdust mulch. The weeds will be smothered out, but this takes about a year to happen.

Herbicidal weedkillers will do the job more quickly. One type, called *Roundup,* is non-selective and kills both grasses and broad-leaved weeds. It works slowly, so don't expect weeds to look dead for a week or two. A second application may be needed for such persistent weeds as Bermuda grass, Japanese honeysuckle and poison ivy. There are other weedkillers for specific types of weeds, as well as pre-emergent herbicides that prevent weed seeds from germinating. The pre-emergent kinds also prevent germination of self-sown perennial seedlings you may want. Many weedkillers have a waiting period after application before you can plant. Handle all weedkillers with caution and follow label directions for applying them.

DRAINAGE
You'll get as bored with reading "needs well-drained soil" as we got writing it, but more plants are killed by soggy soil than in any other way. Most plants can tolerate short soggy periods while in growth, but not when their roots are inactive in winter. Avoid locating the border in low-lying

Above: A raised bed assures good drainage for plants that would rot in waterlogged soil. Perennials shown include *Coreopsis verticillata,* gaillardia, daylilies, butterfly weed *(Asclepias tuberosa),* with annual cosmos.

areas that are subject to flooding during the rainy season.

Improving the structure of clay soil to make it more porous is often all that is needed to promote drainage. But under both clay and sand there may be an underlying impervious layer, sometimes referred to as *hardpan.*

Usually, a drainage problem can be solved by deep digging to break up clay soil or an underlying hardpan layer, if it isn't too thick. However, if only one area is dug, it may act as a sump for the surrounding ground, leaving the area worse off than when you began. A raised bed is often the easiest and best solution. A raised bed can be edged with bricks, stone, railroad ties or planks. For curved beds, you can use benderboard or 1x6 redwood strips.

For more serious drainage problems, you may have to install a system of underground drainage pipes or gravel-filled trenches that lead to a sump or dry well. This is best done by a qualified landscape contractor or soils engineer. It is not acceptable to direct water to your property boundary and let it flood the neighboring garden.

SOIL STRUCTURE

This is far more important than fertilizer for plant growth. If the structure of the soil is good, nutrient deficiencies or excessive acidity or alkalinity are less likely to be a problem. If your soil does not contain abundant organic matter—few soils do—the structure needs improving.

How can you tell if the soil has sufficient organic matter? It should be possible to make a planting hole for a young plant with your bare hands. We don't advocate doing this because it is hard on your fingernails—but it should be possible. Also, when you turn over a spadeful of moist soil, you should see earthworms. They feed on the organic matter in the soil and, in turn, aerate it. Some companies sell earthworms, but you'd be wasting your money buying them for the garden. If organic matter is present, they'll turn up of their own accord. If it isn't, they won't stay.

If you have the ideal rich, dark, crumbly loam, you are one of the lucky few. However, most soils need improving. At the one extreme is clay soil—puttylike when it's moist, as hard as the bricks made from it when

it's dry. At the other extreme is sandy soil, which trickles through your fingers. Stones in the soil, unless of such size and quantity that they impede cultivation, need not be removed. They may be a nuisance to the gardener but they help more than hinder the plants.

Clay—This is composed of tiny particles that adhere to each other and exclude the air roots need. Clay is usually fertile and moisture retentive, but once dry it resists wetting, and when rain is prolonged it may get waterlogged. Clay soils take longer to warm up in spring. If clay soil is worked or walked on when wet, it will compress, destroying the soil structure. Plant roots find clay hard to penetrate, whether it's wet or dry, and so does the gardener with a garden fork or spade.

Sand—Sandy soils are well-aerated and a pleasure to dig. They can be worked or walked on at any time, and warm up quickly in spring. Water penetrates sand rapidly with none lost to runoff. Roots spread through sand easily—sometimes *too* easily—so it is more important to avoid potentially invasive plants on sand than on clay. On the debit side, sand is low in nutrients and dries out quickly.

Loam—This soil is a mixture of clay, sand, rock particles and organic matter. It is the best soil for plants because it is well aerated and retains water and nutrients in the root zone, yet drains well.

IMPROVING SOIL

The soils just described are the three basic kinds. There are many in-between types. But all are improved in the same way—by incorporating decomposable organic matter into the top 1 foot of soil. If the soil can be amended to twice this depth, known as *double digging,* so much the better. But rotary tillers don't work the soil that deep and few gardeners are willing to double dig a large border with a spade. To double dig soil, first remove soil to a depth of 1 foot, or the depth of your spade. Then loosen or turn over the soil beneath that with the spade or a garden fork, adding organic amendments.

If double digging is too much work, compromise by preparing the entire border to the 1-foot depth sufficient for most perennials. Then prepare planting holes 2 feet deep for those that will be left in place for many

years—peonies and *Dictamnus albus,* for instance. Double digging greatly increases drought resistance because roots are encouraged to go deep.

Organic Amendments—The ideal organic amendments are those that also contain nutrients. These include well-decomposed manure—fresh manure might burn plant roots—compost, leaf mold or shredded leaves, seaweed and such byproducts as spent hops from breweries and old mushroom compost. Other organic amendments include fir bark, redwood bark, sawdust and peat moss.

Some sanitation districts sell a black, peaty substance, called *sewage compost.* It is made by composting sewage sludge with wood chips. It is excellent for improving both texture and fertility of the soil. The analysis varies—sewage compost used in the Harper garden contains 2.6% nitrogen, 0.6% phosphorus, 0.3% potassium, 2.0% calcium, 2.0% iron, 0.3% magnesium and traces of several other elements. Sanitation authorities selling sewage compost also advise on the quantity to be incorporated into the soil. Sewage compost is usually not recommended for vegetable gardens.

Sawdust is good for improving soil texture, but as it decomposes it takes nitrogen from the soil, so fertilizer must be added to compensate for this. Most organic matter, especially sawdust and bark, makes soil more acidic.

FERTILIZER

If organic matter containing nutrients is used to improve soil structure, fertilizer may not be needed. If peat moss or sawdust is used, fertilizer will probably be needed for clay soils and certainly for sandy ones.

Soil Test—The only way to know for sure whether fertilizer is needed, and how much, is to have the soil tested. Most states have county agents, a cooperative extension service or department of agriculture that provides this service free or for a small charge. They aren't always easy to locate in the telephone directory. Look under United States Government or state government listings. In some states, they are affiliated with colleges or universities.

The cooperative extension service will tell you how to take the soil samples, then will perform the tests.

A mulch of bark and wood chips helps control weeds in border and path. Mulch will eventually decompose, adding organic matter to the soil, improving its texture. Wood and bark mulches make soil more acidic. This shrub border includes the low-growing perennials, *Dianthus deltoides, Geranium dalmaticum* and *Campanula* 'Elizabeth Frost'.

They will then advise the kind and quantity of fertilizer to use and when to apply it. If your state does not have such a service, have an arboretum or horticultural department of a nearby university recommend a private testing laboratory. You'll also find soil-testing laboratories listed in the Yellow Pages under the heading, Laboratories, Testing.

If you prefer to garden "by guess and by gosh," a system that has served gardeners well for a good many generations, rake 5-10-5, 5-10-10 or 10-10-10 fertilizer into the surface of the soil at the rate recommended on the bag. Do this 1 to 2 weeks before planting time and water it well into the soil.

The numbers refer to percentage of nitrogen, phosphorus and potassium (abbreviated N-P-K) in the fertilizer, always listed in that order. The K in the abbreviation stands for potassium. As an example, 5-10-5 fertilizer contains 5% nitrogen, 10% phosphorous and 5% potassium. The remaining 80% of the bag's contents is a spreader material.

One element likely to be lacking in the soil—and the most important one for flowering plants—is phosphorous. That is why we recommend a general fertilizer with a middle number no lower than the others. Phosphorous does not wash down to the plant's root level quickly, so if soil tests reveal that your soil needs phosphorous, spread 1/4 pound of superphosphate over each square yard of soil surface and mix it in at the same time as the organic matter. Read the bag label carefully, as the contents may be *double superphosphate,* in which case you use 1/2 as much, or *triple superphosphate,* in which case use 1/3 as much. Alternatively, for spot treatment, mix a handful of bone meal into the planting hole for each plant.

There are a number of general-purpose and specialized fertilizers on the market—many more than can be covered in this book. In addition to the general advice offered here, seek advice from a local county extension agent, nursery or garden society. They will be familiar with specific soil requirements in your area.

Chemical fertilizers include dry or granular fertilizers and liquid (soluble) fertilizers. Dry fertilizers are either fast-release or slow-release, which refers to the rate at which they release nutrients into the soil. Slow- or timed-release fertilizers are often too expensive for extensive use. On the other hand, fast-release fertilizers wash from the soil quickly and periodic booster feeds may be required. Natural fertilizers such as bone meal, blood meal and cottonseed meal may also be too expensive for extensive use.

In subsequent years, a spring mulch of organic matter, supplemented with a sprinkling of 10-10-10 fertilizer should keep the soil sufficiently fertile. Apply dry fertilizer when the soil is moist but plant foliage dry. Dry fertilizer sticking to wet leaves may burn them. Water dry fertilizer into the soil—plants can absorb its nutrients only in liquid form.

ACID OR ALKALINE SOIL

The term *pH* is used to indicate the acidity or alkalinity of soil. Acid soils predominate in areas of heavy rainfall, alkaline soils in areas of low rainfall. The pH scale ranges from 1 to 14. A pH reading of 7.0 is neutral, lower numbers progressively more acid, higher ones more alkaline. A soil test is the only accurate way to determine how acid or alkaline the soil is. When you get the test results, find out how much of which amendment is required to bring the soil into the desired pH range.

Few plants will grow in extremely acid or alkaline soils. Either condition can lock up soil nutrients necessary to plant growth. The majority of perennials do best in a neutral to slightly acid soil—between 5.5 and 6.5. Japanese irises will not grow in alkaline soil. A few perennials—gypsophila for one—prefer alkaline soil. If needed, lime can be given to these plants individually to increase alkalinity, using dolomitic limestone, wood ashes or crushed oyster shells.

Acid Soil—If you know your soil to be overly acid (pH 5 or below), lime will probably be beneficial. The most commonly used form is dolomitic limestone, which also supplies magnesium. Lime is not in itself a fertilizer, but when used on acid soils it releases nutrients that might otherwise be unavailable to plants. Lime also improves the structure of clay soil, provides calcium and makes soil more alkaline. To improve the structure of clay soil without making it more alkaline, use gypsum. This also provides calcium. Wood ashes make soil more alkaline and, if stored dry, provide potassium and a small amount of phosphorous.

If using dolomitic limestone, start with about 1/2 pound for each square yard of soil surface. It's better to use too little than too much—it works fairly quickly and more can always be added later, if necessary. Usually, one application is effective for about 3 years. Lime washes down quickly into the soil, so it can be applied as a surface dressing. If you use manure as a soil amendment, apply the manure in

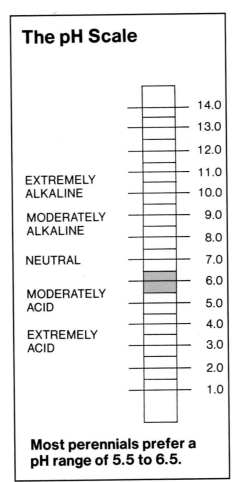

The pH Scale

- 14.0
- 13.0
- 12.0
- 11.0

EXTREMELY ALKALINE
- 10.0

MODERATELY ALKALINE
- 9.0
- 8.0

NEUTRAL
- 7.0
- 6.0

MODERATELY ACID
- 5.0
- 4.0

EXTREMELY ACID
- 3.0
- 2.0
- 1.0

Most perennials prefer a pH range of 5.5 to 6.5.

fall, and the lime in spring. Used together, they nullify each other.

Do not use lime unless you know that your soil needs it. A soil test is the only way to be sure whether your soil would benefit from lime. When having the test made, make it clear that you want recommendations for perennials—a vegetable garden, for instance, has a greater need for lime.
Alkaline Soil—A wide range of perennials can be grown in moderately alkaline soil, but most will do better if the soil pH is lowered by adding organic matter, such as peat moss or sawdust. The only perennial we have never known to succeed in a soil even moderately alkaline is Japanese iris *(Iris ensata),* but likely failures in soil at a pH higher than 6.5 include butterfly weed *(Asclepias tuberosa),* baptisia, turtle-head *(Chelone), Kirengeshoma palmata,* Louisiana irises, the "blue poppies" *(Meconopsis)* and *Opuntia humifusa.* Astilbes and border phlox also do poorly, but alkaline soils tend to be dry and failure may be as much due to lack of moisture as to alkalinity.

We know of no plant that demands an alkaline soil, but some show a preference for it, provided it is rich and moist. A list of these plants appears below. For most others, dig in plenty of organic matter and try them.

SALINE SOILS

In some arid parts of the country, rainfall is not sufficient to leach salts from the soil. If you live in such an area, get advice from your county extension agent on the best way of minimizing the problem. One solution is to plant in raised beds containing soil mixed with liberal quantities of organic matter, such as peat moss or sawdust. Sulphur may be added to make the soil less alkaline. Watering copiously will help wash excessive salts from the soil.

WHEN TO PREPARE SOIL

If you live in a cold-winter region, garden in clay soil and intend to hand-dig the border, fall is the best time for digging. Clay dug over and left in rough clods exposed to frost will be more crumbly by spring, and soil amendments will then be easier to dig in. If lime is needed, apply this in fall to help break down the clay. Gypsum also breaks down clay, but will not change the pH of the soil.

PERENNIALS THAT PREFER ALKALINE SOIL

All these also do well in moderately acid soil.

Bergenia
Centaurea
Centranthus
Clematis (if soil is moist.)
Delphinium (garden hybrids, not species.)
Dianthus
Dictamnus
Echinops
Eryngium (most)
Geranium
Gypsophila
Iris (bearded only—most others prefer acid soil.)
Paeonia
Primula
Scabiosa

Planning the Bed or Border

In cool-summer regions, an ideal site for the majority of perennials would be one with a sunny, southeastern exposure and with deep, well-drained soil. If this means running a border catty-corner across the yard, it will win no prizes for design, so you may prefer to put the bed or border where it looks best, then tailor the plants to the exposure. There are plenty of perennials for sunny, south or west-facing borders, as well as many for shady borders facing north or east.

Climate will influence your choice of a site. Which direction do prevailing winds come from? Do flowers fade fast in hot, afternoon sun? In hot or dry regions where most bloom is over by July, consider an east-facing border of spring and early-summer flowers that like afternoon shade.

Above: Double border in author McGourty's garden. Main border to right of wall faces south. The part closest to camera receives less than 6 hours of sun a day. Shade-tolerant perennials include astilbes, daylilies, ferns, hostas and *Pulmonaria* 'Mrs. Moon', as well as annual impatiens. Pachysandra carpets the ground in the deep shade rear left.

Another option is a sunless, north-facing border of foliage plants such as hostas and ferns—certainly more pleasant to care for in climates where a summer stroll resembles a Turkish bath.

If trees cast too much shade on the border, the lower limbs can be pruned off to let in more light and allow better air circulation. Afternoon shade from tall trees some distance to the west of the border helps prevent some perennials—ligularias, for example—from wilting in hot sun. But when trees are so close that their roots encroach on the border, you must either dig out the roots and repeat the process every few years, or plant tenacious perennials that can compete with the tree roots. These might include wild asters, epimediums, hostas, liriope and Solomon's seal. Wild asters are often seen growing along wooded roadsides.

In hot climates, the ideal place for perennials would be beneath a combination of pergola and lath house 6 to 8 feet wide, running north to south on a west boundary. If you build an open structure 8 feet tall, with spaced lath strips overhead and at the back, small

vines such as clematis could be trained up the supporting posts. Vines overhead might cast too much shade. This would provide the dappled shade enjoyed by most perennials in hot regions, without relying on trees that cause problems with root competition. It would also provide a measure of winter protection for marginally hardy plants.

BORDERS

Nothing sets off flowering perennials better than a mellow, old masonry wall or a tall, dark green hedge—traditionally yew—behind the border, and a well-tended, bright green lawn in front, with or without a paved path between lawn and border. This description brings to mind the time-honored English herbaceous border. However, this may not be the most practical approach for your garden. Some people are fortunate enough to have an existing old wall, but in hotter parts of the country, the reflected heat would be hard on plants. Yew hedges take several years to reach an effective height, and they have to be clipped. Faster growing hedges—privet, for instance—need more frequent clipping and have roots that encroach on the border.

Narrow borders look skimpy against tall walls and hedges. Plants at the back of the border may get leggy from lack of light and may require staking. Poor air circulation near walls and hedges encourages fungal and mildew problems. Rain doesn't always fall straight down—wind may blow it at such an angle that it misses plants close to a wall or hedge.

A picket or similar low, open fence behind a border will enhance its appearance without excluding light and air. A white picket fence lends a formal look. One stained brown or allowed to weather naturally is more informal. Post-and-rail fences have an even more casual look. Chicken wire tacked to them is almost invisible and keeps out wandering dogs. Such open fences can be used to support climbing plants such as clematis, jasmine, non-invasive kinds of honeysuckle or rambler roses.

Wide borders—with a path at the back so that plants can be tended and the hedge cut—are often out of scale in average-size gardens. Large borders may also require more work than the gardener is willing to do.

ISLAND BEDS

Borders backed by hedges, walls or solid fences have another disadvantage: You can't view the flowers in all their dimensions as the sun strikes them at various angles throughout the day. An island bed allows you to view plants from all sides. A bed not much more than 6 feet wide can be tended from one side or the other without stepping on plants. Also, plants in sunny island beds usually grow stockier than those in borders, so they are less likely to need staking. Air circulates freely, which helps control mildew. Plants that do best with their roots shaded can be positioned to the north or east of other plants.

Round or square beds in the middle of a lawn seldom look right and can be an eyesore when bare in winter, unless mercifully concealed by snow. Island beds will be more pleasing visually if three times as long as wide and if placed nearer the edge than the middle of the yard.

Controlling Creeping Grasses—A border more than 3 feet wide needs a path behind it—or at least a catwalk—if only to keep stoloniferous

Plants spill over a stone path in this mixed border at Great Dixter, England. Included are *Sedum* 'Ruby Glow', *Hydrangea* 'Preziosa', *Crocosmia* 'Citronella', *Allium christophii* and *Rosa moyesii*.

grasses, such as Bermuda grass, from creeping through from your neighbor's yard. If a solid, paved path is not practicable, a thick layer of newspaper topped with mulch will help control creeping grasses and ground covers.

What about the Bermuda grass on *your* side of the border? If lawns in your region are made of creeping grasses, this might be the deciding factor between a border and island bed. A paved path between lawn and border not only controls creeping grasses but looks attractive and provides dry footing. Spreading plants such as lamb's-ears, most pinks, or 'Ruby Glow' sedum can tumble onto

the path without being at risk from the mower. A path surrounding an island bed looks like a bicycle track, and if you have young children, may become one. A sunken row of bricks or flat stones, cemented into place, is less conspicuous. While it won't stop creeping grasses entirely, it will make them easier to keep in check.

FORMAL OR INFORMAL?

Whether a border is formal or informal is somewhat determined by the site, but mainly by the shape of the border itself. Geometric shapes are formal, free-form curves informal.

Wide border has access on all sides. Narrow path separates it from hedge in background.

Perennials in island bed include *Ligularia stenocephala*, bee balm (*Monarda* 'Croftway Pink'), yarrow (*Achillea* 'Coronation Gold') and purple coneflower (*Echinacea purpurea*).

A garden can never be entirely natural—if it is, it isn't a garden. The degree to which control is apparent helps determine whether a garden looks formal or informal. Many bedding annuals have been bred into compact, floriferous uniformity that gives them a formal look. Most garden perennials—clipped cushion chrysanthemums and asters excepted—still look much like the wild plants from which they were bred. But the traditional clipped yew hedges, straight borders and velvety, neatly edged lawn, lend them an air of formality.

A hedge need not be tall nor at the back of the border. For a formal look in a small garden, round or rectangular beds, or corner triangles, could be surrounded by a low, clipped hedge. Suitable evergreen hedges include dwarf boxwood (*Boxus sempervirens* 'Suffruticosa'), dwarf Japanese holly (*Ilex crenata* 'Helleri'), and dwarf yaupon (*Ilex vomitoria* 'Nana'). Where these are not hardy, germander (*Teucrium chamaedrys*) could be used.

Conversely, a rectangular border with a wall behind and a paved path in front becomes less formal when vines climb the wall and flowering plants spill over the path—seemingly uncontrolled, though this is usually a carefully created illusion.

To be successful, formal gardens must be kept neat—which is why most of us who garden without help opt for informality.

If you decide on a curved bed or border, sweeping, generous curves are more pleasing than tight squiggles. A power mower is a good way to lay out the curve—it can't be steered into tight curves that look fussy. If the adjacent lawn also follows the curve, mowing it will be easier. A flexible garden hose is also useful for making the curve. When you've got the border laid out to your satisfaction, look at it from an upstairs window or the roof—you may find you need more-sweeping curves.

Whether your choice is a bed or border, you'll need to water it. You may want to install hose bibs nearby to reduce the length of hose that has to be dragged around the garden. Plan for this at the design stage, not after the border is planted.

If you decide to make twin borders, don't attempt a mirror-image—it never works because there is too much difference in the way light strikes the plants.

ARRANGING PLANTS

Not every beautiful border began with a detailed plan on paper, so don't feel that you need one to start yours. However, one or more drawings can be a useful tool during the initial planning stages. Planning on paper can crystalize ideas, clarify options and help avoid mistakes. But remember that you are not bound by the plan. Realize that it is only a beginning, and your border five years hence will probably bear little resemblance to the initial plan. You'll probably want to rearrange plants after observing their height, spread, habit, health, color and flowering time *in your garden*. Unlike trees or shrubs, most perennials are easily moved.

Because the United States has such varied soils and climates, no plan provided by this book would fit all circumstances. There are some basic design principles you can employ when making your own plan, which are discussed here. Before you make the plan, use the plant encyclopedia, starting on page 40, to become familiar with the growing habits of the plants you've chosen.

Scale Drawing—To make a scale drawing, use a sheet of graph paper and draw in the outline of your proposed bed or border to a predetermined scale—for instance, each 1/2-inch square equals 1 square foot of garden space. Then mark out the positions of your chosen plants to the same scale. When you plant, transfer information on the scale drawing to the actual ground, using string, or a dusting of lime or flour to mark the outline of plant groups. Or, use sticks or labels to indicate the position of each plant.

Plant Height—Border plants are usually arranged by height, starting with the tallest at the back of the border, down to the shortest at the front. In an island bed, the tallest plants will usually go toward the middle. There are exceptions. The handsome, gray leaves of some verbascums, or the lush, silvery ones of *Salvia argentea*, shouldn't be hidden behind other plants. Their tall flower spikes are slim and will not obscure the plants behind them. *Verbena bonariensis* is best displayed as a "see-through" plant placed toward the front of the border.

Grouping Plants—Plants are customarily set out at least three to five of a kind, or sometimes in larger groups or drifts for dramatic effect. Too many different kinds create a busy picture, and too few mean long periods without flowers. Don't plant in rows. Stagger the plants. Groups of three, five or seven make more pleasing arrangements than groups of four, six or eight, but if you happen to have an even number of plants, offsetting them avoids a blocky look.

Some perennials, such as large-leaved, spreading kinds of hosta, look best as single specimens. Others, such as *Baptisia perfoliata,* gypsophila and sea lavender, grow wider than tall, and one plant may be enough for the border.

Spacing—How far apart to plant perennials causes new gardeners more concern than is necessary. Most perennials are portable and their spread can be controlled by division. There is no ultimate width for a perennial—if not divided, it will get a bit wider each year. How rapidly it does so varies with the plant, the soil and the climate. Spacing is a compromise: Widely spaced clumps may take several years to meet up;

Many unusual perennials are grown in wind-protected corner with yew hedges on two sides. Plants include *Astrantia, Geranium psilostemon, Campanula latifolia alba, Morina longifolia,* penstemons, *Eryngium alpinum,* verbascum, and at the front, *Nepeta govaniana.*

closely spaced clumps may require thinning in a year or two. As a rough guide, space front-of-the-border plants 1 foot apart, those of intermediate size—the majority—1-1/2 to 2 feet apart and the larger ones about 3 feet apart.

Allow generous spacing for those that don't transplant or divide easily, and allow a bit of extra space between groups. With most perennials, mistakes are easily remedied the next planting season. For quick results, those within a group can be planted closer together, with the intention of removing alternate plants when they start to crowd each other.

We recommend starting small. Don't make your bed or border wider than you can reach across—or, in the case of an island bed, to the middle of. Remember that you'll need to weed, remove dead flowers and otherwise care for individual plants.

What to Plant—Start with big groupings of a few kinds, choosing those known to do well where you live—but not too well! Regard with a wary eye the barrowful of plants offered by a neighbor—if there's such a surplus to

give away, the plant is probably invasive. With large groupings, the effect is good from the start, and it is comparatively easy to see where additional plants will best fit into your scheme.

Some of the plants you first choose may not take to your garden, and some that do you'll probably dispense with later for one reason or another. If you want anything at all unusual, you may have to order by mail. The nursery you order from may be out of stock of some kinds and, unless you tell them not to, may substitute something else. Occasionally, a purchased plant turns out not to be what the label says it is.

In the end, the only way to know plants is to grow plants. Your final plan will have to be worked out on the garden slate, moving the plants around until the result is satisfying to you. Much of the pleasure of growing perennials comes from experimenting with different combinations of color and texture. If you don't want to experiment in the bed or border, you can start a nursery bed as described on page 26.

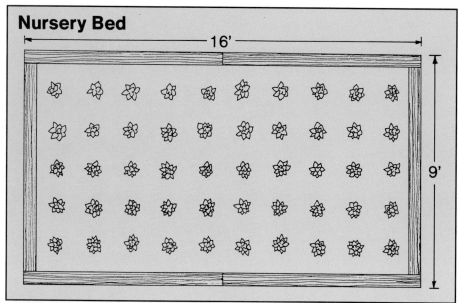

Nursery Bed

← 16' →

9'

A raised nursery bed can be used to grow many individual specimens without regard for design or appearance of the bed. The one shown here is made of 8-foot lengths of 6x6s and will hold about 50 plants.

NURSERY BED

We both wish we'd started a nursery bed many years ago. Slightly raised beds edged with 6x6 lumber look neat, ensure good drainage, and give you something to sit on when caring for or studying the plants. The lumber should be resistant to decay and termites. Redwood, cypress and red cedar are naturally decay-resistant woods. You can also use lumber treated with copper napthanate or other preservative that is non-toxic to plants. Use 8-foot lengths to form the bed, as shown in the drawing above. A bed this size holds about 50 plants, spaced 18 inches apart.

The main advantage of a nursery bed is that it allows you to collect a number of different species without regard to esthetics or design. You need grow only one plant instead of the groupings of three or more usually required for the border. The nursery bed can also serve as a holding area for plants that will later be moved to the bed or border. Gardeners who have moved Paul to make way for Peter, then wandered around the garden seeking a new home for Paul—unearthing the dormant and unseen Penelope in the process—will find a nursery bed their salvation. At least until it overflows!

One plant of each kind can go into the nursery bed. Within a year or two, most can be divided to make a group of five or more for the border—a con-siderable saving in money. Meantime, you'll have observed how tall they grow, how fast they spread, whether they sprawl, how much work is involved in removing dead flowers or spraying for pests and diseases, and which colors and combinations appeal to you most. A few, by dying or looking as if they wished they could, will make it clear that they don't like your soil or climate. It's better to find this out in the nursery bed, with one plant instead of a group, but if it's a plant you really like, try growing it at least three times.

If you can restrain yourself when initially ordering or buying plants for the nursery bed, it will leave space for plants you'll acquire in the future. As time goes by, you'll probably be given plants, grow them from seed, root them from cuttings, or be tempted by new kinds when you visit garden centers.

A few plants—*Dictamnus albus,* for example—don't move easily. You can still start these in the nursery bed by planting them in a container of generous size and plunging it into the ground to a depth just below the container rim.

SEASON OF BLOOM

One day, a magazine editor called one of us, asking for photos of a perennial border in bloom during spring, summer and fall. What was wanted was the same border, pho-tographed from the same place, massed with color in each of the three seasons. No such border exists, except in large public gardens, where plants past their prime are continually being replaced with fresh ones grown in a holding area or hothouse behind the scenes. The home gardener will have to make a choice between massed bloom for a month or two—maybe three in cool-summer regions—or more scattered bloom from early spring through late fall. This is done by growing plants that all flower at the same time or ones that flower at different times during the growing season.

Climate will affect your choice. The authors' gardens are examples. The McGourty garden is in northwestern Connecticut, where the growing season is barely 6 months long and summer temperatures seldom reach 80F (26C). Flowers get off to a slow start in May, reach a crescendo of color in July and August, and taper off in September. Early October blooming *Cimicifuga simplex* only manages to flower before frost about 1 year in 3. It took years of planning and experimentation to achieve peak color when the weather is at its best.

The Harper garden is in coastal Virginia. Bills for summer air conditioning are higher than those for winter heating. All plants flower 4 to 6

In author Harper's garden in coastal Virginia, peak bloom comes in May and June, mainly from shrubs. Here, a border of azaleas is edged with *Iris cristata* and primroses.

Peak bloom in the McGourty garden (Connecticut) comes in July and August. Perennials shown here include *Astilbe* 'Fire', feverfew (*Chrysanthemum parthenium*), *Echinops ritro*, balloon flower (*Platycodon*), *Heliopsis* 'Gold Greenheart', regal lilies and *Phlox* 'Sir John Falstaff'.

This border of cool colors includes *Salvia* × *superba*, campanulas, anchusa, delphiniums, *Thalictrum speciosissimum*, and hybrid musk rose 'Buff Beauty'.

weeks earlier than in the McGourty garden, and from June through September flower for only half as long. There are perennials in bloom during most of the year—from the hellebores and winter irises of February (sometimes January) to the chrysanthemums that may linger into December. In July and August the garden is almost bare of flowers, except for annuals. Peak bloom is in late April to June, but there is never at one time the massed color found in the McGourty garden in midsummer.

COLOR

Color preference is a personal thing. Trust your own instincts as you look at pictures and visit gardens. The only general advice we offer is to make large color groupings, not a spot of this and a spot of that.

Certain color combinations are generally considered more pleasing than others. This should not necessarily influence your choices, but most of us want our garden to be admired. Giving talks around the country has enabled us to gauge general reactions to various color combinations. Seldom is there total agreement. For instance, audiences are equally divided on whether or not yellow and pink are a good combination, but nobody feels strongly about it. Only one combination is consistently disliked. 90% of all audiences dislike orange with bright pink or magenta. Yet just that combination is used by some of the most artistic gardeners to add excitement to their

gardens. The surroundings and the quality of the light also make a difference—what looks right in sunny Virginia may look wrong to the same person in foggy Seattle.

The orange geum of spring won't clash with the pink physostegia of fall, but this kind of planning is complicated until you become familiar with a wide range of plants. If in the meantime you decide to omit either pink or orange, remember that a great many flowers are pink, but few are orange.

There are two effective ways of using orange—either combined with blue or combined with red and yellow. A bed massed with flowers of orange, pure red (scarce among perennials), scarlet and bright yellow has more impact than any other non-clashing combination. Most people like this combination but it may not be right for every garden. In small gardens it might be visually too close to beds of pink and magenta flowers.

Another way to use orange is to surround it with blue—'Enchantment' lily among veronicas, for example. Salmony colors are even more difficult to place than orange because they don't have the same impact, but don't blend well with most other colors either. As with orange, salmony colors can be combined with blue.

There are many pleasing color combinations, based on the general principles of color theory. Rather than discuss these principles in detail, we offer the following tips: *Cool* colors—blues and mauves—recede visually. *Warm* colors, especially

orange, advance. Cool colors are calming, warm ones exhilarating. If you want to bring a distant corner closer visually, use yellow and orange there—you may enjoy these colors better at a distance anyway. If you want the illusion of greater distance, or a feeling of calm, use misty blues and mauves. Clear, sparkling white also advances visually—try the white forms of peach-leaved bellflower (*Campanula persicifolia*) in a woodsy corner. White and pale yellow flowers take on an ethereal quality at dusk.

White flowers are excellent intermediaries between warring colors, but white doesn't always tone down brightness. Creamy whites do, and so do plants with small, white flowers mixed with abundant green foliage—feverfew for example. Irridescent whites take on the character—calm or exhilarating—of their companions. Gray foliage is always calming.

Sedum 'Ruby Glow' with blue-green grass (*Helictotrichon sempervirens*) and orange marigolds makes an interesting, if unconventional, color combination.

27

Buying, Planting and Aftercare

When we asked the makers of a beautiful cottage garden where they bought their perennials, they said that most were given to them by friends, or grown from seed or cuttings. At the time they made their garden, they had no choice—perennials were "out of fashion" and few nurseries sold them. Today, there are hundreds of different kinds being sold by local nurseries or through the mail, and more are being introduced each year. You can probably get starts of the more common kinds from friends and neighbors. For information on starting perennials from cuttings or seed, see pages 35-39. But if you want some of the finest selected forms or the latest introductions, you'll probably have to buy them.

This chapter offers some suggestions on what and where to buy, and how to care for the plant so it will give you many years of pleasure.

Above: The correct way to plant bearded irises: Leaves of divisions are cut back and rhizomes are planted near the soil surface, with all "fans" pointing in the same direction.

HOW PLANTS ARE SOLD

Garden centers sell perennials in containers of various sizes. Mail-order nurseries usually ship either bare-root plants or cell-packs of smaller ones. Each type has its advantages. These are points to consider:

Large plants from garden centers give instant results and you see exactly what you are getting. The plants do not have to endure several days in a shipping carton and you get them at a time of your own choosing. They tend to be expensive, the selection limited and the time of your choosing may not be the best planting time. Perennials are often sold in flower during the summer months. This may not accurately indicate their flowering time in your garden—the plants may have been started in a greenhouse, or have come from a warmer or colder region.

Containerized Plants—Local nurseries and garden centers sell most of their plants, including perennials, in various-size containers. It is often said that containerized plants can be planted any time the soil isn't frozen, but this is poor advice where summers are hot or dry. Most containerized plants sold at local nurseries are pampered, and not fit to fend for themselves in the garden without a period of acclimation.

Containerized plants are usually sold in peat-based potting mixes and these quickly dry out. After transplanting, the plant will need to be watered as often and as thoroughly as if it were still in the container. Use a watering can or hand-held hose to soak the root ball. Sprinkler watering wets the surrounding soil but may leave the peat-encased roots of the plant dry. The roots of plants in peat-based mixes have difficulty spreading out into the soil unless the root ball is cut or loosened. But doing this puts extra stress on a perennial planted during hot or dry weather.

If you plant in summer, check every other day to see that soil remains moist and water plants when necessary. Provide temporary shading. By all means, buy the plant when you see it—only the runts may be left by fall. If you buy plants in summer, it may be easier to care for them if you leave them in the pots and group them together in light shade, postponing planting until cooler, moister weather.

If you decide to do this, first check to see whether or not the roots have completely filled the pot. If they have, repot plants into a larger size container. Watering is less likely to be overlooked if plants bought in summer are kept together instead of being spread around the garden. To keep the roots cool, bury containers up to the rim in sand or mulch.

A cell-pack of small perennials often costs less than a single plant in a gallon can. They dry out more rapidly, but the roots usually move out into the surrounding soil faster than those in large containers. Plants in cell-packs are usually grown from seed, but most named cultivars are clones that do not come true to type from seed. For this reason, the plants are often mislabeled and not true to name.

Regardless of where you buy your plants, the catalogs make good reading. By and large, we've learned more about plants from nursery catalogs than from books. Catalogs from some of the larger nurseries are profusely illustrated, but don't neglect the simpler lists from small ''Mom and Pop'' nurseries—they often have choice plants at modest prices.

WHEN TO PLANT

The ideal planting or transplanting time is a cool, calm, drizzly day followed by several weeks without extremes of heat, cold or wind, and with frequent but not persistent rain. Such ideal conditions are hard to predict, but get as close as you can. Spring is the safest planting time in the coldest regions, especially if the soil is wet in winter—soggy soil when roots are dormant is a major cause of death. Spring is also best for marginally hardy plants. Where summers are hot and dry, plant in fall, or not later than mid-April.

Most growers consider late summer or fall the best planting times for daylilies, bearded irises and peonies, and some growers ship these plants only during that time. All other things being equal, give the plant as long as possible to settle in before it flowers. Plant spring-bloomers in fall, late-season bloomers in spring. Often you must try to outguess the weather: Are the plants more likely to suffer from a bitter winter, or from a dry or sizzling summer? Some experienced growers favor these planting times:

Northeast Coast (Boston to Philadelphia): April to May, September to mid-November.
New England (inland): April to May, September.
Mid-Atlantic Coast: October to November.
Southeast: October to November, February to early April.
Midwest: April to May, late August to September.
Plains States: April to May, September to mid-October.
Central (eastern slope of Rocky Mountains): April to May.
Pacific Northwest (coastal): March, September to October.
California: February to April, October to November.
Southwest: February to April.

If planted in the fall, small plants will be more susceptible to *frost heave* than larger ones. Frost heave is soil movement caused by alternating freeze and thaw, which can push smaller plants out of the ground. Spring is usually a better planting time for small plants.

HARDENING OFF

The term *hardening off* means the gradual exposure of a plant grown in a greenhouse or cold frame to outdoor conditions. Most annuals bought at garden centers require hardening off, but perennials are hardier plants and usually don't need this.

Occasionally, small perennial plants received by mail early in the year have come from a greenhouse. Also, if growing plants are a long time in transit, they may have produced new growth while in the darkness of their packaging. Such plants are vulnerable to wind, strong sun and frost. Plant them in pots and put them in a lightly shaded place for a week or two, plunging pots to their rims in sand or mulch. Cover plants if frost is expected. If plants received by mail have not started new growth, hardening off is not necessary.

Chain stores and supermarkets often sell plants in cardboard tubes, boxes or plastic wrappers. These are dormant when shipped by the grower, but have often made pale, soft and sappy growth before they're sold. These plants are really not a good buy, but will usually survive if hardened off as described above. Don't plant them in the garden until any pale, soft growth has turned to a healthy, green color.

Buying Plants by Mail—Mail-order nurseries usually offer a larger selection of plants than local garden centers. Sometimes these are shipped in small pots, but usually are shipped bare-root. Most of these nurseries ship by UPS, and we've found plants so shipped are delivered promptly and in good condition.

Provided you've received a healthy plant with its roots protected from drying out, and you plant it at the optimum time, bare-root plants often establish more rapidly than containerized plants that were grown in peat-based mixes. Reputable mail-order nurseries guarantee their plants and will replace those received in poor condition or later found to be untrue to name. Prices for mail-order plants vary greatly—but because one nursery charges more for a particular plant than another doesn't necessarily mean it's a better plant.

Send for several catalogs and spend a few winter evenings comparing what is offered. Check what is said about shipping times. Most mail-order nurseries ship in spring, sometimes also in fall. But field-grown plants cannot be lifted when the ground is frozen, and plants from Northern nurseries may arrive when it is already late for planting in the South. Some nurseries lift all plants in fall and store them through the winter. Obviously, it would be better for the plant to be saved the stress of storage if fall is a suitable planting time in your region and the nursery offers the plant at that time.

A list of mail-order nurseries appears on page 156. Catalog prices have not been included because these change frequently. First send a reply-paid postcard asking what each catalog costs.

HOW TO PLANT

If the plant is in a metal can, have the nurseryman cut it open. To remove plants from plastic pots, first soak the roots with water. Then place your hand around the base of the plant, invert the pot and rap it on a hard surface. Gently remove the plant from the pot. If the pot is so densely packed with roots that the plant can be dropped without the rootball shattering, slice the rootball across the bottom and spread it out in the soil like butterfly wings. Don't let plant roots dry out while waiting to

Planting From Containers

1. If roots have compacted in pot, use knife to slice into bottom of root ball.

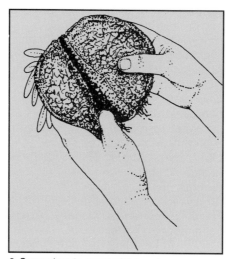

2. Spread roots apart with hands.

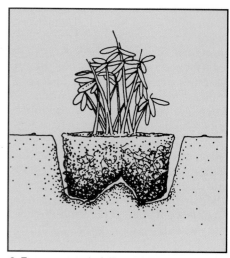

3. Form a mound of dirt in bottom of planting hole and "butterfly" roots over mound.

plant. Keep them covered with mulch, plastic or wet burlap sacks, and put them in the shade.

Plant the plants to the same depth they grew in the container, allowing for recently dug soil to settle. With bare-root plants, it isn't always easy to judge the correct planting depth. It's better to err on the shallow side, but make sure that all the roots are below the soil surface. Dig a planting hole of sufficient size so roots can be spread out without kinking, first cutting away damaged roots or those of excessive length that don't have small, white feeder roots at their tips.

If the soil is dry, fill the hole with water and allow it to drain away before planting. Before planting bare-root perennials, it helps to soak them for 1/2 hour in a pail of water to which a teaspoon of water-soluble fertilizer has been added.

Firm the plant gently into place, then water thoroughly. Mulch with a 2-inch layer of porous organic matter, such as shredded leaves or bark, buckwheat hulls or compost. Some perennials have their foliage raised well above ground level. Others make rosettes or tufts of leaves at soil level, often referred to as the *crown* of the plant. Don't pack mulch closely around the crown or the leaves and growing point may rot. Bearded irises are usually left unmulched.

After planting, water once or twice weekly for a month, unless rain does this for you. If planting has to be done on a hot or breezy day, shade the plants for a few days after planting. For information on spacing, grouping and positioning plants, see pages 24-25.

DIVIDING ESTABLISHED PERENNIALS

The best time for dividing established perennials is either early spring, when plants are 2 or 3 inches high, or in fall when foliage starts to die. If plants are divided in full growth, re-establishment is slow and plant losses high. Methods of division are described on page 34.

If a mature plant needs to be transplanted, it is usually best to divide it. Older plants may no longer have a fibrous root system and are often slow to re-establish if moved intact. Most perennials can be divided, but a few are best left alone once mature. The latter include monkshood (*Aconitum*), baptisia, gas plant (*Dictamnus*), some euphorbias, gypsophila, Christmas-rose (*Helleborus niger*), sea holly (Eryngium), sea lavender (*Limonium*), oriental poppy (*Papaver orientale*) and thermopsis. Most perennials with stout, thonglike or woody roots lend themselves to division only with a struggle. In this category are goatsbeard (*Aruncus dioicus*), bugbane (*Cimicifuga racemosa*), globe thistle (*Echinops*) and some filipendulas, with the exception of *F. vulgaris*, which moves easily. Fortunately, these seldom or never need dividing. A few plants, such as coral bells (*Heuchera*), tend to grow themselves out of the soil and should occasionally be divided and replanted a little deeper than they grew before.

Planting and follow-up care are the same as for newly purchased plants, pages 29-30.

Some plants develop bare centers as they increase their circumference. If you don't want to curtail the spread of such a plant, it can be rejuvenated without division by slicing out a section from the center, filling the hole with fresh soil, and inserting a small division from the outside of the clump. Slicing is best done with a tool called a *border spade*, which has a blade only 6 inches wide. This method works well with bee balm (*Monarda*). In general, if a plant is growing and flowering well, and is not unduly crowding its neighbors, division is not necessary.

WINTER PROTECTION

In cold-winter regions, newly planted perennials, shallow rooting kinds such as chrysanthemums and Shasta daisies, and marginally hardy kinds such as leadwort (*Ceratostigma*), stokesia and goldenstar (*Chrysogonum*), require winter protection. Use a light cover of such non-matting material as evergreen boughs, pine needles or salt hay, applied around Thanksgiving Day. This helps keep an even soil temperature over winter and helps prevent plants being heaved out of the soil by alternating frost and thaw. Remove the cover gradually during early spring.

Some gardeners like to leave dead foliage on the plants until spring as a kind of protective mulch for the roots. But dead foliage also harbors disease spores and looks untidy—it's better to remove it at the end of the growing season. Having protected plants for the winter, don't ignore them entirely. Check regularly to see if they have been disturbed by frost heave—if they have, firm them back into the ground.

MULCHING

Mulching enriches the soil as the mulch decomposes, lessens the need for watering, keeps roots cool, cuts down on weed-seed germination, and makes weeds that do grow easier to pull out. The bed or border should be weeded before mulch is applied. Use any decomposable plant matter that's available and affordable—compost, shredded leaves and shredded bark are popular mulches. Don't use peat moss because it cakes and then sheds water—it is also expensive.

A 2- or 3-inch layer of mulch is usually enough. Leave a small unmulched area around the base of the plant or it may rot where the stem and root meet (called the *crown).* Mulch can be applied at any time. Add a sprinkling of 10-10-10 fertilizer in spring to compensate for nitrogen taken up by the mulch as it decomposes.

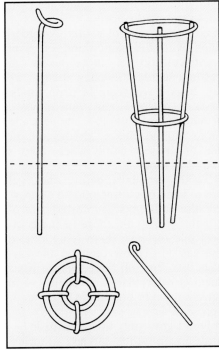

Three types of wire plant supports. Top left is nickel-plated support for individual stems, available from White Flower Farm. Support at top right has two rings spaced 12" apart, available from A.M. Leonard Inc. Support at bottom consists of concentric rings supported by three removable legs, available from Walter F. Nicke. Addresses of above firms are on pages 156-157.

STAKING

Many tall-growing plants need staking, especially in windy or partly shaded sites or in rich soil. Garden centers sell a variety of stakes and other supports. Twiggy brushwood inserted around the plant, or cylinders of chicken wire anchored with stakes, provide adequate support for most sprawling plants. Tall, heavy plants such as the taller gypsophilas need stronger support. Use either stout wire rings, or *corseting.* See drawing below right.

Get supports into place as soon as growth starts in spring. Once a plant becomes floppy, it is too late to do the job neatly. For staking individual stems, or encircling those to be corseted with string, use bamboo stakes, or their more expensive but longer-lasting steel counterparts. These steel stakes have green-plastic coatings that blend well with plant foliage. You'll also need some coarse, dull-colored twine or soft nursery jute. Twist-ties of plastic-covered wire can be used for attaching individual stems to a stake.

PINCHING AND DISBUDDING

Some plants can be kept bushy and self-supporting by pinching back new growth so they don't have to be staked or allowed to sprawl. Pinching is the removal of tips of growing shoots to make the plant branch, re-

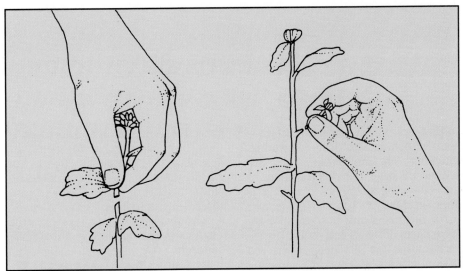

Left: Pinching back new growth helps keep plant more compact. *Right:* Disbudding involves selectively removing buds so remaining ones produce larger flowers.

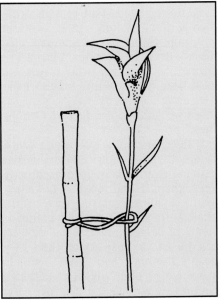

When staking individual stems, use soft jute or nylon pantyhose. Form tie into a figure-eight.

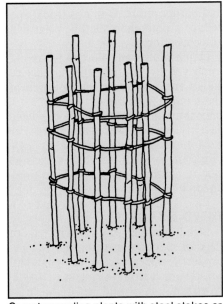

Corset sprawling plants with steel stakes or bamboo canes and string. Insert canes at least 9 inches into the ground.

Kathi is *dead-heading* the border—removing dead flower heads. It is done not only to improve appearance of plant but to prevent flowers from setting seed, and encourage extended or repeat bloom.

sulting in a more compact, floriferous plant. Pinching also delays flowering. Pinching chrysanthemums is described on page 71. This technique is the same for all plants. Pinching is done in May or June in the cooler parts of the country, sooner where spring gets off to an early start. Chrysanthemums are pinched or sheared several times during the growing season, most other plants only once. Plants that respond well to pinching include asters, heleniums, physostegia and border phlox. Don't overdo it and reduce a potentially elegant plant to a graceless glob of color.

Delphiniums and border phlox are improved by thinning the number of stems they produce, taking some of them out at the base.

Disbudding—less often practiced except by flower arrangers or exhibitors—involves selectively nipping out some of the flower buds so that remaining ones make larger flowers on longer stems.

DEAD-HEADING

Dead-heading is the removal of dead or spent blooms. It is done to improve the appearance of the plant and to prevent it from setting seed if self-sown seedlings would be a nuisance.

One thing to consider when choosing perennials is how often they require dead-heading, if at all, to remain attractive. Some perennials dispose of their own garbage, so to speak, by dropping their petals or florets, or curling them up neatly. Such plants include blackberry lily (*Belamcanda*), threadleaf coreopsis, flax (*Linum*), *Gaura lindheimeri*, purple loosestrife (*Lythrum*), *Salvia azurea grandiflora*, sundrops (*Oenothera fruticosa*) and tradescantia. Tradescantia petals become liquid—melt away—a fascinating process to watch. Some, such as yarrows and Sedum 'Autumn Joy', have flower heads that remain ornamental for a long time without attention. Some have attractive seed heads—or at least ones that won't shame the gardener who forgets to dead-head the plants. Bee balm (*Monarda*), butterfly weed (*Asclepias tuberosa*) and gaillardia are among these.

Others, including *Coreopsis lanceolata*, daylilies and Shasta daisies demand almost daily dead-heading to keep them from looking unkempt. With daylilies, you do have some choice—those with heavily branched stems of comparatively small flowers can be left to dispose of their own dead flowers and still remain attractive. The daylily 'Golden Chimes' is among the best of these. Generally, the more opulent the flower, the less attractive it looks if not removed when dead.

With some perennials, cutting back the flowering stems after the main flush of bloom induces a second flowering. If you do this, the plant may not set seed. Some perennials produce seedlings in such abundance that they make weeds of themselves, notably some of the ornamental onions. If you want plants to self-sow to provide additional or replacement plants, allow flowers to set seed. However, remember that the offspring of *species* will come true from seed but those of most *cultivars* will not.

PESTS AND DISEASES

An evergreen shrub with leaves chewed by insects will look unsightly for several years, but the top growth of most perennials dies down in winter so they get a fresh start each year. Remove this dead growth in fall because it is likely to harbor pests over the winter. Here are other ways to minimize pests and diseases:

● Give the plants the growing conditions they need. Red spider mites, for example, are far more likely to attack plants that are dry at the root or growing in too much sun. Botrytis—a powdery mildew—is encouraged both by dryness and by inadequate air circulation around the plant.

● Grow a variety of plants. A garden filled with the same kind of plant (monoculture) is more likely to become severely infested. Just as we do, bugs have their favorite foods. Look at it from their point of view: Would you rather grab a bite here and there around the neighborhood, or stay and raise a family where there's abundant food?

● Tackle problems before they get out of hand by cutting off and destroying diseased or insect-infested parts of a plant. Don't add these to the compost pile or leave them lying around the garden. Throw them in the garbage can. Pick off large, visible pests such as caterpillars and beetles, and squash them or drop them into a jar of kerosene.

● Don't grow only the man-made hybrids with the largest, fanciest flowers—they are often less pest-resistant than the parent species from which they were bred.

If a particular kind of plant is consistently unhealthy, it is either ill-suited to your soil or climate, or so attractive to a pest prevalent in your area that it is not worth growing. However, pests are often seasonal, and infestations are worse in some years than in others. If a certain kind of plant gets infested with a pest or disease, try it several times in different parts of the garden. If it remains consistently unhealthy or damaged, get rid of it and grow something else.

The occasional chewed leaf or flower does little harm to the plant and is scarcely noticeable. But severe infestations ruin the effect you've worked so hard for and have to be dealt with.

Insects—There are literally hundreds of kinds of insect pests that damage plants. But only a few kinds are likely to be prevalent at the same time in any one garden. What kinds these are depends on where you live. There are many ways of controlling insects with or without the use of insecticides. Specific and general controls for the many insect pests is a complex subject and beyond the scope of this book.

The use of insecticides—which to use, how often to use them or if you should use them at all—is a controversial matter. It is generally agreed that non-chemical controls are preferrable if they solve the problem. This book neither advocates nor advises against the use of insecticides or other pesticides, but provides general information on their use.

Aphids are one of the most common pests to attack perennials. These soft-bodied, green or black sucking pests are often present in great numbers on young tip growth. They can be washed off with soapy water or a strong spray from the garden hose. Spittle bugs can be sprayed off plants with a strong jet from a pistol-grip hose nozzle. Earwigs will hole-up in flower pots stuffed with straw, which can be used to trap and dispose of them.

Insecticides—From a gardener's point of view, insects that damage foliage and flowers are foes, and those that prey on other bugs, such as lady bugs and praying mantis, are friends. Most insecticides kill friend and foe alike, so the end result may be *more* pests next year, not less. No insecticide is entirely selective in what it kills. Among the safest are those made from plants, such as pyrethrum and rotenone, both of which are, however, toxic to fish.

Before using chemical sprays or other insecticides, we suggest that you seek the advice of your local extension agent to find the safest effective method of control. The list of approved chemicals changes every year, and new products are being developed with more emphasis on biological control. Japanese beetle traps are one of these, and they work well. These traps use a sex attractant to lure male beetles to their death, but they may pause for a final meal, so the best place for the trap is well away from the plants you intend to protect.

Slugs and Snails—Non-chemical remedies for slugs and snails range from grit or ashes spread around plants, to slug hunts by torchlight at night, to saucers of beer in which they supposedly die happy. Try such simple remedies first, turning to snail bait or other bug killers only as a last resort. If you use slug or snail bait in pellet form, hide pellets under pieces of board or broken flower pots, out of sight of birds and animals. Puppies often eat these pellets. If a pet does find and eat poison bait, rush the animal to the vet. Some of the flake or powder products, though equally harmful to pets, are less likely to be eaten—they are also effective to some degree against pillbugs, sowbugs, ants and earwigs.

Other Pests—The most disheartening damage to plants is that done by slugs and snails, deer, rabbits and other rodents. Deer and rabbits will eat almost anything if hungry enough, though they usually dislike aromatic plants. A deerproof fence is the only certain solution to deer damage. Wiremesh fences will help control rabbits, but to be truly effective, the mesh must extend far enough underground to prevent rabbits from burrowing under it.

There are many methods used to reduce the population of gophers and moles in the garden. A few of these are poison bait, smoke bombs and poison gas, various kinds of traps, and flooding tunnels with the garden hose. However, where these pests are common, most gardeners will admit that they have never found a truly effective method of removing *all* gophers and moles in their yards.

Cats will keep rabbits, gophers and other rodents under control but also, unfortunately, take their toll of birds. Ordinary female alley cats, unpampered, make the best hunters.

Diseases—Most common plant diseases are fungal in nature. Common fungus diseases include: *Botrytis* attacks leaves, stems and flowers, causing a blackening of plant tissue. *Powdery mildew* appears as powdery, gray or white patches on leaves. *Rust* is a fungus that appears as powdery, orange or brown pustules on leaves or stems. *Wilt* is a catch-all name for a number of bacterial and fungus diseases that cause plants to wilt. *Damping-off disease* is caused by a fungus found in unsterilized soil. It attacks young seedlings at the soil line, killing them.

Fungal diseases are less likely to occur when growing conditions are right for the plant—neither too wet nor too dry. To keep disease from spreading, diseased portions of plants should be removed and disposed of. Fungicides are used to prevent or control infestations.

WATERING AND FEEDING

Supplementary watering is necessary from time to time in most parts of the country. The ideal hose has yet to be invented. Soaker hoses and drip or trickle irrigation are good for the plants and the least wasteful of water, but they impede cultivation and don't always work well if water pressure is low. In large gardens, soaker hoses are messy to move around, and drip-irrigation systems are expensive to install. Underground sprinkler systems require the least amount of effort to use, especially if they are on a timer. They are also the most expensive systems to install. Most do not give complete coverage, so you'll still have to hand-water spots the sprinklers miss.

Most of us still rely on the hose sprinkler and hand-held hose. The main thing is, when you water, water thoroughly. Because it has rained, don't assume that no watering is needed. Move the surface mulch to see if rain has wet more than the top inch of soil. If you live in a drought area, it makes sense to grow mainly those plants that get by with minimal watering.

Feeding Plants—If beds are mulched each year, and a sprinkling of 5-10-5 or 10-10-10 fertilizer is applied at the start of each growing season, that should suffice for most gardens. If the soil is poor, or the growing season long, a second sprinkling of fertilizer in mid-summer may be beneficial—let the look of the plants be your guide. For more information on fertilizers, see pages 19-20.

Propagating Perennials

Nearly all perennials can be propagated in one or more of three main ways—by *division, cuttings* or *seed*. Commercial growers have long used grafting for selected kinds of gypsophila. These and other plants are now being propagated by tissue culture—but few home gardeners have the facilities or expertise to use these methods, nor do they need such quantities of plants as to make it necessary. Raising plants by division or cuttings has the advantage that the new plant will be a replica of the old one, which is not always so with plants raised from seed.

DIVISION

Division is the simplest and most certain method for novice gardeners, and is feasible for most perennials. For best performance, many perennials need frequent dividing anyway, and you get all the extra plants you need at the same time. For the best time to divide, see page 30.

Above: Tradescantias (spiderwort) are easily divided by slicing clumps into sections with a sharp spade. Shown here is *T. hirsuticaulis.* See page 152.

Perennials that make strong, dense clumps can be divided by lifting the clump, inserting two digging forks back-to-back in the center, then prying the clump apart. Repeat the process as often as required by the size of the clump and the number of divisions you want. It is usually best to discard the center of the clump, which will probably be worn out, woody and lacking in young, healthy shoots.

Alternatively, vigorous clumps can be divided while still in the ground by slicing them into sections with a sharp spade. If done in fall, the task is made easier if foliage is first cut back. This method works particularly well with daylilies and Siberian irises. It has the advantage that one or two sections can be removed with minimal disturbance to the rest of the clump.

Smaller perennials with fibrous roots often can be pulled apart using your hands. Those with woody roots can be divided using a sharp, sturdy knife such as a hunter's knife or steak knife. If you use a knife, first lift the clump and shake or wash off the soil so you can see what you are doing. Then sever it into sections, each with

some roots and at least one growing shoot. Keep replanted divisions well watered. Provide shade if the sun is strong or the weather windy.

If you don't want to risk disturbing a rare or expensive plant but do want to divide it, try sliding your fingers down into the soil at the edge of the clump and feeling to see if there is a rooted shoot than can be detached and grown as a cutting. Or prepare a year ahead by pushing your fingers into the center of the clump and easing the two halves outward. Then work some light loam, compost or a mixture of peat moss and sand into the center of the clump. After doing this, wait a year, then divide the clump in half.

CUTTINGS

Nearly everyone with an interest in plants will have rooted African-violet leaves in soil or water. These are called *leaf cuttings.* Few perennials can be grown from leaf cuttings. Sedums are one exception. Although the leaves of some other perennials will send out roots, all you'll ever have is rooted leaves—they will not grow into plants. Most perennials can be in-

Dividing a Plant

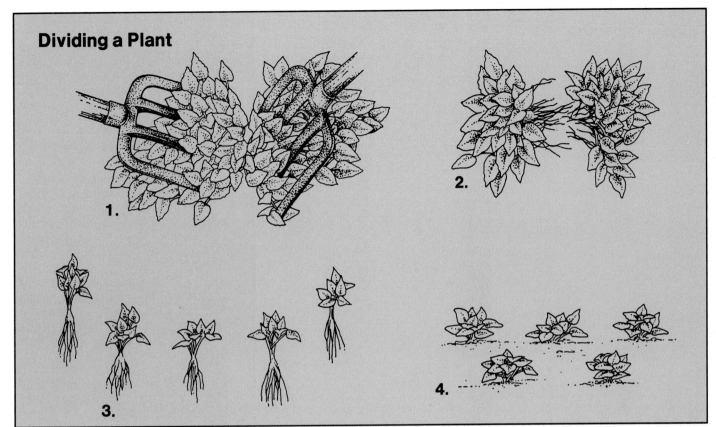

To divide a plant: 1. Insert two garden forks back-to-back in center of clump. 2. Pry plant apart. 3. Continue dividing plant in this manner until you have desired number of divisions. Discard old, woody center part of clump. 4. Replant divisions, water and add mulch. Provide temporary shade if weather is hot.

creased by basal cuttings or stem cuttings—a few are propagated by root cuttings.

Basal cuttings might be described as small divisions without roots—short, young shoots, or tufts of shoots, severed near the base of the clump. *Stem-cuttings* are what your grandmother called "slips." Unlike leaf cuttings, stem cuttings have a *terminal bud* at the end of the stem, and *axillary buds*—those in the angle where a leaf joins the stem. When the cutting has formed roots, these buds begin to grow.

Most perennials are dicotyledons (dicots), which means that when seedlings emerge they have two leaves, or cotyledons. Most dicots can be grown from stem cuttings, but those with hollow stems, and some such as poppies that exude quantities of sap when cut, may fail to root. Grasses, bulbs and perennials of the lily family—hostas and Solomon's-seal *(Polygonatum)*, for example—are monocotyledons (monocots), having a single seed-leaf. Most monocots cannot be grown from cuttings. Daylilies are monocots and cannot be grown from cuttings, but they often

form little plantlets on the stem, which can be removed, potted and grown into new plants.

Knowing just when to take a cutting is a skill that comes with experience. Basal cuttings are usually taken in spring or early summer, using new growth from the base of the plant. Often, new growth suitable for basal cuttings can be induced later in the year by cutting the plant back.

A chrysanthemum basal cutting at the right stage will snap off cleanly in your fingers. Stem cuttings usually need to be a little firmer and call for scissors, pruning shears or—for those skilled in using it—a sharp knife. The stem must be neither old and woody nor so soft that it wilts when cut. If you're not sure when to take cuttings, take a few at weekly intervals until you develop the ability to gauge the right degree of ripeness.

Cuttings need warmth to root, but excessive heat inhibits rooting. Between 65F and 75F (18C and 24C) is about right for most hardy plants, but many root at much lower temperatures. This means that cuttings root well in summer in the cooler regions, but late spring and early fall

are better where summers are hot. Bottom heat from a heating tray or heating cable will speed up rooting during the cooler months, but most cuttings can be rooted without this and without the use of a hormone rooting powder.

When taking a stem cutting, cut it off cleanly just below a *node*. A node is the point where a leaf, or pair of leaves, joins the stem. Pinch or cut off leaves which would otherwise be below soil level. Don't pull them off or you may tear the stem, causing it to rot. If the leaves are large, or the cutting has a tendency to wilt, cut off the tip half of the remaining leaves. A *heel cutting* is a side shoot pulled off with a sliver or *heel* of the main stem attached. It is treated in the same way as a stem cutting.

A 1-to-1 mixture of coarse sand and moist peat moss makes a good rooting medium. The sand should be coarse enough so you can see the separate grains. Sand and gravel dealers are good sources for sand. They will not deliver small quantities but generally will let you pick some up for a charge.

If you need only a small quantity of peat moss, buy a bag of the premois-

35

Stem Cuttings

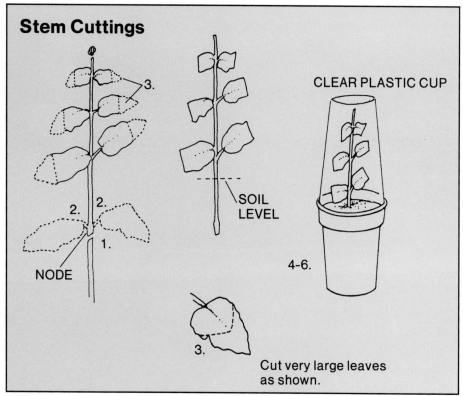

NODE

SOIL LEVEL

CLEAR PLASTIC CUP

Cut very large leaves as shown.

To take a stem cutting: 1. Sever cutting from plant just below node. Cuttings are usually 3 to 6 inches long, but vary with plant. 2. Pinch or cut off lowest pair of leaves, and next pair, if necessary—no leaves should touch soil when cutting is inserted. Be careful not to tear stem when removing leaves. 3. If leaves are large or tend to wilt, remove tip half as shown. If cuttings can't be potted immediately, put them in a glass of water. If this can't be done, put them in a plastic bag, blow air into it, fasten the top and store out of sun. 4. Fill pot to 1/2 inch below rim. A 1-to-1 mix of moist peat and coarse sand works well. Make holes with a stick or pencil and insert cuttings, first dipping them in hormone powder, if desired. 5. Water well. Put on propagator top, or insert sticks for support and fasten plastic bag over top. Stand in well-lit place out of direct sun.

Eryngium is one of a number of perennials that can be propagated by root cuttings. Shown here is *Eryngium alpinum*.

tened kind. If you use large quantities, it is much less expensive to buy dry peat moss in plastic-wrapped bales. Bales usually contain 4 or 6 cubic feet. Dry peat moss does not absorb moisture easily, so keep two bales on hand—one moistened for use, the other being slowly wet down.

To wet the peat moss, remove the plastic from the top of the bale and punch a few holes in the bottom of the bale to allow excess water to escape. Place bale outside and let rain gradually wet down the peat moss, which will take several months during rainy weather. It can be moistened more rapidly by scooping out a hole in the bale and pouring in buckets of water, or by inserting a slowly trickling hose. Newly wetted peat moss is not of the right consistency for propagating cuttings. It needs at least a few days in which to absorb the moisture evenly. There should be no lumps.

Firm the mix into a tray or pot but don't compress it too much. Make a hole with a pencil, insert the cutting and firm it into place. Water well from above, using a sprinkler nozzle on the garden hose or sprinkler-type watering can, to settle the cuttings into place.

To keep the cuttings from drying out, put them in a closed cold frame if you have one. If you don't, you can use one of the inexpensive propagating units that consists of a clear plastic tray or pot with a clear polystyrene cover. If you're starting only a few cuttings, a 4-inch pot covered with a clear plastic drinking glass makes a good individual propagator.

Put the propagator in a well-lit place out of the sun. Moisture will condense on the inner surface of the cover and run back into the rooting medium, so no watering is needed. Apart from occasional removal of cuttings that may have rotted, no further attention is needed until cuttings have rooted. You can tell if cuttings have rooted by gently tugging on them or by lifting them out of the rooting medium with the handle of a teaspoon. New top-growth is not a sure sign because cuttings sometimes start to grow before they have rooted. Procedures for potting and hardening off are the same as those given for seedlings.

Once severed from the parent plant, a cutting starts to die unless transpiration—giving off of moisture by the leaves—is halted or slowed down. A propagator or cold frame

Root Cuttings

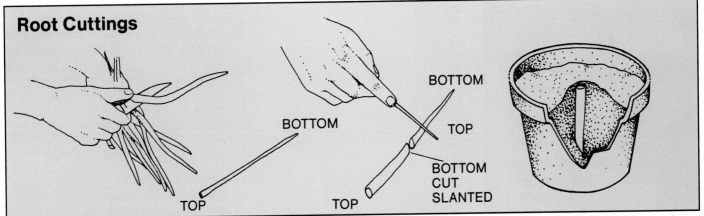

When taking root cuttings, cut top end straight, bottom end slanted. If roots are pencil-thick, such as those of oriental poppies or anchusa, they are inserted vertically in soil. Cover top of cutting with 1/2 inch coarse sand. Place pots in cold frame or propagator. Put in shaded place and keep cuttings moist.

serves this function. For this reason, speed is of the essence when taking cuttings. The well-prepared gardener travels equipped with plastic bags and wire twists. When another gardener offers cuttings, they are put into a bag, some air is blown in to prevent crushing, and the bag is tied.

If you expect to do this often, keep a styrene ice chest in the car in which to place the bags. If kept cool with ice, cuttings will keep this way for a week or more. Except in the heat of summer, cuttings also travel well in the mail if the blown-up plastic bag is packed inside a strong box.

A simple way of rooting cuttings is to put them directly into the garden. If you put them alongside the parent plant—on the shady side—you won't have to label them. Scoop out a hole in the ground, fill it with peat and sand, insert the cutting and cover it with a jelly jar, plastic cup or plastic milk jug with the bottom cut out. All but the milk jug will need shading if afternoon sun strikes these improvised propagators.

Cuttings of plants with hairy leaves may rot in the humid atmosphere of a propagator. The hairiness is itself a means of limiting transpiration and often such cuttings can be rooted in an uncovered tray or pot. Place the tray or pot in an open cold frame or in a shady spot with an improvised cover of window screening. Make sure cuttings do not dry out, but keep water off the leaves.

Root Cuttings—Plants that can be increased by root cuttings include acanthus, anchusa, Japanese anemones, eryngium, oriental poppies and border phlox. If the roots are more than pencil thick, they are cut into 2-

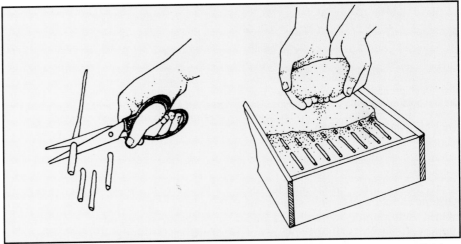

If roots are slender, such as those of Japanese anemones or border phlox, lay them flat in a tray and cover with rooting medium. Put tray in cold frame or propagator. Put in shaded place and keep cuttings moist.

to 4-inch sections, placed upright in trays or pots on a layer of potting compost, then covered with coarse sand to 1/2 inch above their tops. The end that was nearest the crown of the plant must point up. When taking the cuttings, if you cut the top straight and the bottom slanting, you'll be able to tell which end is which. If you do get confused, or if the cuttings are thin, place them horizontally in the sand instead of upright.

Late winter is the best time to take root cuttings. Place the pots or trays in a frame or shaded place and keep cuttings moist until the emergence of shoots and leaves indicates that rooting has taken place. Cuttings are then potted individually and allowed to grow until sturdy enough to plant in the garden.

PERENNIALS FROM SEED

Nurserymen favor seed for growing perennials because it enables them to raise thousands of the same plant quickly. Another advantage is that disease is not carried over in seed, as it may be with divisions or cuttings. More important to the home gardener, seed of uncommon plants may be available when the plants are not. Seed can be used to increase a species such as gasplant (*Dictamnus albus*), which takes several years to make a sizeable clump and is then best not divided.

When the seed of a species is sown, the offspring will look like the parent. This is what is meant when a plant is said to *come true from seed*. However, many garden perennials are not species, but *cultivars*. These are special forms of a species or hybrids between two species. Most cultivars do not come true from seed. If, for example, you let border phlox go to seed, the seedlings will be inferior to the parents. A few seed strains of hybrid plants do come true—or close enough

Individual propagators can be made from plastic pots and plastic picnic glasses. Also shown are manufactured propagators available from Walter F. Nicke.

Seed being raised under fluorescent light in kitchen of coauthor Fred McGourty. Plastic sweater box is used as propagator.

so it makes little difference to the gardener. Examples are strains of hybrid delphinium, columbines and lupines. *Geum* 'Mrs. Bradshaw' is not the best geum available, but because it comes more-or-less true from seed, it is the one preferred by nurseries.

When to Sow—Order seed as soon as the seed list or catalog arrives. If seed can't be sown right away, store it in the refrigerator. The best time to sow *purchased* seed of hardy perennials is late winter and early spring (February to April) and usually the earlier the better. The seed of some perennials—hellebores, for example—does not germinate well unless sown as soon as it is ripe. But for obvious reasons, you cannot buy seed just collected from the plant. Some seed needs a period of exposure to cold before it germinates. Where winters are cold, this happens naturally if seed is sown early and placed outside.

Freezing won't harm seed of hardy perennials. Alternating freeze and thaw helps some kinds to germinate. Seed put outside will not germinate until it is ready to face the weather prevailing from then on, so hardening off is a shorter, simpler process than with plants grown indoors. If seed arrives too late to be exposed to cold, or

if you live in a warm-winter region, it can be sown in a pot, covered with plastic and subjected to 2 to 3 weeks of artificial winter in the refrigerator.

Ask six gardeners what soil mix they use for raising seed and you'll probably get six different answers. Those who raise seed outside often mix loam and compost from their own garden with coarse sand—about one third of each. Seedlings don't need feeding in this mix and they are growing from the start in soil approximating what they'll have to adapt to in the garden. Gauging exactly the right soil texture takes experience. Also, unless the mix is sterilized—not easily done at home—weeds will also germinate and soil-borne fungi may cause seedlings to rot at the base and topple over under the humid conditions otherwise ideal for raising seed. This fungal disease is known as *damping-off.*

All things considered, we recommend that inexperienced gardeners use one of the commercial potting mixes sold under such brand names as Pro-Mix, Jiffy-Mix and Pro-Gro. Damping-off can also occur in these mixes, but a 1/4-inch layer of vermiculite on top of the mix, onto which the seeds are sown, helps pre-

vent damping off. Another way to prevent damping off is to spray the soil surface with a fungicide such as Captan.

Seed germinates at varying speeds, so it is best to sow one kind to a pot, using the square pots that fit together without wasted space. Plastic pots are generally preferred to clay ones. If you use clay pots, soak them in water before using them or they'll draw moisture from the soil. If you sow seed in trays, space the rows well apart so that quick-germinating kinds can be transplanted without disturbing other rows.

Fill the pot or tray and press the mix evenly into place with the bottom of another pot or tray of similar size. Soil should be fairly loose, so don't tamp it hard. If using trays, press a ruler or pencil on the mix to mark the rows. Space seeds about 1/2 inch apart. With fine seed, it helps to fold a piece of white paper to make a channel, place the seeds in it, then ease them off the edge of the paper with the tip of a pointed knife.

Unless the seed is large, do not cover it—just press it lightly into the mix. You can put a light sprinkling of vermiculite over large seeds—better too little than too much. If the seed is to be exposed to rain or watered from above, cover the soil surface with a fine layer of 1/8-inch grit, such as the kind sold by feed stores for chickens. Label each row or pot, with the name running from top to bottom for easier reading. Stand the pot or tray in water to a level just below the rim—a small plastic pot may float and tip over if the water is too deep—and leave it there until moisture can be seen on the surface. Remove pots and allow to drain.

If you have a cold frame, put the pots in this, plunged in sand. If not, use one of the plastic propagating units shown in the photos above. These units ensure that the soil does not dry out. Stand the unit in a sheltered place with maximum possible light but out of afternoon sun. If individual pots are used, put a layer of moist sphagnum moss, peat moss or potting mix into a propagator tray, place the pots on this and cover with the lid. Check once a week to see if the pots need water.

If you'll be away longer than a week, cover pots individually with plastic wrap held in place with rubber bands. If you can remember to water—daily if necessary—and if you'll be there to do it, the pots do not need to be covered. But once seed has germinated, the plants will die if they dry out.

Some seeds have been found to germinate best in the light, others in the dark. Light-requiring seed is usually small. Rather than risk covering it too deeply with potting mix, it is best not to cover it at all. The opposite does not apply because seed needing darkness does, after all, have the night. Park's *Success with Seeds,* by Ann Reilly, describes the individual requirements of many kinds of seed.

In our experience, the seed of most hardy perennials placed outside in February or March will germinate in its own time, usually that spring, but sometimes not for a year from the time it was sown. Don't throw away pots of ungerminated seed. Keep them moist and wait another year, or even 2 years, and they will probably germinate.

Many gardeners have indoor light units that can be used to start plants early. If you try this, put the pots or trays close to the lights. Unless seedlings actually touch the lights, they will not scorch. If they are more than about 6 inches away, they'll probably get spindly.

Once the seed has germinated, expose it gradually to more air, first propping open the frame or propagator top for a day or two, then removing it entirely. Seedlings in a commercial potting mix will now need feeding with a weak solution—about one-third label strength—of such soluble fertilizers as Peters 15-30-15 or Rapid-Gro.

If seedlings are in soil, they can be left until they crowd the pot. If they are grown in a soilless mix, or if some in a tray have germinated and others have not, transplant seedlings when they're no more than 1 inch tall. The handle of a teaspoon is a useful tool for transplanting. Handle seedlings by the leaves, not the fragile stems, and press them lightly into the mix. Place pots in water to dampen soil. Then put them back in a propagator or frame for 1 or 2 days until the roots are re-established. If 1/3 to 1/2 garden soil is mixed with the soilless medium at this stage, it will ease the transition when the plant is transferred to the garden.

The best place for seedlings after

Gasplant *(Dictamnus albus)* is best raised by seed because it takes several years to make sizeable clumps, then is best not divided.

transplanting is a cold frame or a *plunge bed* (a topless frame). Plunge pots in sand up to their rims. Where summers are hot, the cold frame or plunge bed should be located away from afternoon sun, or shaded in some way. Snow fence and window screens provide shade but let through air and rain.

Small plants put out in the garden can be damaged by dogs, cats, birds and the gardener's own clumsy feet, but none of these bring death as certainly as pots left to dry out. If you won't be around to water young plants in the cold frame every day or two, put them out in the garden. To protect plants from animals and people, surround each plant with a cylinder of chicken wire with its base just under the soil, or held in place with stakes. If temporary shading is needed, sheer nylon drapes or nursery shade cloth can be hung over the cylinder. Whether in pots or out in the garden, small plants are especially susceptible to slugs and snails. Use slug or snail bait, if necessary. A full-grown plant can survive a lot of slug or snail damage but a little one deprived of all its leaves will probably not recover. Campanulas are particularly vulnerable to slug and snail attack.

Gallery of Garden Perennials

The following encyclopedia includes more than 250 garden perennials. The emphasis is on available, adaptable, hardy perennials for the border. Regrettably, for lack of space, only a limited number of woodland-type perennials could be included, but the list on page 13 includes some others. At time of publication, every plant in this book is available from nurseries, most from mail-order nurseries. More are becoming available every day.

HOW TO USE

Major plant entries in this encyclopedia are listed in alphabetical order by the botanical name of the genus, followed by the common name, if the genus has one, and the family name. Under each entry, the popular species and cultivars of that genus are described. Each has a heading that lists the species name of the plant, its common name—if it has one—approximate hardiness, approximate height, usual flower colors, and flowering time. Symbols are used to indicate whether the plant is likely to do best in full sun, part shade or full shade. Where two symbols are shown, the plant usually does well in either, with a preference for the one shown first. In hot climates, choose the shadier site.

BOTANICAL NAMES

Botanical names are changed from time to time. Some plants have suffered many name changes. This encyclopedia uses the species names in most common use today, to enable you to find the plant in nursery catalogs. Species names shown in parentheses are either earlier botanical names or the latest name not yet in general use.

If you want to look up a plant, and know only its common name, refer to the index on pages 158-160. You'll note that some of the entries do not list a common name under the genus name. In such cases, the genus name for these plants is also the common name—iris, aster and geranium, are examples. For more information on understanding botanical names, see pages 10-11.

HARDINESS

In the United States, two hardiness zone maps are in common use—that of the USDA and that of the Arnold Arboretum. This book uses the Arnold Arboretum map, with a table of USDA equivalent temperatures. See page 42. When nursery catalogs give zone numbers, check to see whether they are Arnold Arboretum or USDA numbers, because there are some differences.

The zone number given for each plant indicates the *coldest region* in which that plant is reliably hardy. This is the best means we have of suggesting likely hardiness, but often it is only an educated guess, and at best a rough guide. Many of the perennials listed have not been fully tested for hardiness in all parts of the United States and Canada. Also, many other factors, singly and in combination, affect longevity.

Above: *Aquilegia caerulea* is one of several species of columbine native to western North America.

Soggy soil when roots are dormant is a major killer of perennials. Many plants considered tender in England—the source of most information on perennials—will survive much colder, but drier winters in parts of the northern United States. Winter mulch often helps plants through winter, but may cause some to rot. A healthy, well established but comparatively young plant will survive greater temperature extremes than one that is newly planted, diseased, or worn out and in need of dividing.

Many perennials can be grown in Zones 1 and 2, but this book seldom gives zone numbers lower than Zone 3. This is because snow makes so much difference in whether or not a plant will survive the winter. Plants are less hardy where winters alternate between freeze and thaw, without snow cover, than they are in colder regions where they remain frozen under a protective blanket of snow. For gardeners in Zones 1 and 2, this book includes a list of perennials usually successful in Alberta and Manitoba, Canada. See page 43.

For many gardeners, there are considerations other than cold hardiness. Plants such as peonies, Russell lupines and border phlox *need* the winter rest triggered by cold weather, and do poorly without it. These plants do poorly in mild-winter areas. Others flower themselves to an early death. Summer drought is a limiting factor, unless water can be provided artificially. See page 43 for a list of perennials that do particularly well in dry climates, such as those found in Southern California and the Southwest.

Humid heat and the pests that thrive in it account for many losses in the South, especially among gray-foliage plants. The most limiting climates for perennials are those subtropical regions with warm winters and hot, humid summers. Few traditional perennials do well in those regions—see page 43 for a list of some found satisfactory in Florida.

If there are limitations inherent in a plant, these are mentioned. But with so many variables, it is often hard to guess why a plant has died. Almost every experienced gardener has been humbled by seeing a plant die in his or her garden, or by discarding the plant as a failure, even though the same plant may be the picture of health in a neighbor's garden a block away. There is no substitute for local knowledge, observation and individual experiment. If you want a particular plant, try growing it three times, in different locations.

APPROXIMATE HEIGHT

Heights listed are the average ones for plants growing in adequately moist, moderately fertile soil, with sun appropriate to their needs. A plant growing in poor, dry soil and full sun may attain only half the height of the same plant grown in rich, moist soil, and shade. Except where noted, heights given are for plants in bloom.

FLOWERING TIME

The time and duration of bloom varies greatly from one region to another, so the suggested time is necessarily vague. A perennial in peak bloom in Boston in August will reach its peak in July in Philadelphia, June—for a much shorter time—in Charleston, and even earlier in parts of California. Nor is the sequence of bloom always the same. If the flowering time is listed as spring *or* summer, this means that the plant flowers in spring in warm regions, summer in cooler ones. Spring *to* summer means the plant flowers continuously during this time.

SUN OR SHADE

All perennials need good light. A few, hostas among them, tolerate gloomy corners—but none need sun all day long. Few flowering perennials do well in completely sunless sites, but a great many benefit from light shade.

Where you live makes a difference. The hotter the climate, the greater the plant's *transpiration*—the plant equivalent of sweat. Most plants prefer some shade when the temperature exceeds 90F (32C), and they also require more water. In dry regions, shade helps compensate for a shortage of water. Symbols are used to indicate sun and shade requirements of the plants. The symbols, ○◑, mean to give the plant sun in cool regions, light shade in hot or dry ones. If the symbols are reversed, ◑○, the plant will prefer light shade in almost all climates but will tolerate full sun in cool regions.

A plant's physical makeup often contains a clue to its needs. The hair-covered surface of most gray leaves indicates an adaptation to drought. So does the narrowing of leaves, the reduction in size or rolling-under of leaf edges to expose less surface to the sun, or succulent, water-storing leaves or tuberous roots. Large leaves usually indicate a need for shade or abundant moisture.

Many perennials lean toward the strongest light and some turn their flowers toward it. Unless blocked by trees, hedges or buildings, the strongest light comes from the south and west.

There are many permutations of sun and shade, but these are the main ones, represented by the symbols:
○ **Full Sun**—Sites that offer full sun include:
1. Beds in the middle of a lawn or borders on either side of a sunny path.
2. South or west-facing borders backed by walls. West-facing borders will be shaded by the wall in the morning, but there is ample sun for full-sun plants.
3. South or west-facing borders backed by trees, shrubs or hedges.

Site 1 is ideal for full-sun plants. Site 2 is satisfactory, but reflected heat from a wall will fade plants quickly in hot regions—a wood fence would be better. Site 3 is usually unsuitable because plants needing full sun are less able to compete with tree roots than those adapted to shade. This makes it difficult to grow sun-loving or shade-loving plants.

The description, *drought resistant*, can be a trap for inexperienced gardeners. It usually means drought resistant only in deep soil. Plants that survive drought by delving deep for moisture—butterfly weed, for example—are less able than most to compete with surface-rooting trees.

If the only place for perennials is a root-filled sunny border, it may be necessary to dig out a trench at least 3 feet deep and insert a root-proof barrier such as corrugated fiberglass. However, by limiting the root spread of a nearby hedge or tree, it will then require more feeding and watering than before.

◑ **Some Shade**—This includes sites shaded part of the day (part shade), light shade, dappled shade and filtered shade. Sites include:
1. East-facing borders backed by walls. These provide morning sun only.

Hardiness Zones of the United States and Canada

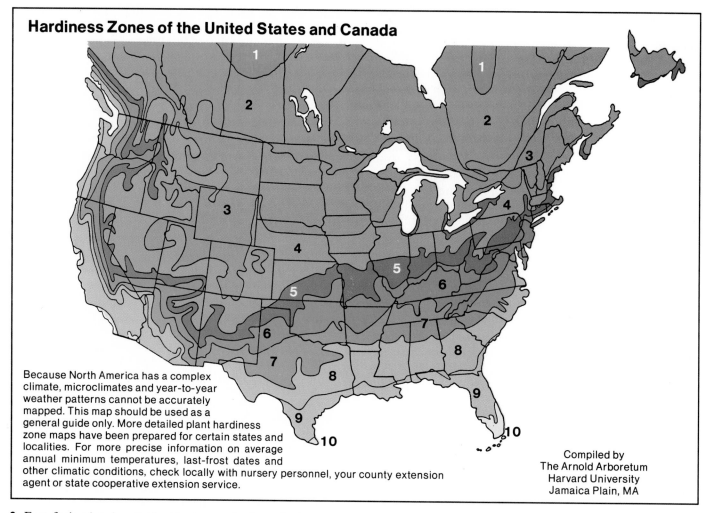

Because North America has a complex climate, microclimates and year-to-year weather patterns cannot be accurately mapped. This map should be used as a general guide only. More detailed plant hardiness zone maps have been prepared for certain states and localities. For more precise information on average annual minimum temperatures, last-frost dates and other climatic conditions, check locally with nursery personnel, your county extension agent or state cooperative extension service.

Compiled by
The Arnold Arboretum
Harvard University
Jamaica Plain, MA

2. East-facing borders backed by trees, shrubs or hedges.
3. Dappled, filtered or shifting shade in clearings between widely spaced, high-branched or thinly branched trees.
4. Lath shade.

Site 1 is suitable for plants that need full shade and for most of those with the ◑ symbol, but not those with the symbols, ○◐. Site 2 is slightly less satisfactory because of root competition from trees and shrubs, but shade plants can usually tolerate this if kept well mulched, fed and watered. Site 3 is a good one in hot regions for most plants that require light shade, provided root competition is not too severe.

Site 4 is potentially the perfect kind of shade for all but full-sun plants, especially in hot regions. We say "potentially" because we know of no gardeners growing perennials under lath structures—it's a brand new plant game waiting to be played. The amount of shade could be varied by varying the spacing of the lath strips.

● Full Shade—Sites that offer full shade are:
1. North-facing borders backed by walls.
2. North-facing borders backed by trees, shrubs or hedges.
3. Dense woodland. If trees are deciduous, site will get sunshine in spring and full shade in summer.

Site 1 would be a good place for perennials adapted to full shade, such as hostas, hellebores, ferns and many woodland wildflowers. Site 2 is also satisfactory if plants are kept well mulched, fed and watered. Site 3 is unsuitable for most perennials, but woodland wildflowers that go dormant in summer could be grown under deciduous trees.

Arnold Arboretum Hardiness Zone	Range of Average Annual Minimum Temperature (°F)	USDA Hardiness Zone
1	Below −50F	1
2	−50F to −45F	2a
	−45F to −40F	2b
	−40F to −35F	3a
3	−35F to −30F	3b
	−30F to −25F	4a
	−25F to −20F	4b
4	−20F to −15F	5a
	−15F to −10F	5b
5	−10F to −5F	6a
6	−5F to 0F	6b
	0F to 5F	7a
7	5F to 10F	7b
8	10F to 15F	8a
	15F to 20F	8b
9	20F to 25F	9a
	25F to 30F	9b
10	30F to 35F	10a
	35F to 40F	10b

PERENNIALS FOR SOUTHERN CALIFORNIA

A West Coast landscape architect, Philip E. Chandler, considers these the best perennials for Southern California. They do well in climates where summers are dry and winters are mild.

Achillea
Agapanthus
Anemone—Japanese
Anigozanthus flavidus
Aquilegia hybrids
Armeria hybrids
Aster × frikartii
Aurinia saxatilis
Bergenia ciliata, Bergenia crassifolia
Campanula species and cultivars
Catananche caerulea
Ceratostigma
Chrysanthemum frutescens
Chrysanthemum morifolium
Chyrsanthemum × superbum
Clivia miniata
Coreopsis auriculata 'Nana'
Coreopsis lanceolata
Coreopsis verticillata
Dianthus
Dietes (some formerly known as *Moraea*.)
Echinops
Erigeron
Eryngium
Felicia amelloides
Francoa ramosa
Gaillardia
Gaura lindheimeri
Gerbera
Geum
Gypsophila
Helianthus angustifolius
Hemerocallis
Heuchera
Iberis sempervirens
Iris (many)
Kniphofia
Limonium perezii
Linum
Liriope gigantea
Liriope muscari (if snails are controlled.)
Nepeta mussinii
Ophiopogon jaburan
Physostegia virginiana
Platycodon
Rudbeckia
Salvia farinacea
Scabiosa
Stokesia
Thalictrum dipterocarpum
Tulbaghia violacea
Veronica

PERENNIALS FOR HOT, DRY CLIMATES

The perennials listed here can survive a combination of sun, heat and drought. They can survive 2 months without water, in full sun with the temperature often exceeding 90F (32C), but only if the soil is deep and free from tree and shrub roots. Under such conditions, mulching is important. A little shade, without root competition, would extend the number of plants listed. Many more perennials are drought-tolerant where summers are comparatively cool.

Achillea
Armeria pseudarmeria
Asclepias tuberosa
Baptisia perfoliata
Callirhoe involucrata
Ceratostigma plumbaginoides
Chrysopsis mariana
Euphorbia myrsinites
Gaillardia (the dwarfs are less drought-tolerant.)
Gaura lindheimeri
Hemerocallis (not all modern hybrids as tough as older kinds.)
Hibiscus coccineus
Hibiscus moscheutos
Iris (many—see plant encyclopedia.)
Marrubium incanum
Oenothera (most)
Opuntia (all)
Phlox subulata
Platycodon
Santolina
Sedum (several kinds, especially *S. aizoon*. Most sedums are drought resistant, but not all are heat resistant.)
Verbascum
Verbena
Yucca (all)

Metric Chart

When You Know:	Multiply By	To Find
LENGTH		
inches	2.54	centimeters
feet	30.48	centimeters
yards	0.91	meters
TEMPERATURE		
Fahrenheit	0.56 (after subtracting 32)	Celsius
VOLUME		
quarts	0.95	liters
gallons	3.79	liters
WEIGHT		
ounces	28.35	grams
pounds	0.45	kilograms

PERENNIALS FOR THE COLDEST ZONES

Most perennials are hardy and a great many can be grown in Zones 1 and 2. Evaluations have been carried out and recommendations made by the University of Alberta, Edmonton, Alberta, Canada T6G 2E9, and by the University of Manitoba, Winnipeg, Manitoba, Canada R3T 2N2. The following are a few of the most popular:

Achillea
Anthemis tinctoria
Bergenia cordifolia
Campanula glomerata
Campanula persicifolia
Chrysanthemum leucanthemum (Shasta daisies—*C. × superbum* (*C. maximum*)—are not reliable.)
Delphinium
Dicentra eximia
Dicentra spectabilis
Doronicum caucasicum
Eryngium maritimum
Filipendula
Hemerocallis (not all)
Liatris
Ligularia
Lychnis chalcedonica
Lythrum
Paeonia
Papaver orientale (orange kinds reliable, others less so.)
Primula—many
Pulmonaria
Trollius
Yucca glauca

PERENNIALS FOR FLORIDA

The heat and humidity of Florida summers do not suit many perennials. The following have proved adaptable:

Asclepias tuberosa
Aster laevis
Canna
Chrysanthemum × superbum
Chrysanthemum morifolium ("mums")
Dietes
Gerbera
Hedychium
Hemerocallis (evergreen kinds excellent.)
Iris—Louisiana
Physostegia virginiana
Rudbeckia laciniata
Salvia azurea
Salvia farinacea
Stokesia laevis
Verbena

Acanthus mollis latifolius

ACANTHUS
Bear's-breech
Family: Acanthaceae

A. mollis latifolius (also sold as A. lusitanicus)
Zone 8, 3 to 4 feet, mauve, late spring or early summer ◑

This is a stately plant of shrublike proportions. Its large, glossy leaves are thought to have been the inspiration for the sculptured leaves on Corinthian capitals. Acanthus is sometimes scanty with its great, lupinelike spikes of purple-bracted flowers, especially in the moist shade it needs in the South. Sun and drier soil are satisfactory where summers are fairly cool.

In coastal regions of California, the roots spread rapidly underground if not confined. Slug and snail damage is readily apparent on the handsome leaves, so baiting should be a routine task if these pests are a problem.

Propagated by division, root cuttings or seed. Acanthus is not a plant to shift around, because every piece of fleshy root left in the ground grows into a new plant.

Other Species—*A. spinosus,* considered the finest species by many plantsmen, is not readily available in the U.S. The leaves are thistlelike—matte, deeply cut and spiny. The flowers are similar to *A. mollis* but more freely borne. The somewhat similar, but smaller *A. perringii,* 18 inches tall with gray-green leaves, is the best for small gardens.

ACHILLEA
Yarrow
Family: Compositae

Creamy-flowered *Achillea millefolium,* a naturalized European plant, is a common wildflower of field and roadside. Those recommended here have similar flat heads of yellow or pink flowers. Yarrows need sunshine and moderately fertile soil, free of tree and shrub roots. They are fairly drought resistant when established and most are self-supporting. Flowers are long-blooming and do not require daily dead-heading. They are excellent for cutting and drying. The finely cut leaves are attractive all season, and sometimes evergreen.

Yarrow is easily increased by division and any invasive tendencies can be curbed at the same time. If cut before the pollen forms, dried heads of yarrow keep their color. Cut later, they turn brown.

'Coronation Gold' (a hybrid)
Zone 3, 3 feet, yellow, summer ○

This is the most often seen of all garden yarrows. It has gray-green leaves and bright, mustard-yellow flowers on stems that seldom need staking.

A. filipendulina **'Gold Plate'**
Zone 3, 4 to 5 feet, yellow, summer ○

Similar to 'Coronation Gold' but taller, with larger flower heads—as much as 6 inches across—on taller stems. It needs support. 'Parker's Variety' is similar. Better as a specimen than massed.

Achillea 'Gold Plate' with orange *Helenium, Helianthus* and *Rudbeckia* 'Herbstsonne'

'Moonshine' (a hybrid)
Zone 3, 2 feet, yellow, summer ○

A lovely combination of bright yellow, fully opened flowers with paler, primrose-yellow buds and fading flowers. It has gray-green, feathery leaves. *A.* × *taygetea* is similar, the flower heads smaller.

A. millefolium 'Fire King'
Zone 2, 2 feet, bright pink, summer ○

This is the most popular of the pink-flowered selections of wild yarrow. Individual florets are larger than in the yellow yarrows, and conspicuously white-eyed. 'Rosea' is a paler pink. All have rapidly spreading mats of bright green, feathery leaves.

Other Species — *Achillea ptarmica,* (Zone 3, 2 feet, white), is invasive and sprawling. The allergy-prone should note its common name, sneezeweed. Double-flowered kinds such as 'The Pearl', with a mass of tiny white pompons, are popular with flower arrangers. *Achillea tomentosa* (Zone 3) is baby brother to the yellow-flowered yarrows. It makes dense, ground-hugging mats of ferny, green leaves topped by flat clusters of pale or bright yellow flowers.

Achillea 'Moonshine'

ACONITUM
Monkshood
Family: Ranunculaceae

A cautionary note: All parts of the plant are poisonous if eaten.

The hooded flowers of monkshood are usually blue, in upright spikes, but in some species they are more loosely clustered and white, shell-pink or yellow. The leaves are fingerlike.

Most are cold hardy, but they need rich, moist soil and do poorly in hot, dry or windy locations. In cooler regions they do well in sun or light shade. Clumps increase slowly and can be left undivided for many years. Propagated by division in fall—monkshood is not easily propagated from seed. The two described here have the best combination of good qualities among those available.

A. bicolor (A. × cammarum)
Zone 4, 3 to 5 feet, blue, summer ◑ ○

The name covers a hybrid group. 'Bressingham Spire' has violet-blue flowers on sturdy, 3-foot spikes. 'Bicolor', with two-tone blue-and-white flowers, is taller with looser flower clusters, so it may need staking.

A. carmichaelii (A. fischeri)
Zones 2 to 3, 3 feet, blue, late summer or early fall ◑ ○

Good, upright spikes with clear blue flowers and attractive dark, glossy leaves. In the Northeast, this is one of the last flowers of the season, combining well with *Sedum* 'Autumn Joy' and *Sanguisorba canadensis*.

Aconitum × *bicolor* 'Bicolor'

45

Aegopodium podagraria 'Variegatum'

AEGOPODIUM
Goutweed
Family: Umbelliferae

A. podagraria 'Variegatum'
Zone 3, 1 foot, foliage plant ◑ ●

Goutweed (*A. podagraria*) is one of the worst weeds known to man. The form 'Variegatum' is also one of the most beautiful foliage plants available to gardeners. It is often suggested that rampant plants be kept out of small gardens. We think the opposite. Let loose in a large garden, this plant will certainly become a nuisance, but the caring owner of a small garden can keep its exuberance curbed. It might be contained within a large sunken tub, or used to beautify a narrow strip between foundation shrubs and a solid concrete path. Unless bricks and paving stones are laid on concrete, goutweed will find its way along the cracks. It also makes a handsome container plant.

The flowers are white and of little ornamental value—cut them off to prevent self-sowing. Remove any unvariegated shoots that appear. Propagated by division.

AGAPANTHUS
Family: Alliaceae

In frost-free regions, evergreen kinds sold as *A. africanus, A. orientalis* or *A. umbellatus* are handsome year-round. In Zone 7 and below they are not hardy, but make excellent container plants and are often grown this way, being moved indoors for the winter. Use wood or plastic containers for these plants—the fleshy roots are so strong they can crack a clay pot.

Headbourne hybrids
Zone 8, 3 to 4 feet, blue, summer ○

Although so far little grown, these are superb perennials for the Southeast. The Headbourne hybrids have proved fully hardy, but *not* evergreen, in the Zone 8 Harper garden. Here, they are vigorous and healthy in low fertility soil, drought resistant, and floriferous for about a month during June and July. They do best in full sun—otherwise, the tall flower stalks lean toward the light.

The Headbourne hybrids are of two types. Those of the *A. orientalis* type have upwards of 100 flowers of Wedgewood-blue, in rounded umbels measuring 8 inches across. The strap-shaped leaves, 1-1/2 inches wide, try to be evergreen but collapse into tawdry mush with the coming of hard frost. For this reason, they should not be placed where conspicuous during the winter months.

The other type, seemingly derived from *A. campanulatus* or *A. inapertus,* is fully deciduous and the narrower leaves die away sooner and more neatly. The 5-inch umbels contain fewer flowers—61 in one head counted. The flowers are a darker blue, held on stalks that tend to angle at the top.

It may not be practical for nurseries to separate out the different kinds from seed-grown strain, so you'll probably have to take potluck. You can then propagate those you wish to increase by division of the rhizomatous roots. But there is no reason why agapanthus should not become as common in Southeastern gardens as they are in California.

Agapanthus; selection from Headbourne hybrids.

ALCHEMILLA
Lady's Mantle
Family: Rosaceae

Alchemillas are grown mostly for their pleated, gray-green rounded leaves, so beautiful when pearled with glistening dew drops. There are several smaller species, some with more-silvery leaves. All have similar requirements.

A. mollis (sometimes sold as *A. vulgaris*)
Zone 3, 12 to 18 inches, yellow, late spring or summer ◑ ○

This beautiful foliage plant is easy to grow—even weedy—in cool, moist climates, where the foam of tiny chartreuse flowers lasts for several weeks, starting in early summer. Light shade is preferred but full sun is tolerated in cooler climates. In hot or dry regions, a moist, rich soil and light shade are needed for good results—or even survival—and the flowering time is short. Propagated by division or seed.

Alchemilla mollis in flower with *Geranium psilostemon*.

ALLIUM
Ornamental Onion
Family: Alliaceae

Onions are bulbs, and although bulbs *are* perennials, they are usually treated separately. The three we recommend for the border are clump-forming and can be lifted, divided and replanted just like any other perennial. You need not search in the soil for scattered bulbs, as you must with daffodils. The species described here all flower for a long time and the foliage stays attractive throughout their long growing season. They smell oniony only if squeezed.

A. senescens
Zone 3, 1 to 2 feet, mauve or lilac, summer or fall ○ ◑

At least three distinct forms are grown. The first grows 1 foot tall, has bright green leaves similar to those of daffodils and lilac-pink flowers in umbels about 2 inches across. It is sterile—a distinct advantage that saves much work in weeding out unwanted seedlings. This form is sometimes called *A. montanum.* The second form is taller, with gray-green leaves and slightly larger heads of pale mauve flowers. Plants and seeds supplied as *A. narcissiflorum* invariably turn out to be this form of *A. senescens.* Both flower in summer. The third, *A. senescens glaucum,* is distinct. The mauve flowers, which come a month later, are held over low swirls of gray-green leaves. The dense clumps make an excellent border edging.

A. tuberosum (Garlic Chives)
Zone 4, 2 feet, white, late summer ○ ◑

White lacecap flowers bring a dainty touch to the border later in the season. You can, if you wish, snip the leaves for use in lieu of chives. A pretty and trouble-free plant, provided it is dead-headed before it goes to seed. If this is overlooked, seedlings will crop up all over the garden.

Other Species—Those described above are the best for borders. Runners-up include pink-flowered shooting stars (*A. pulchellum),* the similar, but shorter, yellow-flowered *A. flavum,* and *A. cernuum* with nodding umbels of mauve flowers. A lovely white form of *A. pulchellum* is also available.

Allium senescens with *Monarda* 'Croftway Pink', feverfew, *Chrysanthemum parthenium* and *Achillea ptarmica* 'The Pearl'.

Aloe striata with *Yucca elata.*

Society garlic *(Tulbaghia violacea)* is a somewhat similar "oniony" plant well suited to borders in the warmer regions. It is illustrated in the HPBook, *Bulbs: How to Select, Grow and Enjoy,* by George Harmon Scott. One attractive form has white-striped leaves.

ALOE
Family: Liliaceae

A. striata
Zone 9, 3 feet, orange, spring ○

For the varied climates of the United States, we need to rethink our notions of what a perennial is. Succulents, such as the aloes and similar agaves, are among the most valuable ornamental plants for frost-free regions, especially in the Southwest. *Aloe striata* hybrids are among the showiest. They have wide basal rosettes of evergreen leaves and branched clusters of orange or coral-pink flowers in spring. Aloes need well-drained soil. They usually require full sun, but light shade is appreciated in the hottest regions. They do not survive more than a light touch of frost, but they thrive in dry-summer, mild-winter climates where many a cold-hardy perennial would succumb to summer drought. Other aloe species have flowers of cream, yellow or red. For more information on aloes, agaves and other succulents, see HPBooks', *Plants for Dry Climates, How to Select, Grow and Enjoy,* by Mary Rose Duffield and Warren D. Jones.

AMSONIA
Blue Stars
Family: Apocynaceae

As an easy-care perennial, amsonia is hard to beat. Native to the East Coast, it is accustomed to sunny summers but tolerant of a little shade. The subtle color of the flowers has a cooling effect on adjacent brighter colors. Propagated by division, stem cuttings or seed.

A. tabernaemontana
Zone 3, 2 feet, blue, spring or early summer ○

Neat bushes of willowy stems and leaves, seldom marred by insects. Each stem is tipped with a loosely rounded cluster of soft, steely blue, star-shaped flowers. Clumps increase quickly enough to please the impatient, yet slowly enough that they seldom need dividing. Soil need be only moderately fertile. If, in richer soil or shade, growth gets loose and open, stems can be cut back by half after flowering to induce bushiness.

A. t. salicifolia has even narrower leaves. For the front of the border, seek out the plant known as *A. t. montana,* 15 inches tall with pearly blue flowers of a bit more substance.

A. ciliata
Zone 6, 2 feet, blue, spring or early summer ○

This species has narrow leaves—mere slivers—giving the plant a feathery appearance. Narrow leaves are a common characteristic of plants adapted to dry soil, and this species grows on sunny sand hills. Dry soil is by no means essential, but where such soil exists, *A. ciliata* is more likely to do well than *A. tabernaemontana.*

Amsonia tabernaemontana (top) and *A.t. montana* (bottom).

ANAPHALIS
Pearly Everlasting
Family: Compositae

A. triplinervis
Zone 3, 1 to 1-1/2 feet, white, summer or early fall ○ ◑

Closely related to pussy-toes (*Antennaria*), and similarly subtle, this plant never occasions ecstatic "oohs and aahs." But it does have an important quality—it will grow in soil too moist for other gray-foliage plants, though not in sopping-wet soils.

A. triplinervis has spear-shaped silvery leaves and heads of tiny, white "strawflowers." When used in substantial groupings, these plants play the role of supporting cast for brighter flowers. 'Summer Snow', a shorter cultivar, makes a hummock of gray leaves that is attractive throughout the growing season and excellent for border edging. This clump-forming species is not drought resistant. Propagated by division.

Other Species—Native to North America, pearly everlasting (*A. margaritacea*) has slender leaves that are gray and downy on the undersides, green or gray above. It grows 8 inches to 2 feet tall and does well in either moist or dry soil. *A. yedoensis* (*A. cinnamomea*), from the mountains of India, grows 2 feet tall, and also does well in moist or dry soil. Both species have spreading roots and can be invasive, but they would be a better choice for regions of summer drought than *A. triplinervis*. Both are hardy to Zone 3. Flowers and flowering times are similar to *A. triplinervis*.

Pearly everlastings are excellent for drying. They should not be cut while in bud because the stems are still immature and will not take water. Cut the flowers when the centers can be seen. Give flowers a drink of water before hanging them upside down in loose bunches.

Anaphalis triplinervis 'Summer Snow'

ANCHUSA
Italian Bugloss
Family: Boraginaceae

Note: For *Anchusa myosotidiflora*, see *Brunnera macrophylla*. This leaves only one available perennial species, *A. azurea*. The well-known Cape forget-me-not (*A. capensis*) is an annual or biennial.

A. azurea (A. italica)
Zone 3, 1-1/2 to 5 feet, blue, summer ○

Sheaves of brilliant-blue flowers and willingness to grow in most well-drained soils, in sun or light shade, compensate for some less appealing characteristics. Plants are of ungainly habit, the foliage is coarse and most cultivars require staking. Plants are short-lived, and like many short-lived plants, have a propensity to self-sow too abundantly.

Division will be needed after about 3 years, if the plant lives that long. Cultivars can be increased by division or from root cuttings. Among the best of them are the deep blue, 18-inch 'Little John', and gentian-blue, 3-foot 'Loddon Royalist'.

Anchusa azurea (A. italica)

Anemone vitifolia 'Robustissima'

ANEMONE
Family: Ranunculaceae

Most anemones do best in rich, moist soil with afternoon shade. *A. pulsatilla* is one exception.

A. pulsatilla (Pulsatilla vulgaris) (Pasqueflower)
Zone 5, 1 foot or less, pale purple, spring ○

Much of the beauty of this plant lies in the glistening silken hairs that coat young leaves, stems and emerging flower cups. Few perennials have prettier seed heads, resembling those of clematis. There is a white form of enchanting purity, and hybrids in varying shades of pink and purple.

In cool climates pasqueflower is drought resistant, but in hot regions it needs some water and shade during the summer. It is easily raised from seeds and color forms often come true from seed.

Special forms can be propagated by root cuttings or by careful division, best done early in the growing season. The best way to do this is to soak the soil around the plant then slide your fingers down into the root zone and feel for a rooted piece to break off. If the weather is hot or dry or the division has few roots, plant it in a pot and keep it shaded until established.

A. × hybrida (Japanese Anemone)
Zone 5, 1 to 5 feet, white or pink, late summer or fall ◑ ○

Under this name we include Japanese anemones sold as *A. japonica* and *A. hupehensis.* Japanese anemones dislike wind, summer drought and soil that gets soggy in winter.

Anemone pulsatilla (Pulsatilla vulgaris) with doronicums, violas, and forget-me-nots.

Under ideal conditions, most spread fairly fast. Propagated by root cuttings or careful division.

These are among the loveliest of late-season flowers. Cultivars about 3 feet in height include single white 'Alba', semidouble white 'Whirlwind', semidouble rosy pink 'Queen Charlotte' and semidouble bright pink 'Margarete'. Single silvery-pink 'September Charm' is somewhat shorter, and semidouble deep-pink 'Profusion' shorter still. The smallest is 15-inch, single rosy-pink 'September Sprite'. All will grow taller in rich, moist soil.

A. sylvestris (Snowdrop Anemone)
Zone 3, 1-1/2 feet, white, spring ◑

A dainty white colonizer for a woodland setting or partly shaded site. Satiny flowers of good size, sometimes nodding, over divided leaves. If you enjoy this European species, you might want to add the similar but taller North American species, *A. virginiana* and *A. cylindrica*. Both are known as thimbleweed, the common name referring to the shape of their seed heads.

A. vitifolia 'Robustissima' (Japanese Anemone)
Zone 4, 2 to 3 feet, pink, late summer ◑ ○

If growing conditions are less than ideal, the plant sold under this name (probably incorrectly) is the one to start with. It is the most tolerant of heat, cold, sun and drought. A typical Japanese anemone, with silvery pink single flowers, it blooms a month earlier than the others. It can be highly invasive, but it seems a pity to restrict such a willing and lovely plant—you may want to allow it to naturalize among shrubs in light shade. The same plant is sometimes sold as *A. hupehensis*.

Anemone × hybrida with Shasta daisies.

ANIGOZANTHOS
Kangaroo Paw
Family: Haemodoraceae

A. flavidus
Zone 9, 5 feet, green, yellow or orange, late spring to fall ○

This Australian plant needs well-drained soil and a sunny site. A single plant is usually enough, and more effective than a group. Forms with bright yellow or orange flowers are recommended because they are more striking than green-flowered forms. The branched flower spikes rise over clumps of evergreen, swordlike leaves. Flowering continues for several months during summer if the weather is not excessively hot, and if spent spikes are cut out. *A. manglesii* is a shorter plant with green-and-red flowers.

Anigozanthos flavidus

Anthemis tinctoria

ANTHEMIS
Golden Marguerite
Family: Compositae

A. tinctoria
Zone 3, 2 to 3 feet, yellow, summer ○

Golden marguerite—not to be confused with *Chrysanthemum frutescens,* also called marguerite—is a long-suffering, sun-loving perennial. It is able to grow in low fertility soil, withstand drought and survive neglect.

In rich soil and shade, golden marguerite grows leggy and flowers less abundantly. Still, it follows the general rule—the longer and hotter the summer, the greater the need for moisture-retentive soil and a little shade. The clumps of neat, gray-green, ferny leaves—evergreen in the warmer zones—get bare in the middle unless divided annually, but this is no great chore.

Golden marguerite has yellow, daisy-type flowers, up to 2 inches across. Punctilious dead-heading prevents unwanted inferior seedlings and may extend flowering into fall. Popular hybrids include pale yellow 'Moonlight', golden yellow 'Kelwayi', and 'E.C. Buxton', which ought to be pale lemon yellow but, as distributed by nurseries, is white-rayed as often as not. Propagated by division or stem cuttings. Seed of cultivars does not produce plants identical to the parent.

Other Species—*A. nobilis* is the carpeting chamomile, its name now changed to *Chamaemelum.* Silvery-leaved *A. biebersteinnii* is best suited to the rock garden, and so is *A. cupaniana* with its white flowers. *A. sancti-johannis* has vivid orange flowers. It was crossed with *A. tinctoria* to produce some of the hybrids.

AQUILEGIA
Columbine
Family: Ranunculaceae

Columbines are hardy perennials, flowering in spring or early summer. They range in height from under 3 inches to over 3 feet. They have smooth-textured green or gray-green ferny leaves, and flowers in colors that are soft or bright but never garish. The flower spurs differ in length—short or inward-curving and knuckly in the European "granny's bonnets" (*A. vulgaris),* occasionally non-existent, as in 'Clematiflora', or, in most North American species, long and elegant.

Many of the species self-sow abundantly. Hybrid strains are easily raised from seed and come surprisingly true, but they tend to be short-lived and need frequent replacement. Columbines have deep, thonglike roots and do not transplant easily except when very small. They often suffer leaf-miner damage, and while this does not kill nor even seem to weaken the plant, it badly disfigures the foliage.

Species
Zone 3, 1 to 3 feet, many colors, spring or early summer
◑ ○

Attractive species native to western North America, except where otherwise indicated, include the following:
- *A. caerulea,* blue-and-white, 1-1/2 to 3 feet.
- *A. canadensis* (East Coast), red-and-yellow, 1 to 2 feet, and the similar but taller *A. formosa* from the West Coast.

Aquilegia caerulea

- *A. chrysantha,* yellow, 3 feet.
- *A. vulgaris* from Europe, short-spurred, 2 to 3 feet, single or double, cloudy blues and dark pinks, occasionally white.

The yellow Texan *A. longissima* has the longest spurs, over 4 inches, but plants sold as this are often *A. chrysantha.*

The best of the columbines for the rock garden or front of the border are the 15-inch *A. flabellata* from Japan and its smaller dwarf forms, such as white-flowered 'Nana Alba' (under 1 foot), and the chunky, 6-inch blue-and-white columbine sold as *A. flabellata* 'Mini Star', which comes true from seed.

Hybrids
Zone 4, 1 to 3 feet, colors vary, spring ◑ ○

The many hybrid strains include such separate colors as 'Snow Queen', 'Crimson Star' and yellow 'Maxi Star'. The McKana hybrids, graceful plants with bright, clear colors, remain among the most popular of the mixed-color strains. But there are many other good ones, some with double flowers, some in pastel colors. The 'Biedermeier' strain is only 1 foot tall and stiff in habit, making it suitable for smaller gardens. 'Nora Barlow' is unusual, having double flowers of pink and red, tinged with green.

Aquilegia hybrids

ARABIS
Rockcress
Family: Cruciferae

Among the arabis species there are little gems for the rock garden, and sprawling, sometimes invasive plants for the rockery or front of the border. Most need porous soil and a generous ration of sun. Flowers are white or shades of pink and some species have variegated leaves. The two described here have special merit.

A. caucasica (A. albida) 'Flore Pleno'
Zone 3, to 1 foot, white, spring ○ ◑

Fancier flowers come and go while the old-fashioned double arabis, with its perky, pure white flowers and gray-felted leaves, never goes out of style. A foot tall when in bloom, it is otherwise low and sprawling.

The flowers are excellent for cutting. This species is enduring and endearing where summers are relatively cool. In hot, humid climates it may rot in summer, as do so many plants with woolly leaves. Propagated by division or cuttings. *A. procurrens,* described below, is reliably permanent under such conditions.

A. procurrens
Zone 4, to 1 foot, white, spring ○ ◑

This plant is not as well known as double arabis, but is becoming increasingly popular. It makes a tightknit mat of tiny, shining evergreen leaves, above which rise numerous sprays of single flowers. It spreads steadily outward without ever becoming a nuisance. It will grow in full sun and poor, dry soil, also in richer soil and light shade. *A. sturii* is much smaller and more compact, otherwise identical. Both are easily increased by slicing clumps into sections.

Arabis caucasica 'Flore Pleno'

Armeria plantaginea 'Royal Rose'

ARMERIA
Thrift, Sea Pink
Family: Plumbaginaceae

Thrifts do particularly well in seaside gardens. They dislike soggy soil, do best in sun and sandy soil. Both species listed here are propagated by seed—with mixed results—or by division of selected forms.

A. maritima
Zone 3, under 1 foot, pink or white, spring ○

So fine and dense are the leaves that clumps of *A. maritima* look like mossy cushions. When the cushions get ragged, it is time to divide the plants. Peak bloom comes in spring, but plants often flower sporadically through summer. Brick-red 'Corsica' makes a pleasant change from such vivid pinks as 'Vindictive', but it is not as hardy and will be killed or badly damaged at temperatures 5F (−15C) or below. If a border of mixed perennials is to be edged with thrift, the white 'Alba' would avoid color clashes.

A. pseudarmeria (A. formosa, A. latifolia, A. plantaginea)
Zone 6, 15 to 24 inches, pink or white, spring or early summer ○

Under these names will be found taller thrifts with tufts of wider leaves. They vary in hardiness, but most are not successful in zones colder than 6.

'Bees' Ruby' (Zone 5) has globular, carmine heads on tough, wiry 15-inch stalks. It was not named for the honeybee, but for an English seed grower whose slogan used to be "Bees' seeds that grow," so the apostrophe is in the right place. There are also scarce white forms of *A. pseudarmeria,* and a seed strain called Formosa hybrids that yields a proportion of terra-cotta colors along with the more-usual pink shades.

ARTEMISIA
Mugwort
Family: Compositae

These are daisy-family plants that don't look the least like daisies. With one exception, *A. lactiflora,* the flowers are dingy and unimpressive. These are foliage plants grown for their silvery leaves. Like most gray-foliage plants, the roots rot in wet soil and the foliage may rot in regions of high humidity. Gray-foliage plants combine enchantingly with white, pink, pale yellow, blue or lavender flowers. They also enhance brighter colors. They blend well with most other plants, but are sometimes wasted on each other.

The genus includes such invasive plants as mugwort *(A. vulgaris)* and Roman wormwood *(A. pontica).* Several artemisias are included in HPBooks', *Herbs, How to Select, Grow and Enjoy,* by Norma Jean Lathrop. These include three woody-based perennials of great ornamental value: *A. abrotanum,* or southernwood, (Zone 5), *A. absinthium,* or wormwood, of which 'Lambrook Silver' is a fine selection (Zone 3), and *A. arborescens,* among the prettiest of silvery plants, but frost-tender (Zone 9).

Artemisia 'Silver Mound'

The species listed below are the best of the hardy kinds. *A. lactiflora, A. ludoviciana* and *A. stellerana* are easily divided and the others can be divided with care. When striking cuttings of silvery plants, give them plenty of air, or they may rot.

A. canescens, A. splendens
Zone 4, 1 foot, gray foliage ○

These are two similar plants, often sold under the name "versicolor." They have lacy, cut-and-curled leaves and look like huddles of silvery wire netting.

A. lactiflora
Zone 3, 4 to 6 feet, cream, summer ○ ◑

This artemisia is grown for its sheaves of tiny creamy flowers on slightly arching but usually self-supporting stems. It is useful for lightening the effect of more brightly colored flowers. It has deeply notched, dark green leaves. It needs moister, richer soil than most artemisias and tolerates light shade.

A. ludoviciana (Silver King Artemisia)
Zone 4, 2 to 3-1/2 feet, gray foliage, deciduous ○

A variable species, *A. ludoviciana (A.l. gnaphalodes)* grows little more than 2 feet tall and has simple lance-shaped leaves, some with a notch or two. It is exceptionally hardy. 'Silver Queen' is almost identical, the leaves being a bit more heavily felted. *A. ludoviciana* 'Silver King' *(A. ludoviciana albula, A. albula),* slightly less hardy, is sometimes called ghost-plant. At maturity, it has a skeletal look, with slender, upright branched stems to about 3 feet in height. The upper leaves are lance-shaped and the lower ones sharply lobed.

All cultivars have running roots that can be controlled on heavy soils and in cool climates if regularly lifted and replanted. Gardeners in warm climates who plant them in sandy soil may come to regret it.

A. schmidtiana 'Silver Mound'
Zone 3, 1 foot, silvery foliage ○

A. schmidtiana is a Japanese species, 'Silver Mound' a cultivar of unknown origin. It is shorter than the species, but taller than *A.s.* 'Nana'. Where it does well, it is the pick of the artemisias, and among the best of all silvery-foliage plants. The hummocks of finely cut foliage form cloudlike mounds about 18 inches wide. Use 'Silver Mound' in quantity, in drifts or as a border edging. In all but the poorest soils, it grows taller than 1 foot if left alone, and clumps then open out in the middle. You can forestall this habit by trimming clumps back before they flower. The foliage may rot in hot, humid climates.

A. stellerana (Beach Wormwood)
Zone 2 to 3, 2 feet, silvery foliage ○

This is one of the toughest and most adaptable "grays," and often found on the seaward side of the dunes on Northeastern beaches. It is less inclined than most to rot in humid summers. Except when in flower, it is about 1 foot in height and, being rhizomatous, makes a good carpeting plant. It has white-felted, staghorn-lobed leaves. Its pale yellow flowers, appealing through a magnifying glass, are dingy in overall effect.

Artemisia ludoviciana

Artemisia lactiflora with *Hydrangea* 'Preziosa'. This is the only artemisia grown for its flowers.

ARUM
Family: Araceae

A. italicum 'Pictum' (Painted Arum)
Zone 6, 12 to 15 inches, foliage plant ◑ ●

This is the hardiest of the available arums. Do not confuse it with the less hardy *A. pictum*, which grows only in warm-winter regions. Arums are related to the calla lilies (*Zantedeschia*) and the flowers are somewhat similar but less ornamental. In this species, flowers are followed by stocky spikes of red fruits, striking when freely borne, but it is primarily a foliage plant and eagerly sought by flower arrangers. The new leaves emerge in fall and, if the weather is not too severe, remain attractive through to the following summer. If excessive winter cold does kill the leaves, new ones emerge the following spring. Each glossy, arrow-shaped leaf is bordered with darker green and patterned with white.

Painted arum thrives in light shade and humus-rich soil that stays moist while the plant is in growth. It goes dormant in summer and needs no watering then. Propagated by division of tubers while dormant, or by seed. *A. italicum* 'Marmoratum' has larger leaves and grows a little taller, but the leaves are only faintly marbled with white and much less attractive.

ARUNCUS
Goatsbeard
Family: Rosaceae

A. dioicus (A. sylvester)
Zone 3, 4 to 6 feet, cream, early summer ◑

Think of this hefty plant, which resembles a giant astilbe, as an herbaceous shrub. Give it plenty of space—plant about 4 feet apart. Try to plant it where you want it to begin with, because moving it later will be hard work. It can be divided, but this is seldom needed. Goatsbeard is *dioecious* (male and female flowers on separate plants). The male plants are more attractive, but this is somewhat academic, as nurseries do not identify and sell the plants by sex.

Goatsbeard usually looks best as a single specimen, placed away from other perennials. It requires light shade. In moisture-retentive soil or areas of heavy rainfall, it can stand some competition from tree roots, which helps to keep it compact. Staking isn't needed, but heavy rain when the plant is in flower will bear the great plumes to the ground. *A.d.* 'Kneiffii' is smaller (3 feet) with leaves cut into narrow segments.

If these are too big for your garden, look for the charming little *A. aethusifolius* from Korea, a small mound of bright green ferny leaves with 1-foot-tall spires of creamy flowers. It is just right for the edge of a woodland path or the front of a lightly shaded border. Known to be hardy to Zone 4, hardiness in colder zones not established.

Arum italicum 'Pictum' berries with lungwort *(Pulmonaria)* behind and periwinkle *(Vinca minor)* in front.

Arum italicum 'Pictum' leaves

ASCLEPIAS
Milkweed, Butterfly Weed
Family: Asclepiadaceae

There are many beautiful milkweeds native to North America, some of them deserving the name ''weed'' by reason of their invasiveness, others of localized adaptability. Blue butterfly weed is *Oxypetalum caeruleum,* a beautiful, short-lived but often self-sowing perennial in the warmest zones, elsewhere an annual. *Asclepias tuberosa* is the undisputed star of the genus.

A. tuberosa (Butterfly Weed)
Zone 3, 1-1/2 to 3 feet, orange, summer ○

Butterfly weed is a rugged, sun-loving plant. Few soils are too infertile for it, and few plants are more drought resistant. However, it is native to areas of fairly high rainfall with no dry season, so give it water if drought is prolonged.

Butterfly weed will not long survive soggy soil, nor can it compete with surface-rooting trees, but it can compete with grass and is a good choice for meadow gardens. Height varies. So does flowering time—anywhere from late spring to early fall, but usually during summer.

As sold, it is orange or sometimes coral in bud. Yellow forms are not uncommon in the wild, where it also approaches scarlet. A seed strain, 'Gay Butterflies', was bred to include red and yellow, but is mostly orange. Commercially, butterfly weed is grown from seed and is easily raised this way if seeds are sown in a sandy bed outdoors. Fine forms can be divided in spring—that this method seldom succeeds is a fallacy. If you dig deep when lifting clumps so you don't slice off the roots, you should have no problem. It is also possible, but not easy, to increase plants by root cuttings in spring. Butterfly weed makes an unusual and long-lasting cut flower.

In rich, moist soil, *Aruncus dioicus (A. sylvester)* will grow taller and looser than this specimen.

Asclepias tuberosa

Aster 'Alma Potschke', a compact hybrid Michaelmas daisy, with *Sedum alboroseum* 'Variegatum.

Aster × *frikartii* 'Wonder of Stafa' with the ferny, gray-green foliage of *Dicentra eximia*.

ASTER
Michaelmas Daisy, Hardy Aster
Family: Compositae

The semishrubby plant grown in California as "Aster fruticosus" is *Felicia fruticosa*. Aster 'Goldflake' is *Aster linosyris*, an English species. It is well adapted to hot summers, its clothing reduced to a minimum with mere slivers of gray-green leaves along wiry, unbranched stems tipped with a few rayless flowers that look like little yellow shaving brushes. For yellow-flowered Aster 'Golden Sunshine', see *Chrysopsis*. China-aster is *Callistephus*, an annual.

Wild asters are as plentiful in the U.S. as goldenrods—there is a bigeneric hybrid between the two, called × *Solidaster*. Both belong to the daisy family (Compositae). Daisies are so enduring and adaptable, and such efficient self-perpetuators, that they are often considered weeds. There are unappreciated beauties among them, some with flowers of a size to rival any in cultivation. The majority have graceful sprays of small flowers, usually white or lavender. *A. ericoides* is one of these.

If there is a wild aster you admire growing near your home, you can collect it without a qualm—daisies will be among the last to become endangered species. Just bear in mind that an aster able to colonize the roadside will be even more vigorous in good garden soil. Wild asters can be found in meadows, woods, swamps and marshes.

Garden hybrids generally dislike drought when growing, and soggy soil when dormant. They dislike intense heat and do best in cool, moist climates, where they need only moderately fertile soil. Most grow fast into sizeable clumps and get gappy in the middle unless divided every year or two. The foliage often mildews—this is more likely to occur in dry soil than in moist. All can be increased by division. Here are just a few of the best available:

A. × *alpellus* 'Triumph'
Zone 4, 1-1/2 feet, violet-blue, summer ○
Said to be a hybrid between the shorter, spring-flowering *A. alpinus*—best in the rock garden—and the hairy-leaved, drought-resistant, 2 foot, fall-flowering *A. amellus*. It combines the good qualities of the two. In cool regions, the yellow-disked flowers are often borne from summer to frost. It increases rapidly without being invasive.

A. × *frikartii*
Zone 5, 2 to 3 feet, lavender-blue, summer and fall ○
This is the name for hybrids between *A. amellus* and the 3-foot *A. thomsonii*. Only the cultivar 'Wonder of Stafa' is commonly available. It is considered by many the best of all asters. It needs winter protection in Zone 5 and will not survive wet soil while dormant. Evergreen boughs are better protection than mulch, because if buried deeply, the plants will rot. It begins to flower in summer and continues to hard frost. In regions of brilliant sunshine, the flower color shows best in light shade. Only fussbudgets feel compelled to stake the tumbling stems. This hybrid can be kept slightly more compact by cutting back the stems early in the season, but attempts to reduce it to graceless gobs of color will fail. Unlike most asters, *A. × frikartii* does not require frequent division. Propagated by division or stem cuttings.

58

A. tartaricus
Zone 3, 7 to 8 feet, aster blue, fall ○

This rugged Siberian species is perfectly suited to the long, dry, sunny fall of the Southeast, where it is often found in old gardens and frequently thought to be a native plant. It has both height and grace, with loose sprays of large, blue daisies in September and October, topping sturdy 7-foot stems that rise over clumps of leaves that are shaped like canoe paddles and sometimes as large. It will grow in soil extremes, from wet clay to dry sand. Unless the soil is moist and rich, plants stand upright without support. *A. tartaricus* spreads rapidly in light soil. It is one of those durable, shareable plants seldom bought but handed from neighbor to neighbor.

MICHAELMAS DAISIES
Zone 4, 6 inches to 6 feet, many colors, late summer and fall ○

These are the hardy asters with which most gardeners are familiar. Grouped under this name are selections and hybrids that at first involved mainly the New England aster, *A. novae-angliae,* and the shorter New York aster, *A. novi-belgii.* New England aster is a good choice for wet soils. 'Harrington's Pink', a 4-foot, bright, clear pink selection, needs less frequent division than most asters. It is also the best for cutting, despite its habit of closing its flowers at night. Many selections of New York aster were made in England, none lovelier than the 3- to 4-foot, soft blue 'Marie Ballard'.

An early English development was the crossing of *A. novi-belgii* with the bushy *A. dumosus* to produce dwarf hummocks solid with flower, of which white 'Niobe' is typical. American and Canadian hybridizers have also selected or bred for particular climates and purposes. A West Coast species, *A. subspicatus (A. douglasii)* was used in such compact Oregon-Pacific hybrids as 'Persian Rose' and 'White Fairy'. The beautiful, mounded 'Royal Opal' is one of the Royal Gem series developed in Canada for rust and mildew resistance and cushion habit.

Because hybrids vary in hardiness, it makes sense to buy plants from a grower in a region with a climate similar to your own. Heights now range from 6 inches to over 6 feet. Colors encompass white, pinks, blues and purples, with some, notably the compact 'Winston Churchill' and 3-foot 'Alma Potschke', close to red. There is no orange, and no bright yellow, but *A. ericoides* has yielded small-flowered, creamy-buff selections.

Michaelmas daisies bought at garden centers may have been sheared to make them compact. Many benefit from pinching tips early in the season, but whether you shear, how much and how late depends on the plant, your climate, the soil and what you are trying to achieve. Not everyone is entranced by compact lumps of color. Shearing retards bloom, which may be desirable in areas where the fall season is long, but not where frost comes early. Buy plants that approximate what you want, then experiment to find the amount of pinching or shearing that gives you exactly what you want. Taller kinds usually have to be staked, whether pinched or not.

Most Michaelmas daisies need frequent division—the compact mounding types to keep them healthy, some of the taller ones to control rapid spread. Small divisions from the outside of the clumps soon grow into large plants. The mounded kinds are susceptible to mildew in some regions.

Aster novae-angliae 'Harrington's Pink'

Aster tartaricus

Astilbe chinensis 'Pumila'

ASTILBE
Family: Saxifragaceae

Note: Astilbes are sometimes called Spirea in old books and catalogs.

Astilbes dislike soils that are poor, dry, alkaline or soggy during the dormant season. They also dislike extremely hot sun and drying winds. Other than these few negative factors, astilbes are long-lived, low-maintenance plants when located in lightly shaded parts of the garden. They are beautiful perennials with upright or arching plumes in soft or vivid shades of pink, red and magenta, also white and cream. The ferny foliage, dark or red-tinted in most red-flowered kinds, is attractive all season in cool regions. In hot regions, it looks shabby by midsummer—less conspicuously so if tucked in bays between shrubs, rather than featured in the border. Though astilbe is not entirely overlooked by slugs and snails, damage is less apparent than on such undivided leaves as those of hostas.

Astilbes yield so many divisions that there's soon enough for the groupings of five or more in which most look best. Some taller ones look best alone. Division is not needed for the well-being of the plants more often than every third year. Even in rich, moist soil, plants respond to a handful of slow-release fertilizer scattered around the clump in spring, or a sprinkling of a quicker-acting 5-10-5 fertilizer, repeated later in the season. Flowering is not prolonged by dead-heading, but with a careful choice of varieties, you can have bloom for most of summer in the cooler regions.

Midgets for the rock garden include *A. × crispa, A. glaberrima (A. japonica), A. simplicifolia*, 12- to 15-inch white-flowered *A. thunbergii* 'Fujisanensis', and, one of the most robust, 9-inch 'William Buchanan', with red-tinted, finely dissected leaves and creamy flowers. Some of the daintiest hybrids of *A. simplicifolia* are regrettably scarce, but the arching characteristic is present in a few available hybrids. All take light shade.

The 4- to 6-foot *A. biternata* is an attractive species from the wooded mountains of the Southeast, available in wildflower nurseries. It is called false goatsbeard because it has white plumes resembling those of goatsbeard, *Aruncus dioicus*.

The following astilbes are the most important border plants:

A. × arendsii
Zone 4, 18 inches to 4 feet, many colors, early to late summer ◐

The popular hybrids are usually grouped under *A. × arendsii,* though not all of them belong there. Upwards of 20 are readily available. Our favorites might not be yours, but a cross-section might include: 'Europa', 2 feet, pale pink, early summer; 'Fanal', 2 feet, dark red; 'Pink Curtsey', 18 inches, arching plumes of soft pink; 'White Gloria', 2 feet, dense plumes of creamy white; 'Bridal Veil', 2-1/2 feet, graceful sprays of pure white. These look best when planted in groups. 'Erica', 3 feet, with erect spikes of clear pink, could stand alone. The 4-foot 'Professor van der Wielen', with arching white plumes, calls for specimen status, as does the slightly shorter, deep coral-pink 'Ostrich Plume' ('Straussenfeder').

Astilbe 'Fanal'

A. chinensis 'Pumila'
Zone 4, 8 to 12 inches, mauvish pink, late summer ◑

If you are uncertain whether astilbes will do well for you, use this one as your "canary-down-the-mine-shaft." It tolerates drier soil than most. It also differs in that it is densely stoloniferous, making it a first-rate edging plant, well able to fight off encroaching lawn grasses. Flower spikes are stiffly upright and abundantly borne.

Pink-flowered, 15- to 18-inch *A. chinensis* 'Finale' (don't confuse it with red 'Fanal') more nearly resembles the *A. × arendsii* hybrids. It has fluffier flowers, and greater susceptibility to drought than 'Pumila'. It is one of the most delicately lovely of those with upright plumes and, with *A. tacquetii* 'Superba', the latest to flower.

A. tacquetii 'Superba'
Zone 4, 3 to 4 feet, magenta, summer ◑

A knockout with its steeples of vibrant color held well aloft on sturdy stems. It is especially attractive when planted with late-blooming hostas. Fairly heat and drought resistant, but less so than *A. chinensis* 'Pumila'.

AURINIA AND ALYSSUM
Basket-of-gold
Family: Cruciferae

Aurinia saxatilis (Alyssum saxatile)
Zone 3, 6 to 12 inches, yellow, spring ○

This popular plant needs sharply drained soil and is seen at its best hanging over the edge of a raised bed. Its life can be prolonged by cutting plants back by about a third after flowering. It tends to rot in humid climates. The species, the smaller 'Compacta' and double-flowered 'Plena', are brilliant daffodil-yellow. 'Citrina' is a paler lemon-yellow and 'Dudley Neville', of which there is a variegated form, is buff or pale apricot. These are not easily divided, but cuttings root readily. Mountain-gold, *Alyssum montanum,* is a similar plant—smaller and more compact but equally bright and floriferous. It is slightly fragrant and often longer-lived. Another plant commonly referred to as alyssum or sweet alyssum, is *Lobularia maritima,* an annual.

Astilbe taquetii 'Superba'

Aurinia saxatilis, better known as *Alyssum saxatile,* grows well in cracks between paving or garden walls.

Baptisia australis

Baptisia perfoliata

BAPTISIA
Wild Indigo
Family: Leguminosae

Pea-family plants are noted for their ability to grow in low-fertility soil. Baptisia is no exception. There are species and hybrids with flowers of white *(B. alba, B. leucantha)*, buff, yellow *(B. tinctoria)*, blue *(B. australis)*, and violet. *B. tinctoria* (Zone 5, 3 to 4 feet) does well in the deep South. In the wild, it often grows in dry, open woods, but it usually does best in sun. The only well-known species is *B. australis*. With flower arrangers in mind, we describe one other little-known but available species, *B. perfoliata*.

B. australis (Blue Indigo)
Zone 3, 4 to 6 feet, blue, early summer ○ ◑

In the wild, this species is often found in thin woods and alongside streams, but it seems to do best in full sun when in a garden environment. Smooth, gray-green cloverlike leaves are spaced along branched stems. The loosely lupinelike spires of flowers are violet-blue, followed by inflated pods. Clumps need no dividing and should be given about 3 feet of space. One clump is enough for all but large borders. Self-sown seedlings will appear, which are easily transplanted while small. Blue indigo combines well with peonies, which bloom at the same time.

B. perfoliata
Zone 7 (see note below), yellow, early summer ○ ◑

This species tends to form long, sparingly branched stems that arch out sideways, so a clump may be only 2 feet high but 5 feet wide. Native to sand hills of the Southeast, it is drought resistant. It is picked and sold, fresh or dried, as "eucalyptus," which it closely resembles. A dozen or more 2-inch gray-green leathery leaves, rounded and dished, are threaded at even intervals along supple stems. Such leaves are called *perfoliate leaves*. Little yellow flowers in the leaf axils look as if they were sitting on a plate, an impression even more pronounced when they turn to pods resembling small, green gooseberries.

Note: *B. perfoliata* has only recently become commercially available and has not been adequately tested for hardiness in colder zones than 7.

BEGONIA
Hardy Begonia
Family: Begoniaceae

B. grandis (B. evansiana)
Zone 6, 2 feet, pink, late summer or fall ◑ ●

This relatively hardy member of a mainly tropical genus mixes better with shrubs than with other perennials in a border. In the Southeast, it grows well in humus-rich, moist soil in dappled shade, or in east-facing bays between such evergreens as azaleas and camellias. In cooler regions, it can stand more sun. At its hardiness limit, give it the protection of winter mulch.

Loose sprays of candy-pink flowers—white in variety 'Alba'—come late in the season. The pink ovaries of female flowers remain attractive long after the flowers are spent. The large, angel-wing leaves are attractive all seasons, especially when lit from behind to reveal the ruby-red veining. Little bulbils form in the leaf axils, drop to the ground, and emerge as new plantlets around the parent clump the following spring, growing fast to flowering size. The bulbils are the easiest means of propagation. This species does equally well in alkaline or acid soil. Needs no dividing or staking.

Begonia grandis (B. evansiana)

BELAMCANDA
Blackberry Lily
Family: Iridaceae

B. chinensis
Zone 5, 2 to 4 feet, orange, summer ○ ◑

In full sun and low-fertility soil that is on the dry side, *B. chinensis* grows to a height of about 2 feet. In rich, moisture-retentive soil, it grows twice as tall and luxuriant. A modicum of shade is helpful in hot regions. Candelabras of apricot-colored, red-speckled flowers are held above fans of sword-shaped leaves. Flowers last about 2 weeks in hot weather, longer when it is cool. The flowers wither neatly, twisting into a tight spiral, much as one might twist up a paper bag. They are followed by round, green seed pods, opening on blackberrylike clusters of glistening black seeds, effective for weeks, either on the plant or cut. Seedlings spring up in abundance, and it is easier to let these replace the parent after a year or two than to attempt division.

B.c. 'Freckle Face' is shorter and paler than the species. *B. flabellata*—sold as 'Hello Yellow'—is shorter still, little more than 1 foot tall. It has yellow, unspeckled flowers and grayish leaves in less flattened fans. The Vesper iris, *Iris (Pardanthopsis) dichotoma*, flowers at the same time as blackberry lily, and has been crossed with it to produce the multi-colored × *Pardancanda norrisii* hybrids. All of the above are self-supporting and free of pests or diseases.

BERGENIA
(Formerly called Saxifraga or Megasea)
Family: Saxifragaceae

These are stalwart plants, with rounded or oval leathery leaves to 1 foot across, often red-tinted. They have substantial trusses of white, pink or magenta flowers, often starting to open down among the leaves on stalks that elongate to 1 foot or more. All but *B. ciliata* are evergreen. They can be grown almost anywhere—between shrubs, at the front of borders, in containers—and in any soil, including those high in lime content. However, they'll do best if planted in humus-rich soil, watered during periods of drought and, in most regions, given light shade. In hot regions they may not flower. The leaves provide a perfect dark, damp hiding place for slugs, and also a good place to hide slug bait out of sight of pets.

Divide clumps when they get gappy, severing the thick rhizomelike stem with a knife and planting the divisions well down in the ground.

B. purpurascens (B. beesiana) is one of the prettiest bergenias, with relatively large, reddish-purple flowers held on tall stalks, and bronze-flushed leaves. Unfortunately, it is scarce, and perhaps not as hardy as

Belamcanda chinensis

Bergenia cordifolia

some of the others. Those described below are readily available.

B. ciliata
Zone 5, 1 foot, white to pinkish, late winter or spring ◖○

Roots are hardy to Zone 5, but top growth is frost damaged in Zone 8 and usually deciduous in zones colder than 8. This species is popular in the mild-winter regions of California. Short, bristly hairs on the leaf surfaces glisten in the sun. In *B. ciliata ligulata,* only the leaf edges are hairy. Flowers are white with a reddish tinge. 'Silberlicht' ('Silver Light') is a similar, slightly later flowering, white-flowered hybrid.

B. cordifolia
Zone 2, 18 inches, pink, spring ◖○

This species is the most common one on the East Coast. It has rounded to oval glossy leaves up to 1 foot across, and deep pink flowers. *B.c. purpurea* ('Purpurea') has darker pink flowers and markedly purple-flushed leaves. It is the tallest bergenia.

B. crassifolia
Zone 2, 1 foot, pink, spring ◖○

Popular on the West Coast. Similar to *B. cordifolia* but smaller leaves, oval in shape. Sometimes flowers in summer or fall, but mainly spring. Flower color varies among plants sold under this name—some are probably hybrids.

Hybrids

A few of the many fine hybrids are: 'Abendglut' ('Evening Glow'), chunky clusters of deep magenta flowers, some semidouble; 'Morgenrote' ('Morning Blush'), deep pink flowers on tall stems; 'Silberlicht' ('Silver Light'), mentioned under *B. ciliata,* and 'Sunningdale', red-stemmed, carmine flowers, leaves mahogany-tinted in winter.

BOLTONIA
Family: Compositae

B. asteroides 'Snowbank'
Zone 3, 4 feet, white, fall ○

'Snowbank' looks like a Michaelmas daisy (aster) and flowers at the same time. The species is white to pale lilac, can attain 7 feet, spreads fast and needs stout staking. The cultivar 'Snowbank' is a manageable 4 feet, usually self-supporting, bears showers of white daisies on branching sprays, dense enough for impact, loose enough for grace. The sparse, grayish foliage is less susceptible to mildew than that of Michaelmas daisies, and plants are more tolerant of extreme heat and humidity. 'Snowbank' spreads rapidly in moist, sandy soil, but is not a nuisance.

Boltonia asteroides 'Snowbank' with a selected form of *Aster novae-angliae.*

BRUNNERA
Family: Boraginaceae

B. macrophylla
Zone 3, 1-1/2 feet, blue, spring ◑

This plant is usually listed in catalogs as *Anchusa myosotidiflora,* its former name. The name means "the anchusa with forget-me-not flowers," and this is in effect a perennial forget-me-not. When daffodils and forsythias are in bloom, brunnera sends forth loose sprays of bright blue flowers that rise over rough, heart-shaped leaves which continue to grow in size.

Brunnera tolerates dry shade, and one of the best places for it is naturalized among shrubs. This makes an asset of the many self-sown seedlings, which can be a nuisance if in the border. The thonglike roots go deep, so seedlings cannot be yanked out with a flick of the wrist while passing by.

The blue of the flowers softens the effect of orange geums, but this combination works only if the soil is moderately moist, as required by geums. 'Hadspen Cream' and 'Variegata', cultivars of brunnera, have leaves with a creamy variegation that are enchanting with the blue flowers. These cultivars are not as easy to grow well as others. 'Langtrees', with spotted leaves, is a promising recent introduction.

Note: The borage family is rich in plants with bright blue flowers—*Cynoglossum nervosum* (Hound's-tongue) is one of these. Flowers are the same brilliant blue as brunnera, but larger. Unlike brunnera, the leaves are narrow, and this Himalayan plant needs sun. Plants grow 2 feet tall and flowers bloom during summer. Soil should be only moderately fertile; otherwise, plants get floppy. Western Hound's-tongue (*C. grande*) is native to the Western coastal ranges and lower slopes of the Sierra Nevada. It adapts to summer drought by going dormant. It needs a cool, shaded site. *C. amabile,* or Chinese forget-me-not, is an annual, biennial or short-lived perennial.

Brunnera macrophylla

Callirhoe involucrata

CALLIRHOE
Wine-cups, Poppy Mallow
Malvaceae

C. involucrata
Zone 3, prostrate, red-purple, summer ○

Checked against a color chart, the flowers are unequivocally purple, but what the eye perceives is described by its folk name, *wine-cups*. Flowers are cup-shaped, the glowing color of port wine held to the light. If you've been disillusioned by the words, *blooms all summer,* try this plant. From a central crown of much-cut leaves, prostrate stems trail out as much as 3 feet, flowering as they go and impervious to heat. Obviously not a plant to be hidden in the border, but rewarding where a path or rock allows it to bask in the sun.

The carrotlike root delves deep for moisture, so watering is necessary only in periods of prolonged drought. Seed is scattered from flattened, round receptacles, called *cheeses* by children where the plant grows wild. The tiny seedlings can be transplanted during cool weather. Larger plants may not survive transplanting, and division is never needed. The trailing stems do not, as one might expect, send down roots as they go. However, 4-inch lengths of stem cut below a node, taken in early summer, will root quickly if placed in a frame or propagator. Otherwise, it is easily raised from seed. Evergreen Zone 8 and warmer.

Caltha palustris 'Flore Pleno'

CALTHA
Marsh Marigold, Kingcup
Family: Ranunculaceae

C. palustris
Zone 3, 1 to 2 feet, yellow, spring ○ ◑

In some parts of the country this is also, confusingly, called cowslip, a name that belongs to *Primula veris*. Marsh marigold must have abundant moisture all year and grows best in boggy soil or shallow water at the edge of a garden pond or stream. The double form, 'Flore Pleno', is the most popular for the edges of garden ponds and streams. Usually propagated by division.

CAMPANULA
Bellflower
Family: Campanulaceae

The biennial Canterbury-bells *(C. medium)* is probably the best known campanula. There are many rock-garden gems and, at the other extreme, the invasive *C. rapunculoides*—attractive, but suitable only for wild places. Not all campanulas have campanulate (bell-shaped) flowers—some are starry and upward-facing.

Campanulas—otherwise trouble free—are magnets for slugs and snails, so it's best to use bait on a routine basis. Most campanulas do well in moderately fertile, moist but well-drained soil. Light shade is recommended where summer temperatures reach 90F (32C) and above. Elsewhere campanulas can take full sun. Campanulas need only be divided every third or fourth year to keep them

Campanula carpatica

under control. Species can be grown from seed, named kinds propagated by division or cuttings.

Adenophora (ladybells), with its spikes of dark blue bells, is a plant commonly found in older gardens and often mistaken for a bellflower. It is slow to establish but when it is, it is enduring and best left alone.

The campanulas described below are the pick of available border kinds:

C. carpatica
Zone 3, under 1 foot, blue or white, late spring or early summer ○ ◑

If protected against slugs, this is an excellent edging plant, often short-lived but quickly raised from seeds. Cold seldom kills it, but drought or drowning will. Delicate bowl-shaped flowers are held upright on stems about 6 inches tall. Colors include white and several shades of blue.

C. glomerata
Zone 2 to 3, 1 to 3 feet, violet or white, early summer ○ ◑

Large, loose knobs of upward-facing, bell-shaped flowers with pointed petals are borne on the stiff stems of stoloniferous clumps. There are often 12 to a cluster—an old folk name is "twelve apostles." Height varies, from tiny *C.g. acaulis* of rock garden size to the vigorous, dark violet 'Superba', at 3 feet tall. 'Joan Elliott' is a fairly compact 18-inch plant with violet flowers, 'Schneekrone' ('Crown of Snow') a 2-foot plant with white flowers. *C. glomerata* is a plebian but stalwart plant that does well in most soils, including wet ones.

C. persicifolia (Peach-leaved Bellflower)
Zone 3, 2 to 3-1/2 feet, blue or white, early summer ○ ◑

The pick of the bellflowers, combining grace with lustiness. Cup-shaped flowers face outward along unbranched stems rising over rapidly spreading mats of bright green, lance-shaped leaves. It is evergreen in the milder regions. In batches of mixed seedlings, those with white flowers can be recognized before they flower by the paler green of their leaves. Sun tolerant, but welcoming light shade, the single-flowered blues and whites are enchanting among well-spaced, white-trunked birches. Naturalizes by root spread and seed, but not a nuisance. Flowers are white to violet, single or semidouble and of varying height. The single, blue 'Telham Beauty' has the largest flowers.

Other Species—Campanulas for the front of the border include *C. garganica* (6 inches, Zone 5), *C. portenschlagiana (C. muralis)* (Zone 4) and *C. poscharskyana* (Zone 3). *C. portenschlagiana* forms clumps that trickle steadily outward, but remain controllable. *C. poscharskyana* has long, trailing stems of starry flowers and invasive threadlike stoloniferous roots.

Scotch bluebell, or English harebell, *C. rotundifolia* (Zone 2, 1 to 2 feet), also grows wild in other countries, including North America. The compact form called 'Olympica' comes from Washington's Olympic mountains.

Only the basal leaves of harebells are rotund, and these die away early. Stem leaves are linear, giving the plant a deceptively fragile look, an impression reinforced by the dainty blue—rarely white—thimble-shaped flowers. "Warn that it is a terrible weed," says a Seattle friend. Sometimes it is and sometimes it isn't. In hot climates, it is fugitive, disappearing from where it was put, to turn up

Campanula glomerata 'Superba'

Campanula persicifolia comes in white (shown) and several shades of blue.

Catananche caerulea

somewhere else, or not at all. Check locally before deciding whether this might be friend or foe.

A taller campanula of regrettable scarcity is *C. lactiflora*. Masses of pale lilac flowers weigh down the 4-foot stems, which require support. Named cultivars include pale, violet-blue 'Prichard's Variety', pale pink, 18-inch 'Loddon Anna' and pale blue, 18-inch 'Pouffe', shaped as the name suggests.

For naturalizing in light shade, try the spiky, 3- to 4-foot, *C. latifolia*. It is also suitable for sunny areas. It is usually self-supporting and a generous self-seeder. Violet-blue 'Brantwood' is a good selection of this. 'Alba' is a sparkling white.

CATANANCHE
Cupid's-dart
Family: Compositae

C. caerulea
Zone 4, 18 inches, blue or white, summer ○

A prairie-type plant for full sun, its cornflowerlike blooms are the equal of strawflowers for cutting and drying. A "bit player" for border purposes, it flowers on wiry stems over narrow, gray-green leaves. Its effect is insubstantial unless many plants are grouped. Cupid's-dart is drought-resistant, and may not survive the winter if soil is too damp. It is more reliable in humus-enriched sand, but seldom long-lived. Annual spring division helps prolong its life. The range of flower colors—white and varied soft blues—is similar to that of *Stokesia laevis.* Except for drying, or in dry soil, *S. laevis* is usually the better plant.

CENTAUREA
Knapweed
Family: Compositae

Knapweeds are numerous and include two popular annuals—cornflower or bachelor's-button *(C. cyanus)*, and sweet-sultan *(C. moschata)*. Gray-leaved *C. cineraria,* Zone 4, will be found in catalogs among the dusty-millers. It is a perennial but, except in frost-free areas, usually grown as an annual. It is often called *C. gymnocarpa*.

Perennial knapweeds are not a distinguished group. Many are weedy: The great knapweed *(C. scabiosa)* of Europe has naturalized in the eastern U.S. Knapweeds are not fussy about soil, as long as it is neither bone dry nor sopping wet. They are easily propagated by division.

C. hypoleuca
Zone 3, 2 to 3 feet, bright pink, summer ○

The best of the knapweeds grown for their flowers is *C. hypoleuca* 'John Coutts', usually called *C. dealbata* in catalogs. It is a 2-foot plant of fairly rapid spread. The lobed leaves are green on top and gray underneath. It has white-eyed fringed flowers of deep rosy purple, 2 inches or more across, one to each stiff, self-supporting stalk. This knapweed flowers over a long period. The silvery seed heads are also attractive.

Centaurea hypoleuca 'John Coutts', usually called *Centaurea dealbata* 'John Coutts'.

C. macrocephala
Zone 2 to 3, 3 to 4 feet, yellow, summer ○

This robust yellow thistle is a change from yellow daisies, but one plant is probably enough. The flowers measure 3 inches across and are attractive to butterflies. It flowers for only 2 to 3 weeks. Good for drying.

C. montana (Mountain Bluet)
Zone 2 to 3, 2 feet, blue, summer ○

This species has few-rayed, spidery flowers for several weeks, starting late spring or early summer. Only a few flowers open at a time, so it never makes a great impact. The color is the main attraction—a deep cornflower-blue, touched with dark red in the center. It can be invasive.

CENTRANTHUS
Red Valerian
Family: Valerianaceae

C. ruber (Kentranthus ruber)
Zone 4, 2 to 3 feet, pink, white, reddish, flowering time varies ○

This plant is often listed as *Valeriana ruber*. Smooth, gray-green leaves are spear to deltoid shaped. Flowers are in dome-shaped terminal clusters with smaller axillary ones below. Flower color may be white, light pink, a color approaching red ('Atrococcinea'), or a rosy pink with a hint of coral. The rosy pink variety is attractive by itself, but difficult to combine with other colors. You might try it against a background of purple-leaved barberry.

Most plants sold are seed-grown, which means you may have little choice in the colors you get—when you do get the color you like, increase it by basal cuttings. Centranthus can be grown in most soils, as long as soil isn't too wet. Flowering time depends on climate. Where centranthus blooms early, subsequent shearing often results in a second crop. It does best in cool-summer regions, where it self-sows prolifically. Propagated by seed or basal cuttings.

Centranthus ruber in two shades of pink, with hardy asters.

CERATOSTIGMA
Blue Plumbago
Family: Plumbaginaceae

C. plumbaginoides (Plumbago larpentiae in catalogs)
Zone 5 with winter protection, 1 foot, blue, summer or fall ○

Blue plumbago does best in full sun. It tolerates light shade but can't compete with tree roots. Where soil texture is loose and the growing season long, its rapid, stoloniferous spread puts it in the ground-cover category. It does best in light, moderately fertile soil. It emerges in late spring and makes an excellent overplanting for early crocuses.

Blue plumbago has neat, diamond-shaped leaves that alternate along rough, tough, slightly zig-zag stems tipped with clusters of bright blue flowers that open a few at a time. The leaves turn reddish tints with the first light frosts. Where it is marginally hardy, consider planting

Ceratostigma plumbaginoides

Chelone lyonii

plumbago near a stone walk or paving slab under which the roots can creep. This will help protect the roots from frost and give the plant a better chance of survival.

C. willmottianum (Chinese Plumbago)
Zone 8, 3 feet, blue, late summer or fall ○
This species needs the same growing conditions—light soil and sun—and bears similar flowers. The leaves differ only in that they are coarsely whiskered, which seems to give the plant an extra measure of drought resistance. It is a deciduous shrub, staying neatly within its dense, arching clump. You can treat it as a perennial and cut the stems back to the ground in spring. *C. griffithii* is similar but frost tender.

CHELONE
Turtlehead, Snakehead
Family: Scrophulariaceae

Turtleheads need moist, even boggy, humus-rich soil, in sun or light shade. Under these conditions, they are easy-care plants, increasing fairly fast without being invasive. No staking should be needed—stems that straggle suggest too much shade, or too much fertilizer.

C. lyonii
Zone 3, 3 feet, pink, late summer or early fall ◑ ○
This is the most common garden species. It has glossy, dark green, saw-edged leaves, oval in shape and pointed at the tip. Leaves are attached to the stem on 1-inch stalks. The rosy pink flowers form short spikes at the stem tips, and they do indeed resemble the head of a turtle with mouth agape. If a shorter, bushier plant is desired, turtle-heads respond well to tip-pinching when about 6 inches tall.

Red turtlehead *(C. obliqua)* is similar to *C. lyonii,* but has slightly narrower leaves tapering to shorter stalks. It is possibly less hardy than *C. lyonii.* White turtlehead *(Chelone glabra)* has white or pale pink flowers and is hardy to Zone 3. All are native to the eastern United States. The plant often called *Chelone barbata* is *Penstemon barbatus.*

CHRYSANTHEMUM
Family: Compositae

Note: Because this is such a large genus, with well over 100 species, only the best border plants are described here, starting with the "Mums."

GARDEN CHRYSANTHEMUMS ○
Garden chrysanthemums, or "mums" are often grouped under C. × *morifolium.* Most are hardy to Zone 5, the hardiest kinds to Zone 4 with winter protection.

"Mums" are at their best where falls are long and warm. They are all easy to grow, and they flower for many weeks. Northern gardeners should choose those bred for hardiness. The Cheyenne series, developed by the USDA at Cheyenne, Wyoming, is one such group.

Chrysanthemum flowers may measure less than 1 inch across, or more than 6 inches. They come in all colors but blue. Flower forms include single, double, pompons and such fancy-petalled kinds as spoons, quills and spiders. They vary in height and flowering time. Those that flower early are best for the North, and those that flower late are best for the South.

Hobbyists devote daily care to spraying, fertilizing, watering, staking and disbudding the giant-flowered exhibition kinds, or to pinching and training the charming small-flowered cascades. The latter are grown in pots and trained into waterfalls of color. At the other extreme are those who buy the finished product in fall, enjoy the plant while the flowers last and then discard it. Fall is an acceptable planting time in warm climates, but in cold climates the odds are against survival if they're planted at this time.

Those requiring least work are the low-growing "cushion mums," averaging 15 inches in height. You'll need to watch them for mildew, aphids and other pests, and water them during dry weather. Otherwise, the only routine attention needed is division every second spring, replanting single rooted shoots from the outside of the clump, discarding the center. North of Zone 6, a winter cover of evergreen boughs increases their chance of survival.

If you buy "mums" by mail, you'll probably receive rooted cuttings. Don't feel cheated, because that is a good size. Plant them 18 inches apart with roots just below the surface, in deep, humus-rich soil. By fall they'll be big, flowering plants. They are greenhouse grown so don't put them out if frost is still expected. Mid-May is about the earliest safe planting time in the Midwest. In the Northeast, June 1 is safer.

In the South, they should be planted much sooner or they may scorch in early hot weather. For maximum bushiness, all but the cushion types are pinched as shown in the drawing below, nipping out the soft growing tip of each shoot when it reaches 4 to 6 inches in length. This can be tedious if you've got a lot of plants. The results will be almost as good if you top the plants with garden shears. In the North, stop pinching plants in early July or they may not flower before the first frost. In the South, pinching can go on a bit longer. All but the cushion kinds need dividing every spring for best results.

A fine display of garden "mums" in a Virginia garden in November.

"Mums" do well in containers. Behind is *Sedum* 'Autumn Joy', the flowers dead but still attractive.

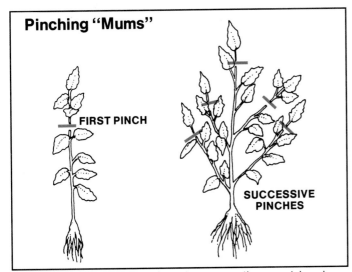

Pinching "Mums"

FIRST PINCH

SUCCESSIVE PINCHES

To maintain proper height of garden mums, they must be given enough room—a minimum of 18" each way—and plants must be pinched as often as necessary up to about July 1.

Chrysanthemum coccineum is an excellent plant for cutting. Flowers of seed-raised plants are often malformed, as shown here. It is best to buy plants in flower.

OTHER KINDS OF CHRYSANTHEMUMS
C. coccineum (Pyrethrum roseum) (Pyrethrum, Painted Daisy)
Zone 3, 1 to 3 feet, white, pink and red, spring or early summer ○

This is one of the best perennials for cutting. Flower forms include single, anemone and double. They are borne one to a stem, height varying from under 1 foot to a lanky 3 feet. Even the taller kinds are best grouped near the front of the border so the dainty, carrotlike foliage is visible. Painted daisies need fertile soil, preferably light in texture, and full sun. They often don't survive being shipped bareroot; otherwise, division or transplanting presents no problems.

After flowering, cut stems to ground level, because this sometimes prompts a second crop of flowers. Mixed seed strains produce mostly single flowers. Seedlings flower in their second year.

C. frutescens (Marguerite)
Zone 9, 3 feet, white, yellow, pink, flowering time varies ○

Marguerite is grown as an annual in most parts of the country. In frost-free regions it is an invaluable woody-based perennial, short-lived but of rapid growth. There are dozens of cultivars with single, anemone-form or double flowers. Cutting back lightly and repeatedly—but not into old wood—prolongs bloom. Named forms are propagated by cuttings.

Two similar semishrubby, yellow-flowered daisies for frost-free climates are *Euryops pectinatus* and the taller *Gamolepis chrysanthemoides*. The latter can stand some frost but is not hardy enough for Zone 8. Both are evergreen in frost-free climates.

C. nipponicum (Nippon Daisy)
Zone 5, 2 feet, white, fall ○

Within just a few years, this broad, woody-based fall-flowering daisy has rocketed into popularity in the Southeast, where the long sunny falls suit it perfectly. It is hardy at −10F (−25C), but where winter comes early, may not have time to flower before the first frost. Rounded bushes, abundantly clad in glossy, spear-shaped leaves, bear a succession of Shasta-type daisies for several weeks.

In the Southeast, plants need pinching or shearing, starting late May and repeated at intervals until mid-July. Without this, buds will be set in July, a period of intense summer heat. Pinching retards bloom, so in areas where it is questionable whether bloom or frost comes first, it might be best to leave plants unpinched—better a September bloom on leggy branches than frost-damaged ones on a compact bush.

Being shrubby, Nippon daisies cannot be lifted and divided, but a few rooted branches can usually be found around the base, which can be cut off to make new plants. Spring-rooted cuttings make better plants and will develop into substantial clumps by fall.

C. parthenium (Feverfew)
Zone 4, 2 feet, white, early summer to fall ○ ◑

Such low, mounded forms as 'White Stars' and 'Golden Ball' (usually sold as *Matricaria)* are annuals or short-lived perennials, though they may self-sow true to type. *C.p.* 'Aureum' (Golden Feather), often called Pyrethrum, is a yellow-leaved perennial usually grown as a bedding plant.

Chrysanthemum frutescens cultivars

Tall doubles such as 'Ultra Double White'—which does come double from seed—are usually short-lived. The species itself lives for several years—forever by means of self-sown seedlings. For this reason, many gardeners consider it a weed. We think it is a desirable weed. Inch-wide, upward-facing gold-disked daisies in branched sprays continue to appear for many weeks, shedding their petals neatly and needing no dead-heading. The foliage is bright green and dainty.

This is a splendid filler plant for any gaps in the border, or for toning down brighter colors. Annual division keeps plants thrifty, but if this is neglected you can usually count on finding seedlings to replace moribund plants. The foliage is evergreen in mild-winter regions. Full sun or light shade suit it equally well. A tendency to legginess can be curbed by shearing plants when they reach 1 foot in height.

C. × rubellum (C. zawadskii latilobum)
Zone 4, 1 to 2 feet, pink, summer or late summer ○

Pink flowered 'Clara Curtis' is the only representative of this group in general circulation. For practical purposes, it is an early-flowering, easy and reliable single-flowered "mum," with leaves more deeply cut and lobed. Spreads rapidly on warm, light soils.

C. × superbum (C. maximum) (Shasta Daisy)
Zone (see note below), 1 to 3 feet, white, summer and fall ○ ◐

Flowers are as much as 5 inches across. Many are of anemone-form, quilled, frilled and neatly or shaggily double. The 1-foot 'Little Miss Muffet' is effectively single, with a few extra petals, 'Aglaya' a popular frilly double, 'Canary Bird' a creamy white deepening to yellow in the center, and 'Thomas Killen'—much used by florists—has the largest single flowers. There are dozens of others. The one sold as 'May Queen' is a selection of the naturalized European ox-eye daisy, *C. leucanthemum* (Zone 2), and flowers 1 month earlier than the others, which makes it a good choice for regions where summer gets hotter than Shastas really like. It is evergreen down to at least 5F. It spreads rapidly, by spreading roots and self-sown seed.

Shastas need rich, moist but well drained soil and frequent division. They do best in cool-summer climates. Light shade is helpful in hot climates, and in most climates for the double forms. Those over 18 inches tall can be kept bushy by pinching or shearing early in the season. This produces smaller flowers in greater number. Disbudding is the opposite of this—a proportion of the flower buds are nipped out so the whole strength of the plant goes into producing larger flowers and longer stems from those remaining.

Note: Shastas vary in hardiness. Few live long in zones colder than Zone 5, but single-flowered 'Alaska' is Zone 4 hardy, and even hardier selections are locally available in some cold regions.

Chrysanthemum × rubellum 'Clara Curtis'

Chrysanthemum × superbum 'Little Miss Muffet'

Shown are two forms of *Chrysogonum virginianum*. The one at right is the most common. The more compact form with dark green leaves (left) is the best one for rock gardens.

Chrysopsis mariana (Heterotheca mariana) is much more resistant to heat and drought than fall asters.

CHRYSOGONUM
Goldenstar, Green-and-gold
Family: Compositae

C. virginianum
Zone 5, under 1 foot, yellow, spring or summer ◑ ○

Goldenstar grows wild on sandy banks and in woodland clearings from Pennsylvania south to Florida and Louisiana. It puts forth a succession of five-rayed stars for several weeks between March and June where spring comes early and summers are hot, all summer farther north. The form usually sold is low and spreading with gray-green spatulate leaves and fairly small flowers on branched stems to about 8 inches high. There are shorter and taller forms, some with smooth or dark green leaves. The flowers are always yellow, but vary in size and in the width of the rays.

Goldenstar is easily grown in moderately fertile soil that is neither soggy nor bone dry, in sun or light shade. It is easily divided and also self-sows, but not invasively. Hardy in Zone 5 three winters out of four, and worth trying in Zone 4, but a severe winter without snow cover may kill it.

CHRYSOPSIS
Golden Aster
Family: Compositae

C. mariana (Heterotheca mariana) **(Maryland Golden Aster)**
Zone 4, 1-1/2 to 3 feet, yellow, fall ○

If you find a bright yellow aster among the Michaelmas daisies at a garden center, it is likely to be *Chrysopsis villosa,* often sold as Aster 'Golden Sunshine'. *C. mariana* is a better plant, being less likely to sprawl. Height varies with soil and rainfall, but in the hot sun and barren sand to which it is so well adapted, its height is under 2 feet. Basal foliage is evergreen down to 15F (−10C).

C. mariana has sturdy, hairy stems encircled by gray-green, lance-shaped leaves that decrease in size as they ascend the stem. Each leaf has a half-twist, giving the compact clumps an appealing curly look. Sprays of clear yellow flowers start opening in late summer and continue into fall. A good plant for full sun or a little shade. It is much better adapted to hot climates than the Michaelmas daisies. It needs no special attention and infrequent division. Removal of unwanted seedlings is about the only chore it creates. Easily propagated by division or seed.

CIMICIFUGA
Bugbane
Family: Ranunculaceae

Compound, ferny leaves are topped by bottle-brush wands of white or creamy flowers in summer or fall. Bugbanes need rich, moist soil and, at least in hot climates, do best with a little shade. Any species you see offered for sale is worth investigating. Only the next two are at all common. They can be divided, but clumps increase slowly and can be left untouched for many years. The species can be propagated by seed.

C. racemosa (Black Snakeroot, Black Cohosh, Bugbane)
Zones 2 to 3, 5 to 8 feet, white, summer ◑

Branched stems of fluffy spires remain in flower for several weeks and are still attractive after they have gone to seed. The foliage needs no staking, but the flower spikes may. This can still be done neatly at flowering time, fastening each spike to a separate, slender stake hidden by the abundant foliage. The flowers are more smelly than fragrant, but not objectionably so. *C. americana* is similar. Both are native to eastern United States and are sold by wildflower nurseries.

C. simplex (Kamchatka Bugbane)
Zone 3, 3 to 4 feet, white, fall ◑

The last bugbane to flower, and October frosts will nip the display in the bud more often than not. The wands of white flowers arch gracefully. 'White Pearl' is a good, named cultivar of this species.

CLEMATIS
Family: Ranunculaceae

It is often said that clematis must have lime added to the soil to decrease acidity. In reality, these plants do well in either acid or alkaline soil. What they *don't* need is hot, dry soil—it should be cool and moist, though never soggy. Add plenty of peat, leafmold or compost to sandy soil. Most clematis are climbers, but there are a few non-vining perennials among them. Only three are readily available.

C. recta
Zone 3, 2 to 5 feet, white or cream, late spring or early summer ○

Recta means upright, and the species is, though it may need some support. The mass of lacy, white flowers comes near the top of leggy clumps that look best if partly hidden behind shorter plants. In *C.r.* 'Purpurea', the flowers are enhanced by leaves the color of oxblood shoe polish. *C.r. mandshurica* does not hold itself erect but sprawls over the ground. This habit can be turned into an asset, if the plant is grown toward the front of a raised bed, letting the foam of creamy flowers cascade down.

Other Species—*C. heracleifolia davidiana* (Zone 3, 3 to 4 feet, blue, summer) is a woody-based, shrub-size bush with delicately scented blue flowers reminiscent of wood hyacinth. Though fairly plentiful, the flowers seem lost against the abundance of large leaves. 'Wyevale' is a fine form of this variable species. Clumps need 4 feet of space.

C. integrifolia (Zone 3, 2 to 4 feet, blue, summer) has wiry, vining type stems. Most books and catalogs list the height as 18 to 24 inches, but it is variable and can reach up to 5 feet. Tall plants require support, which is best provided by a low shrub over which it can drape its stems to display its sparse, nodding, soft blue flowers. These are connoisseurs' plants. *C. recta* is easier to use effectively.

Cimicifuga racemosa

Clematis recta mandshurica with *Dianthus* 'Agatha'.

Coreopsis lanceolata tends to sprawl.

COREOPSIS
Family: Compositae

The annuals known as Calliopsis *(Coreopsis tinctoria)* belong to this genus. The following are the only perennial kinds usually sold. There are numerous other species, some adapted to specific climates. All are easily propagated by division.

C. grandiflora/C. lanceolata
Zone 5, 1 to 4 feet, yellow, summer ○

These plants are characterized by masses of bright yellow daisies on wiry stems in early summer. They bloom longer in cool regions. Hardiness varies, but most do better in warm regions—in cold ones, they may be biennial. They are woody-based plants, easily divided, and more enduring if divided annually.

The leaves are long and slender, occasionally lobed. Except in full sun and poor, dry soil, taller plants usually tumble, but they remain popular for their cutting quality, ease of cultivation, long and abundant flower display and rapid increase.

In 1980, the 1-1/2- to 2-foot, double 'Sunray', which can be grown from seed, became the first perennial to be given the European Fleuroselect Award. However, the outstanding plant in this group is dwarf 'Goldfink'. This cultivar increases fast, but not invasively. It makes such dense tufts of spear-shaped leaves that it could be used as a ground cover on a limited scale. Clumps bear a succession of flowers in such abundance that removing the stalks of dead ones can be time-consuming. Resist the urge to simply pop off the flower heads. Use clippers to cut flower

Coreopsis 'Goldfink' is densly compact.

stalks at the base, or the plant will be left with unsightly stubble. The self-sown seedlings of 'Goldfink' are taller plants, and should be removed if the overall height of the grouping is to be maintained.

The plant known as *C. auriculata* 'Superba' belongs to the *C. grandiflora/lanceolata* group. Each flower has a slight, red stain at the base. Flowers come on bushes less than 2 feet tall. Bushes get leggy only in rich, moist soil; otherwise, they're compact. 'Baby Sun' is similar, but shorter.

The true *C. auriculata* (Zone 4) has short, broad leaves in stoloniferous clumps. Each leaf is triangular in shape, with an egg-shaped terminal lobe and two small lobes of the same shape sticking out like ears directly beneath. The word *auriculata* means "eared." It is usually represented by the form 'Nana', which bears yellow-orange flowers on 9-inch stems over spreading mats of leaves. Though adaptable, *C. auriculata* seems to prefer light, moist soil and some afternoon shade. In cool-summer regions, it may flower from spring to fall if dead flowers are removed. In warm-summer regions, it flowers in spring and early summer.

C. verticillata (Threadleaf Coreopsis)
Zone 3, 1 to 3 feet, yellow, summer ○

This is not only the best species of the genus, but one of the best perennials. 'Golden Shower' is the most common cultivar, with bright yellow, starry flowers blooming liberally and continually through summer. Flowers appear on a 2- to 3-foot airy mound of delicate foliage. 'Zagreb' is similar but only 18 inches tall and spreads less rapidly. 'Moonbeam' is between the two in height and gains added delicacy from its creamy yellow flowers. All are drought resistant and grow well in sun or light shade, in any moderately fertile soil. The running thickets of stems are easily divided. *C. verticillata* can be invasive where moist, sandy soil is combined with long, warm summers.

DELPHINIUM
Family: Ranunculacea

There are three relatively tender species of wild delphiniums that are primarily of interest to gardeners in the cooler regions of the West Coast. They are scarlet *D. cardinale* and *D. nudicaule*, both native to California, and the yellow *D. zalil (D. semibarbatum)* from Persia. Unlike most wild delphiniums, *D. nudicaule* is found in shaded locations. These and others have been used in breeding hybrids with scarlet, orange and yellow flowers, but because they are hard to propagate, these have not yet proved commercially practicable. Hardier species tend to be less showy, but at its best the loosely bushy *D. grandiflorum (D. chinense)* from China and Siberia is a gentian-blue that is unexcelled in brilliance. It seldom exceeds 2 feet in height. It is hardy but short-lived, and usually grown as a biennial. Popular hybrid delphiniums for the garden are discussed below.

Garden hybrids (Elatum hybrids)
Zone 2, 2 to 8 feet, many colors, summer ○

When most of us think of delphiniums, we picture the tall Elatum hybrids, with their stately flower stalks of clear and beautiful colors, especially blue ones. These plants are traditionally associated with lilies and climbing or old-fashion roses, looking most at home in the wide, hedge-

Coreopsis verticillata 'Golden Shower'

Coreopsis verticillata 'Moonbeam'

Delphinium 'Summer Skies'

backed borders of large, old estates. Cold-hardiness is not a limitation, and they live longer where summers are cool and the growing season short. Where summers are long and hot, they grow poorly, if at all. Delphiniums require frequent attention and are not a good choice for the low-maintenance border.

Delphiniums need rich, moist soil—alkaline to slightly acid—and regular fertilizing. They grow best in a a sunny site protected from wind. These plants are highly susceptible to pests and diseases. A complete spray program at 10-day intervals is often recommended, combining insecticide, fungicide and miticide. They also need protection from slugs and snails.

The tall flower stalks require staking. Bamboo stakes work well for this purpose, as do the plastic-coated steel stakes sold at nurseries. These are green in color and have bamboo-like ridges to prevent ties from slipping. The stakes should be two-thirds the final height of the flower stalk when inserted at least 1 foot into the ground—deeper in light soil. Ties made from lengths of old nylon pantyhose or stockings are less likely to snap the flower stalks than string or garden twine. To help hide the stakes, position delphiniums behind other perennials with abundant foliage.

Because they are short-lived but grow quickly from seed, delphiniums are often treated as annuals, especially in Zones 8 to 10. You'll find more information on raising them from seed and on dealing with various pests and diseases in HPBooks' *Annuals, How to Select, Grow and Enjoy,* by Derek Fell.

You can purchase container-grown plants from a nursery, or plant rooted divisions. When planting delphiniums, mix 1/2 cup of superphosphate into the bottom of the planting hole. Do not plant them too deep and handle them gently because the roots are easily damaged. Space the large hybrids 2 feet apart. If mulch is used, keep it away from the crown of the plant.

When the young shoots are 6 inches tall, thin them back to a few of the strongest. This helps avoid overcrowding that makes the plants more prone to disease. Young plants usually produce the best spikes but can sustain fewer of them than can larger clumps.

Delphiniums are seldom overfed. A sprinkling of 5-10-5 fertilizer around the plant at planting time, repeated each subsequent spring, will probably be beneficial. Keep fertilizer off the foliage.

When the blooms of early summer have faded, cut off stalks below the lowest flower. Leave the foliage and remove the remains of the old stalk only when new basal shoots have developed. Water plants thoroughly if soil is dry, and apply more fertilizer if lack of plant vigor indicates the need. New shoots should develop and bear a second crop of shorter spikes.

Choice forms can be propagated by careful division, or by basal cuttings in spring. Vermiculite, kept damper than usual, is a good rooting medium. Under ideal growing conditions, clumps will need dividing in their third year, but delphiniums are so easily raised from seed that you may prefer this method. The following are the most readily available groups of hybrids.

Blackmore & Langdon Hybrids—In the first half of this century, this English firm bred outstanding hybrids in white, cream and yellow as well as blue. Economic realities have resulted in the virtual disappearance of many of these hybrids. Remaining ones are usually offered only as mixed seedlings, in a narrower color range. They are cold-hardy, but less tolerant of heat than the next.

Giant Pacific Series—Bred by Frank Reinelt in California, the first being the *Round Table* series with Arthurian names. These are also now raised from seed. Seed strains come fairly true to color, most of them double, in white, pink, lavender, pale or dark blue, violet and purple. Most florets have a small central cluster of short petals (called a *bee*) of a contrasting color. 'Galahad' is a beeless white. A later addition, 'Summer Skies' is a soft blue with a white bee.

Shorter Hybrids—We think of delphiniums as stately plants, and the shorter ones may never be as popular. However, staking is a lot easier to do neatly and sometimes, if the weather is kind, the stalks may be self-supporting—but this is a gamble. Dwarf Pacific delphiniums resemble the Giant Pacifics but are only 2 feet tall. They are best treated as annuals. 'Blue Fountains' are mixed blues, 'Blue Heaven' sky blue.

The Belladonna hybrids are hardy to Zone 3, and grow 3 to 5 feet tall, with branched stems of flowers in shades of blue or white. If less elegant, they are also less demanding. 'Belladonna' is light blue, 'Bellamosa' dark blue, 'Casa Blanca' white. Connecticut Yankees (Zone 3) are bushy, graceful plants, to 2-1/2 feet with single larkspur-type flowers of white, blue, lavender or purple.

DIANTHUS
Pinks, Carnations
Family: Caryophyllaceae

The common name *pink* is usually applied to the hardier kinds, *carnation* to the tender kinds sold by florists. *Border carnations* are intermediate. These vary in hardiness and usually flower much longer where summer heat is not intense.

Border carnations are front-of-the-border plants, seldom much more than 1 foot tall when in bloom. The plant has mats of narrow leaves, usually blue-green, which in the milder regions are attractive all year long. Clumps cannot be mulched for winter protection or the foliage rots, but evergreen boughs can be used for protection.

Flowers are single or double, white, pink, red and occasionally approaching purple, often with a darker eye or lacing. The one available yellow kind, *D. knappii,* has scant green leaves, small flowers and a gawky habit—not a good border subject. Spring or early summer is peak flowering time, but in cool regions blooms may continue all summer if spent flowers are removed. Pinks are often said to need lime but this is not always so. Sharp drainage is more important, and sandy loam is the ideal soil for most. Lime is needed only on extremely acid soils.

Annuals, biennials or short-lived perennials include *D. chinensis* and the Sweet Williams *(D. barbatus)*—but see under *D. barbatus,* page 80, for hardy kinds. Florists' carnations are grown outdoors in warm-winter parts of California, but they are lanky, disease-prone plants. The

Mixed pinks *(Dianthus)* include 'Doris' (rose pink), 'Margaret Curtis' (white with maroon eye), *D. plumarius* (white) and 'Pink Parfait' (banded pink).

Dianthus plumarius

Dianthus 'Her Majesty'

'Loveliness' strain of *D. superbus* have deeply fringed, almost spidery flowers. They are short-lived and best grown as biennials.

There are a host of hardy, dwarf pinks for the rock garden, raised bed or front of a small border. *D. deltoides* (Zone 3) makes flowing mats of tiny, bright green leaves. In late spring, hundreds of small single flowers of brilliant pink or white are displayed against the mats. This plant self-seeds prolifically, but unwanted seedlings are easily pulled out. *D. gratianopolitanus (D. caesius)* makes neat, gray-green mounds and bears fragrant, pink flowers on stems 4 to 6 inches tall. Good, named dwarfs include 'Little Joe' with single crimson flowers, 'Rose Bowl' with cerise flowers and 'Tiny Rubies', which makes dense, flat mats studded with double, bright pink flowers.

D. barbatus
Zone 5, 12 to 18 inches, late spring or summer ○

This species is usually biennial, occasionally overwintering in milder climates, or self-perpetuated by seed. The common name, Sweet William, is given to those plants usually grown as annuals or biennials. However, there are three cultivars of proven hardiness to Zone 5, and just as tolerant of summer heat farther south. 'White Beauty' and 'Scarlet Beauty' are self-descriptive colors. The most common cultivar is coral-pink 'Newport Pink', which can be grown from seed. These cultivars have somewhat ragged clumps of bright green, glossy leaves, surmounted by stout stems bearing large domes or flattened heads of massed, 1-inch-wide single flowers. Flowers are only mildly fragrant. If cut back after flowering—advisable, in any case, to neaten the clumps—they may repeat flower. These plants need richer, moister soil than most pinks, in sun or light afternoon shade. Frequent division is recommended.

BORDER PINKS AND BORDER CARNATIONS

These excel in fragrance. The most reliable are the old forms of the cottage pinks or grass pinks, *D. plumarius* (Zone 3). One-foot-wide hummocks of evergreen blue-gray lance-shaped leaves bear hundreds of white, rose, pink or maroon-eyed flowers on slender, upright stems. Those sold as *D. × allwoodii* are of this type, though not as hardy as some of the older ones.

D. plumarius was crossed with carnations (*D. caryophyllus*) and other species to produce fancier, often double, pinks and border carnations. Whether you choose single or double forms, plain or fancy, remember that the double-flowered ones most resembling florist's carnations are usually sprawling plants, and not as rugged as the simpler ones. The best places to grow them are the edge of a path or raised bed over which they can tumble. Double white 'Her Majesty', double, soft rose 'Evangeline', and white, maroon-eyed 'Sweet Memory' are exceptionally reliable cultivars.

A simple, old-fashioned way of propagating pinks is by "pipings"—tip cuttings 3 to 4 inches long, taken in summer. These are taken by holding the stem in one hand while pulling from the top with the other, until it separates at a node. Cuttings are rooted in moist sand under a jelly jar, which in hot climates should be located in shade. Heel cuttings—side shoots pulled off with a *heel* of old stem—can also be used, or old clumps can be torn apart and replanted during mild, moist weather. Those with sprawling stems can also be *layered*. A horizontal slit is made through a node on the underside, the stem pegged down with a hairpin into sandy soil and held in place with a stone. It takes practice to do this without severing the stem completely, but if all goes well, a new plantlet will be ready for separation a few months later.

DICENTRA
Bleeding-heart
Family: Fumariaceae

Note: The name *Dielytra,* occasionally seen, arose as a spelling mistake.

All the bleeding-hearts mentioned except the Japanese *D. spectabilis* are native to the United States. Squirrel-corn *(D. canadensis)* and Dutchman's-breeches *(D. cucullaria)* are only suitable for the shaded wildflower garden. The 4-foot, yellow-flowered *D. chrysantha* from the mountains of California will not adapt to other regions, nor is it easy to transplant.

The species listed below are easy to grow in light, deep loam. Soil must be well-drained—plants will not survive in wet or boggy soil. Light shade is advantageous, and essential in hot regions. All bleeding-hearts can be divided, preferably just as new growth appears in early spring. Handle divisions gently—the new foliage is extremely fragile.

D. eximia (Eastern Bleeding-heart)
Zone 3, 12 to 18 inches, pink, spring or summer ◑
The gray-green, finely dissected leaves push through the ground at the first sign of spring. In cool climates, flowering may continue all summer. In warmer climates, flowering stops during hot weather, sometimes repeating in the cool of fall. *D. eximia* does not have invasive roots but self-sows abundantly. It is excellent for naturalizing in woodland gardens.

A beautiful white form of *D. eximia,* known as 'Purity', 'Snowdrift', or 'Alba', comes true from seed. If this and the pink-flowered form are grown together, the pink will probably crowd out the white.

D. formosa (Pacific Bleeding-heart)
Zone 3, 1 foot, pink, spring or summer ◑
Similar to *D. eximia.* In Pacific Coast regions, where the climate suits it best, root spread is rapid, making it a good choice for naturalizing. In many other regions, *D. formosa* spreads slowly. 'Sweetheart' is a dainty, white-flowered selection.

Hybrids—Selections and hybrids of *D. eximia* and *D. formosa* are similar in height and hardiness to the parent species. They outrank their parents as border plants, being more sun-tolerant and less invasive. It is not certain from which of these two species some cultivars are derived. All grow 12 to 18 inches tall, with ferny, gray-green foliage and flowers in varying shades of pink. The plants flower for many weeks. The patented, cherry-red 'Luxuriant' has proved particularly successful where summers are hot or dry, or winters are warm.

Dicentra eximia 'Alba'

Dicentra 'Luxuriant'. Taller plant behind is *Dicentra spectabilis.*

D. spectabilis (Japanese Bleeding-heart)
Zone 2, 2 to 3 feet, pink, spring ◑

Japanese bleeding-heart is taller and wider than the others. Foliage is graceful but less finely divided. The larger rosy-pink flowers swing side-by-side along the top half of arching stems.

White-flowered 'Alba' or 'Pantaloons', is slightly less robust, its bright green leaves lacking the pink tints of the species, as is common in albino varieties.

In hot or dry climates, the foliage of Japanese bleeding-heart soon gets shabby and gardeners there often discard plants after flowering and buy new ones in early spring. When the leaves start to turn brown, plants can be cut down. If large-leaved hostas are grown nearby, their foliage, which develops later, will help to fill the gap. Hostas and bleeding-hearts like the same humus-enriched loam and lightly shaded site. *D. spectabilis* can be propagated by careful division, by root cuttings taken in early spring or by stem cuttings in spring or early summer. Seed is seldom available.

Dicentra spectabilis

DICTAMNUS
Gas Plant, Burning Bush
Family: Rutaceae

D. albus (D. fraxinella)
Zone 2 to 3, 3 feet, white or pink, late spring or early summer ○

This is the only species in cultivation. The flowers are white but there are also pink-flowered forms. The plant got its popular names because on sultry days the old flower heads give off a volatile oil that can sometimes be ignited. That same oil in the leaves has been known to cause a rash similar to poison ivy. *D.a. purpureus* is shown at left. White-flowered *D. albus* is shown on page 39.

Dictamnus is a long-lived, rugged plant that requires little care. Plant it in fertile, humus-rich soil that does not get soggy, in sun or light shade. Then mulch it and leave it alone. It will probably outlive you. No staking or routine care is needed, but an occasional sprinkling of fertilizer is recommended if the soil is not rich. It may require watering during prolonged drought. The spires of flowers are brief in duration, but the elegant glossy pinnate leaves are attractive all through the growing season. The foliage has a faint, lemony scent.

Dictamnus grows slowly, but will eventually become a large bush, so allow 3 feet of space between plants. Seedlings usually flower in their third year.

Division is possible, but in most parts of the country, hot, cold or dry weather will kill divisions before they re-establish. It's best to grow dictamnus from seed, one plant to a pot. Don't disturb the roots when you take it from the pot and put it in the garden.

Dictamnus albus purpureus

DIGITALIS
Foxglove
Family: Scrophulariaceae

Annual and biennial foxgloves are included in HPBooks' *Annuals, How to Select, Grow and Enjoy,* by Derek Fell. The perennial kinds are less showy, perhaps not grand enough for the border, but worth a place on the fringes of a woodland garden, or in a lightly shaded corner. They grow in any moderately fertile, well-drained soil and are evergreen where winters are not severe. If spikes of dead flowers are removed, smaller ones may develop and flower later. Leave some dead flowers if you want plants to self-sow and naturalize. Following are the two most-ornamental perennials:

D. grandiflora (D. ambigua)
Zone 3, 3 feet, yellow, summer ◑

A long-lived, easy-care plant, with spires of 3-inch, creamy-yellow bells. Propagated by seed or division.

D. × mertonensis
Zone 5, 3 feet, pink, summer ◑

Less elegant and only permanent if frequently divided, but the flowers are an attractive and unusual shade of coppery pink. Although a hybrid between *D. grandiflora* and the biennial *D. purpurea*, it comes true from seed.

DISPORUM
Fairy-bells, Mandarin
Family: Liliaceae

There are several North American and Asian species suitable for the woodland garden, including the low, rambling *D. sessile* 'Variegatum'. This cultivar is grown more for its white-striped leaves than its nodding greenish-white flowers. *D. flavum*, below, is an outstanding border plant.

D. flavum
Zone (see note below), 2 to 3 feet, yellow, spring ◑●

This shares with the closely related Solomon's-seals (*Polygonatum*) the uncommon ability to compete with tree roots and dry shade. Extremely sturdy, bamboolike stems branch halfway up from their base. The branch tips bear several small clusters of nodding, lemon-yellow bell-shaped flowers. They last only a week or two, but the bright green, round-to-oval leaves with a silken sheen beneath, have long-lasting textural value. They have the feel of supple leather and their vein channeling resembles the longitudinal lines of a globe. Shoots spear up each spring, forming a patch of steadily increasing circumference. These are easily divided for propagation; otherwise, division is not needed.

Note: *Disporum flavum* is fairly new and not adequately hardiness tested, but proven reliable in Zone 4 and probably hardy much farther north.

Digitalis grandiflora (D. ambigua). This species is a hardy perennial.

Disporum flavum

Doronicum with forget-me-nots and *Alchemilla mollis*.

Echinacea purpurea with Gloriosa daisies (*Rudbeckia*).

DORONICUM
Family: Compositae

There are many yellow, daisy-type flowers among perennials, but nearly all bloom in summer or fall. Doronicums bloom at the same time as tulips—early spring—combining exuberantly with them in cool climates. In hot climates, where they do less well, doronicums need light shade, where they combine beautifully with the blue flowers of Virginia bluebells *(Mertensia),* or clump-forming bugleweed (*Ajuga pyramidalis),* but not the creeping *Ajuga reptans,* which would crowd out the doronicum.

Doronicums are shallow rooters, so the soil need not be deep, but it should be cool and rich. The slowly creeping mats need dividing about every third year, best done in early spring. They usually go dormant in summer. Although most plants that do this are then drought-resistant, doronicums that stay dry all through summer may not come back next spring. Keep soil moist during dry periods.

There are shorter and taller kinds, but only those described here are common.

D. caucasicum (D. orientale)
Zone 3, 1 to 1-1/2 feet, yellow, spring ◑ ○

Low, creeping clumps of heart-shaped, toothed leaves, becoming narrower where they join the upper part of stems that bear single, 2-inch flowers. 'Miss Mason', probably a hybrid, is a popular doronicum, but not all plants sold as such are correctly named. 'Spring Beauty' has double flowers that convey more the voluptuousness of summer than the newly minted look of spring. Flowers of both are excellent for picking. Propagated by division.

ECHINACEA
Purple Coneflower
Family: Compositae

E. purpurea (Rudbeckia purpurea)
Zone 3, 2 to 4 feet, pink, summer ○

In all but color, purple coneflower resembles a gloriosa daisy *(Rudbeckia).* The cone-shaped flowers resemble party hats, with a brim of rosy purple petals (ray flowers) and a coppery or orange crown. Flower arrangers use not only the complete flower, but the tawny cone with petals removed, which also dries well. Purple coneflower is a mainstay of the summer garden, in bloom for many weeks. It is susceptible to Japanese beetles where these pests are common, but otherwise requires little care. Plants need not be staked unless the soil is rich and moist. A plant of prairies and open woods, purple coneflower is used to full sun but tolerates light shade.

Named kinds, some involving other species, are a big improvement over the wild plant. The pink of the petals varies in shade, as does the bronze, yellow or orange of the crown.

'The King', 'Bright Star' and 'Robert Bloom' are recommended cultivars. 'White Lustre' has a coppery orange crown and creamy white, reflexed petals. Seedlings from cultivars, while not exactly like the parent, will be prettier than the wild plant. Space plants 18 inches apart, and divide about every fourth year.

Other Species—There are other species with garden potential, particularly the hardy *E. pallida,* which includes Minnesota in its native range. In the coldest zones, it may survive without the winter protection needed by *E. purpurea* cultivars.

ECHINOPS
Globe Thistle
Family: Compositae

Echinops ritro

E. ritro (also sold as 'Taplow Blue')
Zone 3, 3 to 5 feet, blue, summer ○

Globe thistles belong to the daisy family, but their globular flower heads don't look a bit like daisies. Their unusual form adds variety to the border. Arrangers use the flower both fresh and dried. Cut flowers before they open and hang them by their stems to dry, otherwise, they shatter. All attract bees by day and moths by night.

Plants sold as *E. ritro* are now said to be *E. humilis,* but if names are wrong, they are at least uniformly wrong, and what you will get is a plant that averages 4 feet in height, with steel-blue heads of less than golfball size and thistlelike, but not flesh-piercing, dark green leaves. Plants sold as 'Taplow Blue' are the same as those sold as *E. ritro,* or with only the minor variations one might expect among a batch of seedlings from the same species. Other species are uncommon as garden plants in the United States.

A group of three is usually enough, positioned in the middle of island beds, or toward the back of a border. A plant of strong character, globe thistle looks best associated with plants of softer appearance, such as border phlox.

Globe thistle does best in full sun and fertile soil. Staking will be required if soil is excessively rich. Ideally, the soil should be moist during the growing season, but roots go deep and will endure drought. Plants can be left undivided for years. Digging and dividing is arduous, but often a rooted division can be taken without lifting the plant from the soil. Plants can also be raised from seed.

EPIMEDIUM
Family: Berberidaceae

Epimediums have several qualities that could categorize them as ground-cover foliage plants. Their foliage is graceful yet dense, and sometimes evergreen, depending on species and climate. They have tough, wiry stems, usually under 1 foot in height, and are tolerant of competition from tree roots. Some kinds have a stoloniferous habit.

Many epimediums have attractive flowers on compact clumps. Over a dozen kinds are offered by specialty nurseries. The five described here would make a good selection. Though tolerant of dry shade and of full sun, epimediums are at their most luxuriant in deep, rich soil and light shade. It's best to cut deciduous kinds to the ground in early spring, so that old stem-stubble does not disfigure the new young foliage. Propagated by division.

E. grandiflorum
Zone 4, 1 foot, pink, early spring ◑ ●

'Rose Queen' is one of the showiest cultivars of this species. The large, spurred flowers are a deep, dusky pink,

Epimedium grandiflorum 'Rose Queen'

Epimedium × rubrum

the new foliage reddish, turning to dark green, then dying back in winter. Clumps increase slowly and you'll never have too much—or, indeed, enough of it.

E. × rubrum
Zone 4, 1 foot, bright pink, early spring ◗ ●

The small flowers are carried in abundant sheaves. Flower sepals are almost crimson, with a creamy star within. The red-tinted semievergreen leaves have the dainty, angel-wing leaflets typical of epimediums. Increase is slow, so for use as a ground cover, space clumps no more than 1 foot apart. Often sold as *E. alpinum* 'Rubrum'.

E. × versicolor 'Sulphureum'
Zone 5, 1 foot, yellow, early spring ◗ ●

A grower familiar with many epimediums writes: "If I could grow only one, it would be this. The flowers, 10 to 20 nodding delicately above the foliage, with their pale yellow sepals and butter-yellow spurred petals, are the epitome of graceful beauty. They appear at the same time as forget-me-nots and grape hyacinths, and a planting of the three is one of my favorite springtime pictures."

Need we say more? It is vigorously stoloniferous, tries to be evergreen, but in cold climates looks shabby by year's end.

E. × warleyense
Zone 5, 1 foot, orange, early spring ◗ ●

"Orange" really isn't a fair description for flowers of a glowing, red-streaked apricot. Flowers are held well above the leaves, and are all the more conspicuous because most of the foliage—always scanty and scattered—has died away by flowering time. Spread is rapid but not dense. In dappled shade, the glancing rays of the sun bring brilliance to the flowers.

E. × youngianum 'Niveum'
Zone 5, 8 inches, white, early spring ◗ ●

Small but sturdy, with numerous snowy flowers held well above the leaves. The compact clumps increase moderately fast. They never need dividing, but if you want more of the plant, a clump sliced in quarters, replanted 1 foot apart will fill a given space much more rapidly than a single plant left undisturbed. The cultivar *E. × youngianum* 'Roseum' *(E. lilacinum),* has flowers of pale lilac.

ERIGERON
Fleabane
Family: Compositae

Fleabanes have flowers resembling those of Michaelmas daisies (asters) but with more and narrower rays, giving the yellow-eyed flowers a densely fringed look. There are yellow and orange species, but most are white, blue, lavender, pink or purple.

Hybrids
Zone 6, 1 to 2 feet, many colors, summer ○

Most garden fleabanes are selections or hybrids involving two species: One is the evergreen beach aster *(E. glaucus),* 1 foot or less with lavender flowers. It is native to the beach cliffs of the California and Oregon coast and able to stand some salt spray. The other is the 2-foot, lilac-flowered *E. speciosus* from the Pacific Northwest.

Erigeron 'Sincerity'

The hybrids are at their best in similar maritime climates where they flower for a long time in summer—some all year in Southern California, if cut back between flowerings. In hot-summer regions, they benefit from light shade, but still flower briefly. Double pink, 18-inch 'Foerster's Liebling' (Zone 5) is the hardiest and most widely distributed cultivar. 'Double Blue' is violet-blue, 'Pink Jewel' a bushy 2 feet with single, pale pink flowers. Many others are locally available in regions where they do well. The soil must be well drained, ideally a light loam or humus-enriched sand, only moderately fertile. Propagated by division or basal cuttings in spring.

Other Species— *E. karvinskianus (E. mucronatus)* from Mexico is at home on the West Coast where the dainty pink-and-white daisies are borne over a long period. It is not reliably hardy where the temperature drops below 20F (−6C).

Two pretty East Coast wildlings for naturalizing are the 1- to 2-foot Robin's plantain *(E. pulchellus)* with several 1-1/4-inch, pale mauve to violet flowers in each branched cluster, and the similar *E. philadelphicus.* These do best in light shade. Ten-inch, *E. aurantiacus* has orange flowers.

ERYNGIUM
Sea Holly
Family: Umbelliferae

Sea hollies bear round or teasel-shaped heads surrounded, in the most ornamental kinds, by conspicuous ruffs of spiny bracts. In the prettiest kinds, the stiff stems, flowers and bracts are silvery-gray or tinted blue and violet. The basal leaves are often smooth and rounded in contrast to the thistlelike look of the rest of the plant. Most flower in summer or early fall and they do best in deep, sandy soil of moderate or low fertility in full sun. Most also have carrotlike roots and may not survive moving or division. This limits availability of those that do not come true from seed, though they can be propagated by root cuttings. Most are hardy in Zone 5.

E. giganteum
Zone 5, 1 to 3 feet, gray, bluish-gray, summer or early fall ○

If you are not yet acquainted with sea hollies and unsure whether you'll like them—or they you—we recommend starting with *E. giganteum,* 2 to 3 feet tall and needing no staking. The silvery gleam of the jagged, broad-bracted, prickly ruff is particularly striking at dusk.

It is easily grown from seed scattered in fall or spring. It is *monocarpic* (dies after flowering) but leaves seedlings behind.

Other Species— If you want to explore the genus further, be aware that names are muddled. If you are lucky, the plant sold you as *E. amethystinum*—incorrectly named, according to taxonomists—will be a Zone-2-hardy, 2-foot plant with bluish bracts. If you are not as lucky, it will be the less appealing, 3-foot *E. planum,* with plentiful but small, pale blue flower heads, excellent for cutting. *E. planum* 'Blue Dwarf' is only 1 foot tall.

Some plants that were once sold as species are being grouped under the name *E. × zabelii.* This covers hybrids

Eryngium alpinum

Eryngium giganteum

Eupatorium coelestinum

between *E. alpinum* and *E. bourgatii*, but is also a catch-all for such handsome hybrids of unknown parentage as 'Violetta'.

E. alpinum (Zone 3) is considered by many the most beautiful of all. The feathery blue ruff, soft to the touch, is partially upturned around large, cone-shaped heads. It is usually about 2-1/2 feet tall. *E. alpinum* seems more tolerant of heavy soil and of light shade than most.

Two species are grown as much for foliage as for flowers. Two-foot *E. bourgatii* has wiry, deeply-serrated, white-veined leaves—the flowers are not remarkable. The rounded, glossy leaves of the stocky, 18-inch *E. variifolium* are conspicuously white-veined. All except *E. giganteum* are perennial.

EUPATORIUM
Family: Compositae

Several eupatoriums that flower in late summer and fall are bewilderingly similar. They include Joe-Pye weed *(E. purpureum)*, spotted Joe-Pye weed *(E. maculatum)* and hollow Joe-Pye weed *(E. fistulosum)*, with hollow stems. These are lofty plants, 6 feet or taller, with fluffy dome-shaped clusters of soft, purplish-pink flowers. They are easy to grow but do particularly well at the boggy edge of ponds or streams. All are hardy to Zone 4. White-flowered, white snakeroot *(E. rugosum)* is an invasive weed, growing to 4 feet tall, but valued for its ability to grow under trees and to flower in deep shade. It is hardy to Zone 3. Though less hardy, *E. coelestinum,* below, is the only one to have gained widespread acceptance in gardens.

E. coelestinum (Hardy Ageratum, Mist Flower)
Zone 6, 2 feet, blue, fall ○ ◑

Coelestinum means sky-blue and so it is to the eye but not to photographic film, so make allowances when looking at its picture. The tendency of some blue flowers to photograph pink or mauve is so pronounced in this plant, and in the annual garden ageratum it so much resembles, that this phenomenon is often known among photographers as the ''ageratum effect.''

This plant serves to emphasize the effect various soils and climates have on plants. It had to be removed from the Harper garden because it was too invasive in Southeastern sand, spreading both by seed and creeping, threadlike roots. At its hardiness limit, *E. coelestinum* may not survive soil soggy in winter. On clay soils it is not unduly invasive and is valued by many gardeners for its late-season bloom. In the wild, it grows in full sun or light shade, usually in moist soil.

This plant is attractive to butterflies and produces flowers good for cutting. It looks particularly appealing combined with the goldenrods that bloom at the same time.

Eupatorium fistulosum with zinnias and *Begonia semperflorens. E. purpureum* is similar, but usually has flowers of darker purple.

EUPHORBIA
Spurge
Family: Euphorbiaceae

The best known spurge is the Christmas poinsettia *(E. pulcherrima)*. There are also three well-known annuals—painted leaf *(E.cyathophora*, called *E. heterophylla* in the trade), snow-on-the-mountain *(E. marginata)*, and caper spurge or mole plant *(E. lathyris)*, reputed to repel moles. The showy part of all spurges is the bracts, not the flowers.

A characteristic of spurges is the milky sap that bleeds from cut stems, which can cause skin irritation. Common sense suggests that the sap be kept away from eyes, mouth or open wounds. Spurges do well in well-drained soil of average to poor fertility. In hot-summer regions, all but *E. myrsinites* prefer light shade.

E. characias
Zone 8, 4 feet, chartreuse, spring ○ ◐

This dominating plant deserves a prominent position in the border. It is shrublike and evergreen. Narrow blue-gray leaves are tightly packed around upright stems, giving them a chunky look. Stems bear thick clusters of dark-eyed chartreuse flowers or, in the form *E.c. wulfenii (E. veneta)*, yellow flowers. When spent flower stems start to turn yellow, cut them out at the base of the plant. Difficult to propagate.

E. corollata
Zone 3, 1 to 3 feet, white, summer ○ ◐

Strange that this graceful plant should be so little known. It grows wild from Massachusetts to Minnesota and Nebraska, south to Florida and Texas, in fields, dry open woods and by the roadside. Southern country folk call it Baby's-breath, and like the *Gypsophila* also given that name, it cuts well and adds lightness to bouquets. It is a refreshing sight on a sweltering summer day, with its delicate sprays of 1/4-inch snowy white, broderie anglaise flowers held on wiry stems.

The leaves are also delicate—1/4 inch wide, 1-1/2 inches long, smooth and jade green. For the first year or two the slender stems tend to be lax, becoming more self-supporting as clumps expand. Baby's-breath seldom needs dividing. It is best propagated by seed or by stem cuttings, which, unlike most spurges, root easily.

E. epithymoides (E. polychroma) (Cushion-spurge)
Zone 4, 12 to 18 inches, yellow, spring ○ ◐

This is a good plant in cool-summer regions, but the hotter summer becomes, the less the plant seems to like it. In hot, humid regions, it frequently succumbs to one of the many wilt diseases. In spring, it becomes a chartreuse dome of shocking brightness, turning into a neat, green cushion in summer. It can be divided with care.

E. myrsinites
Zone 5, 6 inches, chartreuse, varies ○ ◐

Perennial, but short-lived in warm-winter areas, this plant is valued more for its evergreen, gray foliage than for its flowers, bright though these briefly are. Scalelike blue-gray leaves overlap along snakelike or partially upright stems.

To accommodate its sprawling habit and preference for sharply drained or dry soil, plant *E. myrsinites* in a raised bed, wall crevice or alongside a rock. Once the plant is

Euphorbia corollata

Euphorbia epithymoides (E. polychroma)

established, it self-sows prolifically. Small seedlings can be transplanted if lifted with a good shovelful of soil. Cut out old flowering stems after the seed has been dispersed—sooner if you want to avoid the seedlings.

The less hardy *E. rigida (E. biglandulosa)* is similar to *E. myrsinites*, but with longer stems, some of them erect. Flowering time for both species varies with climate, between late winter and early summer.

Other Species—The most widespread perennial euphorbia is cypress spurge *(E. cyparissias),* a naturalized European plant with needle-fine leaves and yellow bracts. It is so invasive that it is usually considered a weed. Among desirable perennials, the only hardy, red-bracted kind available is *E. griffithii* 'Fire Glow'. It is 3 feet tall with bright orange bracts in summer. It is not readily available.

Felicia amelloides 'San Gabriel'

FELICIA
Blue Marguerite
Family: Compositae

F. amelloides (Agathaea coelestis)
Zone 9, 1 to 2-1/2 feet, blue, varies ○
Blue marguerite is grown as an annual in most parts of the country, but is one of the best perennials for frost-free regions. It is woody-based, with neat foliage. The yellow-eyed, daisy-type flowers are an azure blue of rare purity. Large-flowered 'San Gabriel' is an outstanding cultivar. 'Astrid Thomas' is a compact form and 'Variegata' has leaves with white variegations.

Soil can be acid or alkaline, but not dry or sodden. If dead flowers are removed, bloom may continue from fall through spring in mild-winter areas. After blooming, plants should be cut back to about half their height. The species is raised from seed, selected kinds by cuttings of young growth.

Filipendula rubra

FILIPENDULA
Family: Rosaceae

In the past, some of these plants have been called *Spiraea*. All but *F. vulgaris* need fairly moist, humus-rich soil and benefit from a little shade. *F. vulgaris* can be gently pulled apart with the fingers, the others divided by means of a sharp knife and a strong wrist.

F. rubra (Queen-of-the-prairie)
Zone 2, 4 to 7 feet, pink, summer ◑
Native to moist meadows and prairies of North America, *F. rubra* is not successful where summers are hot or dry. Clusters of tiny flowers of peach-blossom pink are gathered into fluffy plumes rising over large, jagged leaves. It will probably need some support. The cultivar *F.r.* 'Venusta'—Martha Washington's plume—should have brighter pink flowers, but plants sold as such are usually the species.

F. ulmaria
Zone 3, 4 feet, cream, summer ◑

This less showy European counterpart has an even greater need for moisture and will grow in soggy soil. The foliage may mildew if the roots get dry, and sometimes if they don't. This species prefers cool climates but will grow in hotter ones with compensating shade. The species self-sows freely and is naturalized in parts of the eastern United States. Double 'Flore Pleno' is the better plant, its densely packed flowers giving it a fluffy look. The bright green leaves are lobed and crinkled, whitish beneath. In *F.u.* 'Aurea', they are yellow in spring, becoming light green, and in 'Variegata' a mixture of yellow and green blotches and streaks.

F. vulgaris (F. hexapetala) (Dropwort)
Zone 3, 1 to 2 feet, white, early summer ◑ ●

F. vulgaris is an easily-grown, adaptable species. It prefers a fertile loam, either slightly acid or alkaline, but will grow in poor, dry soil, scattering its progeny around as if to prove its invincibility. Seedlings are easily weeded out. The carrotlike, dark green leaves form a flat, circular mound over which rise slender stalks topped with sprays of small white flowers. The leaves are evergreen in mild-winter climates. In the double 'Flore Pleno', flowers resemble tiny, white roses. The double form is shorter than the single, and makes a good edging plant, but the flowers fall over when heavy with rain. 'Flore Pleno' also self-sows.

Filipendula vulgaris 'Flore Pleno'

FRANCOA
Bridal-wreath
Family: Saxifragaceae

F. ramosa and F. sonchifolia (F. appendiculata)
Zone 8, 3 feet, white or pink, summer ◑

Bridal wreath will do well only in regions where winters are fairly mild and summers are sunny but not excessively hot. It is frost-damaged at 15F (−9C). At temperatures much over 80F (26C), the flower spikes wilt, even though the soil is moist and the site shaded. This makes it ill-suited to most East Coast gardens. Where its needs can be met, it is a desirable and easily grown plant with graceful wands of white or pink flowers and basal clumps of leathery 1-foot-long evergreen leaves. The leaves are described botanically as *lyrate,* or lyre-shaped. The top third of each leaf is egg-shaped and wavy-edged, the remainder narrowly frilled and winged. The flowers show best when backed by evergreen shrubs. Clumps increase slowly and need only infrequent division unless for propagation. Bridal-wreath can also be raised from seed.

Francoa ramosa

Gaillardia × grandiflora

Gaura lindheimeri

GAILLARDIA
Blanketflower
Family: Compositae

G. × grandiflora
Zone 3, 6 inches to 3 feet, red and yellow, summer ○

Perennial gaillardias are now usually grouped under this name, which covers hybrids between *G. aristata* and *G. pulchella,* though some of the most enduring may be selections of *G. aristata* and not hybrids. Flowers are single or semidouble. They vary in longevity. 'Monarch Strain' has proved long-lived in sandy, low-fertility soil that is often dry in summer, full sun and temperatures often exceeding 90F (32C). A friend who does flower arrangements for parties and weddings finds this the only perennial she can count on for cut flowers from late May through September. Gaillardia flowers continuously, even if not dead-headed, and the globular seedheads are themselves attractive.

'Monarch Strain' makes gappy clumps of gray-green leaves, inclined to sprawl, but the long flower stalks turn themselves back upright. The center of the clump tends to die out, and one way of "dividing" is to slice out and discard this center section, using a sharp-edged narrow spade, called a *border spade,* and filling the hole with fresh soil. If clumps are lifted for division, do this in early spring. Soggy soil will kill this plant, but some of the dwarf gaillardias seem to need richer, moister soil.

The flowers of 6-inch 'Baby Cole' and 1-foot 'Goblin' have red petals with yellow tips, and this coloring also predominates among seedlings from the 30-inch 'Monarch Strain'. The cultivars 'Burgundy' and 'Yellow Queen' (2 feet) have solid-color flowers. 'Monarch Strain' is usually grown from seed. The others must be increased by cuttings or division if they are to remain true to type.

GAURA
Family: Onagraceae

G. lindheimeri
Zone 5, 4 to 7 feet, white, early summer to first frost ○

Gaura—the name means superb—is native to Louisiana and Texas, and excels in all the southern states. Through a Virginia summer in the Zone 8 Harper garden, when daytime temperatures usually exceeded 90F (32C), only this and gaillardia flowered daily from June to October. It begins summer as a 2- to 3-foot, vase-shaped bush clad in downy 2- to 3-inch, spear-shaped leaves, sometimes maroon-speckled. Wiry pink wands rise above it, steadily elongating at the tip as lower flowers are neatly dropped until, by fall, it is shoulder high and still bearing flowers that look like flights of small, white butterflies, fading to pink.

Give it deep, sandy soil, raising the bed, if necessary, to ensure that water drains rapidly away. The parsniplike root delves deep for moisture, so watering is needed only after prolonged drought. Easily raised from seed.

Where summers are long and warm, self-sown seedlings reach flowering size in 1 year. To move plants, use a spade and dig deep, to avoid severing the root. Clumps seldom need dividing. Where summers are cool, it does not flower until late summer. It may sprawl in moist, rich soil.

GAZANIA
Family: Compositae

All
Zone 9, 6 inches to 1 foot, many colors, summer ○

Gazanias may overwinter for a year or two in Zone 8, but are usually grown as annuals in this and colder zones. In frost-free parts of California and the Southwest, they are important evergreen perennials, flowering mainly between winter and early summer. The wide range of colors offers both brilliant and pastel shades, including multicolored flowers. Trailing kinds, *G. rigens leucolaena (G. uniflora)*, are used as ground cover, often alongside an even more vigorous spreader of similar appearance, the yellow-flowered, gray-green leaved, evergreen Cape weed *(Arctotheca calendula).* Or they are mixed with purple, mauve and white freeway daisies *(Osteosperum fruticosum).*

Clump-forming gazanias for beds and borders, often called *G. splendens,* include mixed-color seed strains and such splendid named kinds as red-flowered 'Fiesta' and double-flowered, yellow 'Moonglow'.

Seed can be sown in flats in fall, the seedlings transplanted into the garden when of sufficient size. Selected forms are increased by careful division or basal cuttings. As their predominantly brilliant colors suggest—shade plants are usually of subtler color—gazanias need sun. Flowers do not open without it, and most close when the sun goes down, which makes them unsatisfactory cut flowers. They grow well in most soils, including poor, dry ones. They are fairly drought tolerant, but a combination of heat and soggy soil causes root rot.

Gazania hybrid 'Copper King'

GERANIUM
Cranesbill, Hardy Geranium
Family: Geraniaceae

The scientific name for the frost-tender plants popularly called geraniums is *Pelargonium.* True geraniums are often called *hardy geraniums,* though not all are hardy. For example, the magenta-flowered, cut-leaved *G. incanum,* much used in the warmer parts of California, is frost-tender.

There are so many hardy geraniums that only a few of the most versatile can be described here. Some, such as *G. cinereum* 'Ballerina' and *G. subcaulescens* 'Splendens', are scarcely robust enough for the border, best in the rock garden in sharply drained, gritty soil. Those described grow well in most well-drained soils, including those with high lime content. They do best in cool-summer regions and require light shade in hot-summer regions. Hardy geraniums seldom need dividing. If you want extra plants, you can take divisions without lifting the clump, by pushing your fingers down among the roots and separating a piece from the parent plant.

G. dalmaticum
Zone 4, 6 inches, pink, spring or early summer ◑ ○

Flights of 1-inch-wide, pink blossoms hover over tufted clumps of small, glossy, fan-shaped leaves, prettily lobed. There is a less-robust, white-flowered variety with a slight hint of pink in its petals. Three years of growing *G. dalmati-*

Geranium 'Johnson's Blue'

Geranium endressii 'A. T. Johnson'

cum in Virginia's hot sun reduced it to a small, sad fragment, saved from imminent death by moving it to rich, moist soil with afternoon shade, where it does well. In cool-summer climates, it can take full sun and drier soil.

G. endressii
Zone 3, 12 to 18 inches, pink, varies ◑ ○

This plant does best in cool, even climates such as that of the Pacific Northwest, where it flowers all season and remains evergreen. In such climates, it is adapted to sun and tolerant of dry shade. Bitter winters kill the leaves, and flowering stops during hot, summer weather. The species has flowers of mallow pink with purple veining. 'A.T. Johnson' is silvery pink and 'Wargrave Pink' a warmer pink. *G. endressii* is one parent of the hybrid, 'Claridge Druce', a vigorous 18-inch colonizer with pink flowers penciled purple.

G. himalayense (G. grandiflorum, G. meeboldii)
Zone 3, 12 to 18 inches, violet blue, early summer ◑ ○

This species has 2-inch, saucer-shaped flowers of violet-blue with red veins. Flowers rise on 15-inch stems over colonizing clumps of deeply lobed leaves. The cultivar 'Alpinum' is 1 foot tall, and 'Plenum' has double flowers of mauvish blue.

'Johnson's Blue'
Zone 4, 1 foot, blue, spring or early summer ◑ ○

Though of moderate height, this hybrid is inclined to sprawl, but not unattractively. Because it flowers early, 'Johnson's Blue' can take full sun, even in Southern gardens, though it also does well in light shade. The flowers are smaller than those of *G. himalayense,* but borne in greater number.

G. macrorrhizum
Zone 3, under 1 foot, pink, late spring or early summer ◑ ○

This plant makes a good deciduous ground cover. Each leaf is rounded and lobed, the lobes scalloped. Leaves are held horizontally, shading the ground beneath the plant so weeds are discouraged. *G. macrorrhizum* is stoloniferous and soon makes large patches where soil and climate suit it. The flowers, each about 1 inch across, are held in small clusters at the stem tips. Those of the species have been described as "tolerable magenta." The cultivar 'Album' has whitish flowers in red calyces. The most attractive cultivar is baby-pink 'Ingwersen's Variety'.

G. maculatum
Zone 4, 1 to 2 feet, pale lilac, spring ◑ ○

This is the only species included that is native to North America. It grows wild from Maine to Manitoba, south to Georgia, Tennessee, Arkansas and South Dakota, usually in light shade, but in the cooler regions it also grows in meadows. Two white forms are available, one blushed with pink, the other pure white. Within its native range, this plant would be a better choice than its European-woodland counterpart, *G. sylvaticum,* with its violet-blue flowers. These two plants have similar requirements. If you have the space, you may want to try both.

G. sanguineum
Zone 3, 1 foot or less, magenta, spring or early summer ◑ ○

The most robust and adaptable of all geraniums, *G. sanguineum* is able to stand full sun, even in hot climates. The

Geranium sanguineum (top) and *Geranium sanguineum lancastrense.*

magenta flowers of the species are softened by mounds of rounded, starry lobed leaves. The flowers of *G.s. lancastrense* are soft pink with crimson veining. White-flowered 'Alba' forms less-compact clumps, is a bit less robust and does best in light shade. 'Shepherd's Warning' is an attractive new form with sunrise-pink flowers.

If you like the strong magenta flowers of *G. sanguineum*, this color is also found in *G. psilostemon (G. armenum),* rendered striking by the 4 foot height of the plant and the black eye of the flower. This species is scarce.

GERBERA
Transvaal Daisy
Family: Compositae

G. jamesonii
Zone 8, 18 inches, many colors, spring or summer ○

The size of the flowers—as much as 5 inches across—and the clear, bright colors make gerberas the most exotic of the daisies. Colors include white, cream, yellow, pink, orange and red. Flowers are single or double, borne one to a stem and excellent for cutting. They rise to a height of 18 inches over clumps of hairy, lobed leaves, similar in shape to those of dandelions.

Gerberas need rich, moist but well-drained soil and benefit from light shade in hot regions. Mulch should be kept away from the base of the stems and leaves of the plant to avoid rotting. These plants are hardy through the average Zone-8 winter if protected with a nonmatting material such as dried pine needles, salt hay or evergreen boughs. Plants can be carefully divided in early spring. Seed, which must be fresh, should be sown in peat-amended soil and needs a temperature of about 70F to germinate.

GEUM
Family: Rosaceae

All species
Zone 6 (except as noted), 1 to 2 feet, orange, red, yellow, spring or early summer ○ ◑

Geums are excellent, long-flowering, evergreen perennials for cool-summer, mild-winter climates, where they do well in sun or light shade. Hardiness varies, but most are chancy in zones colder than Zone 5. Many are less hardy than that. Geums may survive heat and drought, but the foliage shrivels, making them unattractive.

Geums need fertile soil, moist but well drained. A few are red or yellow, but orange shades predominate. Height seldom exceeds 2 feet. They are among the first perennials to flower in spring, and the taller, orange-flowered cultivars are striking when interplanted with forget-me-nots or brunnera. The leaves are fascinating—small frills of leaf scattered along leaf-blades that spread out and resemble strawberry leaves at the tip. Both sides of the leaf are covered with a glistening down.

Among the best geums for colder regions (Zone 5) are *G.* 'Borisii', with dark orange flowers on 10-inch clumps, 12- to 15-inch 'Georgenberg' with paler orange flowers, and 12- to 18-inch 'Heldreichii' with orange flowers.

Gerbera jamesonii

Geum 'Starker's Magnificent'

95

Geum 'Fire Opal'

Gillenia trifoliata

Gypsophila paniculata 'Pink Fairy'

The tender, scarlet-flowered *G. chiloense* (*G. quellyon, G. coccineum*) is thought to have parented the semidouble, orange-scarlet 'Mrs. Bradshaw' around 1906. A yellow counterpart, 'Lady Stratheden', followed. Both are short-lived in most regions, but widely distributed because they come more or less true from seed. Annual division may prolong their lives. Two more-reliable cultivars, needing only infrequent division, are coppery orange 'Starker's Magnificent', 15 inches tall, and the taller, semidouble 'Red Wings'.

The 9-inch *G. reptans* (Zone 5) is typically yellow but orange color forms are known to exist. This is the only geum in cultivation that spreads by means of runners.

GILLENIA
Family: Rosaceae

G. trifoliata (Bowman's-root)
Zone 4, 2 to 3 feet, white, summer ◑ ○

This dainty native of the eastern United States is more appreciated in England than it is in its homeland. Although in the wild it grows in open woods, in all but the hottest regions it does just as well in full sun, and in any moderately moist and fertile soil. It makes a loosely bushy plant, with sprays of 1-inch-wide, starry flowers of white or pale pink. Propagated by seed or division.

GYPSOPHILA
Baby's Breath
Family: Caryophyllaceae

The clouds of white or pink, single or double flowers are almost indispensible for adding lightness to borders, filling gaps, or hiding dying foliage of early bulbs and such perennials as oriental poppies. One plant of *G. paniculata* makes a huge bush, 3 to 4 feet across and provides all the "filler" you need for bouquets. Dry branches by hanging them in bunches in an airy place. The leaves are small and inconspicuous.

G. paniculata and the shorter *G. repens* are the most familiar kinds. *G. elegans* is an annual.

"Gypsophila" means lime-loving. In overly acid soil, stir a handful of lime into the planting hole, mixing well. If you add a pint of crushed oyster shells, this will be a long-lasting source of calcium, and plants will also appreciate the increased porosity of the soil. Gypsophila requires deep, moisture-retentive but well-drained soil in a sunny site.

Spring is the best time to plant gypsophila. The seed of species can be sown directly into the ground. Plants have long taproots, and once established are best left undisturbed. Selected forms of *G. paniculata* may prove to be longer-lived than they have been in the past, now that nurseries are beginning to propagate them by tissue culture instead of grafting. They can be grown from cuttings, but it isn't easy.

Gypsophilas over 18 inches tall require support. You can support plants with a corset of twine laced around bamboo stakes, to half the final height of the plants. Or, you can buy the sturdy galvanized-wire rings made for this purpose. They are available in four diameters, in heights from 18 to 36 inches, sold by garden-tool distributor Walter F. Nicke—see catalog source list on pages 156-157.

If bushes are cut back before the flowers go to seed, they will usually flower again where the growing season is fairly long. At the limit of their hardiness, they need winter protection unless covered by a blanket of snow.

G. paniculata
Zone 3, 1-1/2 to 3 feet, white or pink, summer ○

The following cultivars are usually listed under *G. paniculata:*
- 'Bristol Fairy'; 3 feet tall, white, double flowers.
- 'Compacta Plena' ('Bodgeri'). Probably a hybrid with *G. repens* 'Rosea'; 15 inches tall, white, semidouble flowers fading to pale pink, blooms early spring.
- 'Dantziger'; New and not yet well tested, but selected for its ability to flower with less light than the others. White flowers.
- 'Flamingo'; 2 feet tall, pink, double flowers. May be a form of *G. oldhamiana.* Not very robust.
- 'Perfecta'; 2-1/2 feet tall, white, double flowers. Flowers larger than 'Bristol Fairy'.
- 'Pink Fairy'; 1-1/2 feet tall, light pink, double flowers.
- 'Rosy Veil' ('Rosenschlier'); Possibly a hybrid with *G. repens* 'Rosea'. 15 inches tall, pale pink, semidouble flowers. Plant is semiprostrate.

G. repens (Creeping Gypsophila)
Zone 3, 6 inches, white or pink, summer ○

Flowers have the familiar misty look common to gypsophilas, but the stems are long and trailing, and plants seldom get higher than 6 inches. It has the same deep root system, making it difficult to get rooted divisions, but can be increased by cuttings taken in summer. The cultivar 'Rosea' has pink flowers.

Other Species—Lesser known perennial kinds, variable in color but usually pale pink, are the 3-foot *G. oldhamiana* (Zone 5), and the ungainly, 4-foot *G. pacifica.* These often do better in the South than *G. paniculata,* as does 'Snowflake', which flowers a month earlier than *G. paniculata.* Seed of 'Snowflake' yields a mixture of single and double flowers.

HEDYCHIUM
Ginger Lily
Family: Zingiberaceae

Ginger lilies are tender perennials, needing warmth and rich, moist soil. Propagated by division of the rhizomes.

H. coronarium
Zone 9, 3 to 6 feet, white, summer ◑

This is the hardiest species available. Leaves are broad and cornlike in appearance. Fragrant, silky flowers are reminiscent of white butterflies. If well mulched, this plant survives short spells of 15F (−10C) temperature. It requires humus-rich soil, in sun or light shade. Under ideal conditions, it may exceed 5 feet in height.

H. gardneranum
Zone 9, to 8 feet, yellow, late summer to fall ◑

The soft, yellow flowers with protruding red stamens are individually small, but are massed in a thick spike over 1 foot long. Just one spike makes a flower arrangement. Flowers are extremely fragrant.

Hedychium gardneranum

Helenium autumnale

HELENIUM
Sneezeweed
Family: Compositae

All heleniums have a prominent "hub" of disk flowers, surrounded by reflexed petals (ray flowers).

H. autumnale
Zone 3, 2 to 6 feet, yellow, orange, mahogany, late summer to early fall ○

H. autumnale is valued for its late flowering time and for the ability to grow in wet soils. This yellow-flowered species grows wild in wet, sunny places over much of the United States and Canada. It has imparted its hardiness to the hybrids. The species is usually a lanky, 5-foot plant.

Some of the following selections and hybrids of *H. autumnale* are compact. Ranginess in taller ones can be literally "nipped in the bud" by pinching out tip growth through spring. This also increases the number of flowers. They are vigorous plants, so space them 1-1/2 to 2 feet apart. Divide clumps about every third year. There are many others, but the following are the most readily available:
- 'Bruno', 2 feet tall, mahogany flowers.
- 'Butterpat', 3 feet tall, golden yellow flowers.
- 'Crimson Beauty', 2 feet tall, mahogany flowers, despite its name.
- 'Gypsy', 3 feet tall, bronze and gold flowers.
- 'Riverton Beauty', 4 feet tall, flowers yellow with maroon eye. Plants sold as 'Riverton Beauty, are not always true to name.

Other Species— *H. bigelovii* (Zone 8), 2 to 3 feet tall, is native to California, and too tender for most of the country, but it has played a part in some of the hardy hybrids. The only other species under cultivation is the early-flowering, 2- to 3-foot *H. hoopesii* (Zone 3) with flowers of deep gold or orange.

HELIANTHUS
Sunflower
Family: Compositae

So many wild sunflowers are scattered over the Americas that many garden-worthy kinds still await introduction. Most have bright yellow, daisy-type flowers. If you decide to try a wild species, remember that many are invasive.

H. annuus, an annual, is the sunflower raised commercially for its edible seeds. The Jerusalem artichoke *(H. tuberosus)* is pretty but invasive, as is shade-tolerant *H. decapetalus.* The plant often listed as *H. decapetalus* 'Flore Pleno' is now considered to be a hybrid and placed under *H. × multiflorus.* Those described here need thinning out or dividing only when performance deteriorates, usually every third or fourth year.

H. angustifolius (Swamp Sunflower)
Zone 6, 3 to 7 feet, yellow, fall ○

Where the fall season is long and sunny, this graceful plant with narrow leaves is a winner. If given summer water, it does well in dry climates. For a plant found wild in low, wet ground, it is surprisingly drought tolerant. Late in the season, seldom before September, the slenderly branched upper part of the plant erupts into a shower

Helianthus × multiflorus 'Triumph de Gand'

of 2-1/2-inch, brown-disked yellow daisies. It is self-supporting in soils that are not overly rich. *H. giganteus* is similar but larger in all its parts, attaining an impressive 10 feet—when it may fall over unless staked.

H. × *multiflorus*
Zone 4, 3 to 5 feet, yellow, summer ○

These, with heliopsis and some rudbeckias, are the forsythias among perennials, as easily grown, and guaranteed visible at 100 yards. 'Flore Pleno' and 'Loddon Gold' are the most common cultivars, similar bushy plants needing 2 feet of space. In summer they produce a mass of bright yellow flowers resembling shaggy, double chrysanthemums. One plant is enough for a garden of average size. These are not invasive, but the similar 'Miss Mellish' is a colonizer to be avoided in light soils or where the growing season is long.

HELIOPSIS
Family: Compositae

H. helianthoides scabra
Zone 4, 3 to 4 feet, yellow, summer ○ ◑

This species is similar to helianthus in flower color, bushy size and foliage. It is usually a little shorter and less likely to need support, more tolerant of shade and poor, dry soil, and has a greater variation in flower form among available selections. The color of most is more yellow-orange than yellow-green. The cultivars 'Karat' (single flowers) and 'Incomparabilis' (full, semidouble flowers), are deep golden-yellow. 'Gold Greenheart', a well-formed double, is nearer to yellow-green, with a green center when newly open. 'Golden Plume' has fully double flowers. 'Summer Sun' is usually grown from seed, therefore variable. The species itself is well worth growing. These are among the best perennials for prolonged summer color. Divide clumps when flowers diminish in size or quantity. Cultivars are propagated by division or cuttings, the species by seed.

HELLEBORUS
Christmas Rose, Lenten Rose
Family: Ranunculaceae

These are not roses at all, but are related to the buttercups. Hellebores are among the best perennials where the weather permits their handsome, usually evergreen leaves and early, long-lasting flowers to be seen at their best. At temperatures below 15F (−10C), bloom is delayed and, unless snow protected, leaves become increasingly scorched.

In most regions, hellebores do best in light shade and humus-rich soil. In deep soil, they are usually not bothered by high summer temperatures. Plants can be divided if done carefully—*H. orientalis* is comparatively easy to divide. However, these plants seldom, if ever, need dividing. Seedlings that spring up under the sheltering umbrellas of mature plants will provide ample new plants. Purchased seed may take 2 years or more to germinate, so you

Heliopsis helianthoides 'Incomparabilis' with the annual or biennial *Malva sylvestris* 'Zebrina' (*Althaea* 'Zebrina').

Helleborus niger

Helleborus orientalis hybrid

may want to start with a purchased plant. Only those described here are readily available.

H. foetidus (Stinking Hellebore)
Zone 6, 18 inches, green, late winter or spring ◑ ●

Name notwithstanding, it doesn't stink. Stinking hellebore has attractive, multifingered, dark green leaves. Flowers are clustered, green bells rimmed with red, 1 inch across. It may go dormant in hot, dry summers, re-emerging in spring.

H. lividus corsicus
Zone 8, 2 to 3 feet, apple-green, winter or spring ◑ ●

A magnificent, shrubby bush, firmly and stiffly upright when not in bloom. Flowering stems often exceed 3 feet in length, leaning under the weight of their great trusses of translucent, apple-green flowers, which bloom for months. Remove flowering stems from the base when no longer attractive. The leaves are among the most striking of all perennials, the three leaflets a softly shining gray-green, netted with paler veins and edged with needle-fine teeth. They are firmly held out on thick, pale stalks.

This species is drought tolerant, can take more sun than most and is the best hellebore for Southern California. Although *H. lividus corsicus* is hardy in zones much colder than Zone 8, it gets so battered at winter temperatures of 5F (−15C) or below that it is hardly worth growing.

H. niger (Christmas Rose)
Zone 3, 1 foot, white, winter or early spring ◑ ●

An almost legendary plant, but where both can be grown, the Lenten rose *(H. orientalis)* is a better plant. Traditionally, the Christmas rose bears its white, salver-shaped flowers singly, but those sold in nurseries more often have two or three pink-flushed flowers to a stem. These flowers seldom open before February, often coinciding with, or even later than, the Lenten rose. The fingered, dull green leaves are less handsome than those of other hellebores. Plants are slow to take hold after division, which is never needed unless you want more plants. Christmas rose self-sows sparingly. A large clump flowering in winter is a rare sight. Protecting plants with a transparent cover, such as a sheet of glass or acrylic plastic propped up on bricks, increases the possibility of seeing unsullied flowers. Christmas rose does not do well in regions with frost-free winters.

H. orientalis hybrids (Lenten Rose)
Zone 4, 18 inches, colors vary, late winter or early spring ◑ ●

For most gardens, this hellebore is the easiest to grow. Flower color ranges from green through cream and pink to dark maroon, usually streaked or speckled.

Each stem bears several flowers, effective as long as 3 months—their only fault is the tendency to nod. Less-nodding kinds have been developed but these are expensive and hard to find. Palm-shaped, glossy leaves are held flat and deeply divided into saw-edged lobes. Prolific self-sowers, excellent for naturalizing between shrubs or deep-rooted trees.

HEMEROCALLIS
Daylily
Liliaceae

Daylilies are among the most adaptable perennials—one kind or another can be grown in all but the most bitter climates. They revel in warm, sunny days, and prefer moist, moderately fertile loam, either slightly acid or neutral. However, the tough, old tawny daylily *(H. fulva)* will grow in almost any soil or site and has established itself as a wildflower in the eastern United States. This is remarkable because it is a sterile form *(H. fulva* 'Europa'), and the thousands of plants by roadsides have got there by root spread.

Tawny daylily is excellent for meadow gardening, and for soil retention on steep slopes. It sets no seed but has been a pollen-parent in hybridizing, as has the double 'Kwanso', which is equally tough. There is a frail form of 'Kwanso' with white-striped leaves. Pink-flowered *H. fulva* 'Rosea' made possible the pink and red shades in modern hybrids. The 3-foot, fragrant lemon-lily, *H. lilioasphodelus (H. flava)* is less of a spreader, but equally robust, common around abandoned New England homesites.

Other species that contributed their special qualities to modern hybrids include:
- *H. aurantiaca*, 3 feet, orange flowers: Evergreen foliage, also lesser hardiness.
- *H. citrina*, 3 feet, lemon-yellow flowers: Fragrance, nocturnal flowers.
- *H. dumortieri*, 2 feet, yellow flowers from brown buds: Earliness, fragrance.
- *H. littorea (aurantiaca littorea):* Fall bloom.
- *H. middendorfii*, 2 feet, orange-yellow flowers from brown buds: Compactness, early flower.
- *H. minor*, yellow flowers: Dwarfness, fragrance, grassy foliage.
- *H. multiflora*, 3 feet, yellow-orange flowers: Small flowers, graceful branching habit. 'Golden Chimes' is of this type.

Of these and other species, only *H. fulva* and *H. lilioasphodelus* are now common. Rock-gardening enthusiasts can be thanked for keeping in circulation *H. minor*, *H. dumortieri* and *H. middendorfiana*.

Nowadays, new daylilies are created by crossing one hybrid with another. At its simplest, this involves only the transferring of pollen from one desirable plant to the pistil of another—something you may want to try yourself. If the cross is successful, seeds of the crossed plant will produce a new hybrid. Sometimes the bees do the crossing for you. On a professional level, hybridizing is more complex, requiring knowledge of which plants will cross successfully to create the exact qualities sought.

A thousand or more new hybrids are now registered each year. The only colors to elude hybridizers are pure white—there are good creamy whites—and blue. Colors are bright or pastel, solid or in numerous two-color combinations, either distinctly zoned or softly bleeding in. Flower form and texture are equally varied. Sizes range from under 3 inches (miniature) to over 6 inches. There may be as many as 30 flowers to a scape (stem), and as many as 12 scapes on a single plant. The yellow 'Green Flutter' is a good example of this multi-stemmed floriferousness.

A border of daylilies *(Hemerocallis)*.

Hemerocallis 'Baby Pumpkin'

A daylily color-matched with 'Crimson Pygmy' barberry leaves.

Most daylilies are 2-1/2 to 3-1/2 feet tall when in flower, but there is an increasing range of dwarf varieties, some less than 1 foot tall. Don't confuse the term *miniature* (size of flower) with *dwarf* (height of plant).

There are hybrids that flower in spring, in early or late summer or in fall. Some repeat bloom. Those with evergreen foliage are ideal for the Deep South and for Southern California, but not very hardy. At their hardiness limit, the foliage on evergreen kinds gets so shabby one wishes the plant would go decently to rest.

Many modern hybrids are less robust than such staunch old favorites as yellow 'Hyperion'. If you favor grace over sumptuousness of flower, sifting through the many available hybrids for this quality can be a lengthy process. Remember that the larger and lusher the flower, the more today's beauty is marred by the tawdry remains of yesterday's blooms. Daily dead-heading is required to keep the plant looking its best, which may detract from the plant's other labor-saving qualities.

There is a daylily for almost every garden, but not every daylily does well everywhere. To get the best of the daylily world, choose from growing plants if possible, or buy those bred and tested in a climate similar to yours. But catalog pictures are often so enticing that most of us succumb to buying a plant that may or may not be suited to our gardens. If you feel unable to make a choice, the American

Hemerocallis 'Green Flutter'

Hemerocallis Society publishes a list each year of those voted the best plants. The society's address is listed on page 157.

Daylily care is relatively easy. They can be planted in spring or fall, but growers usually ship them in late summer. Space them 2 feet apart, slightly less for dwarfs. Dead-head them each day, if required. Cut out the whole scape when flowering is done. Older varieties can be left undivided indefinitely, but modern hybrids should be divided about every third year. Robust clumps can be sliced into sections with a sharp spade. Choice hybrids should be lifted, washed clean of soil and the tubers carefully divided so that nothing is wasted. Each tuber should have a piece of stem attached. Daylilies cannot be grown from cuttings, but little plantlets often appear along the stems and these can be removed and treated as cuttings.

HEUCHERA
AND ×HEUCHERELLA
Alumroot, Coralbells
Saxifragaceae

Note: *Heuchera* (alumroot) is a North American species native to both coasts. × *Heucherella* is the name given to hybrids between *Heuchera* and *Tiarella* (foamflower).

H. sanguinea hybrids (Coralbells)
Zone 3, 1 to 2-1/2 feet, red, pink, white, spring or summer ○ ◑

Most species of Heuchera have sprays of greenish or cream flowers, but those of *H. sanguinea* are bright red. The graceful flower sprays rise on wiry stems over basal clumps of usually evergreen leaves, which are rounded, scalloped and often darkly marbled. Most garden coralbells are selections of *H. sanguinea,* or hybrids between this and the hardy *H. micrantha,* a cross named *H.* × *brizoides.* These are usually hardy to Zone 3.

Hybrids vary in height from 1 to 2-1/2 feet, and in color from white and chartreuse through shades of pink to scarlet. The cultivar 'Queen of Hearts' was one of the first introductions and is still popular today. Rose-pink 'Chatterbox', scarlet 'Pluie de Feu' (Rain of Fire), white 'Snowflakes', tall 'Scarlet Sentinel' and 'Scintillation' with red-tipped pink bells, are just a few of the many excellent cultivars to be chosen on the basis of preferred height and color. The seed of Bressingham hybrids yields a mix of colors and heights.

Coralbells are easy to grow in most soils that are not sodden in winter. Plant in full sun or light shade. Bloom peaks in spring. In cool-summer climates, blooms will continue through summer if spent stems are removed. Clumps are shallow rooted and quickly get bare and woody at the base. Top-dressing with loam or mulch postpones the need for division to about the third year, when the woodiest parts of the clump should be discarded and strong, well-rooted divisions replanted to the level of the leaves.

Other Species—Several species, especially *H. americana* (Zone 4), are valued as foliage plants for the woodland garden. There are selections with mahogany-colored leaves.

Victor Reiter of San Francisco crossed *Heuchera* 'Pluie

Heuchera sanguinea hybrid

The hybrid × *Heucherella* 'Bridget Bloom' was raised by English nurseryman Alan Bloom, and named for his daughter.

Hibiscus coccineus

de Feu' with the tender *H. maxima* to produce excellent, tall hybrids. Similar crosses by Dr. Lee Lenz at Rancho Santa Ana Botanic Garden produced such cultivars as 'Genevieve', 'Susana' and the outstanding 'Santa Ana Cardinal', the finest heuchera for warm West Coast gardens, and possibly for other warm, mild climates. 'Santa Ana Cardinal' makes clumps to 4 feet wide and may flower for 4 months or more, sometimes carrying as many as 100 spikes of bright rose-red, each 2 to 3 feet tall.

× *Heucherella*
Zone 3, 12 to 18 inches, pink, spring to early summer ○ ◐

'Bridget Bloom' is the best known hybrid, a cross between *Heuchera* × *brizoides* and *Tiarella wherryi*. It resembles the daintier cultivars of coralbells, with starrier flowers of a clear, soft pink. It starts to flower a little earlier, needs similar site, soil and treatment.

Tiarella wherryi is a variable species with flowers from creamy-buff to soft pink and leaves that are deeply or shallowly lobed. The main distinguishing characteristic between this plant and the more common, creamy-flowered foamflower *(T. cordifolia)* is that foamflower is stoloniferous and *T. wherryi* is clump-forming. Both are Zone 3 hardy and desirable perennials for acid soil in the shrub or woodland garden, or the front of a shaded border.

HIBISCUS
Rose Mallow
Family: Malvaceae

H. moscheutos hybrids, (Giant Rose Mallow)
Zone 5, 3 to 7 feet, white, pink, red, summer or late summer ○

No hardy perennial has bigger flowers than those of giant rose mallow. Flowers are as much as 1 foot across, resembling outsize single hollyhocks. Colors include white, crimson, in-between shades of pink and rose, and some bicolors. A plant this dominant is best grown alone, perhaps in a courtyard bed. Shorter kinds can be grown in large containers.

These hybrids prefer damp soil in full sun, but drier soil is tolerated—so is some light shade. If seed is sown early, plants flower the first year. Usually propagated by seed.

Other Perennial Hibiscus—If you prefer more graceful flowers, consider the species used in breeding the giants. These are native to swamps and marshes of North America, but tolerant—more so than the hybrids—of poor, dry soil. *H. moscheutos* is white with a red eye, *H.m. palustris* pink, and the less-hardy *H. coccineus* (Zone 6) a bright red. Seashore mallow, *Kosteletzkya virginica*, is a related plant often found in the same brackish marshes as *H. moscheutos*, but exceptionally tolerant of dry, sandy soil. It is a daintier plant with 2-inch, pale pink flowers.

Hibiscus moscheutos hybrid

HOSTA
Plantain Lily
Family: Liliaceae

Species
Zone 3, under 6 inches to 5 feet, mauve or white, flowering times vary, foliage plants ◑ ●

Hostas are cold-hardy plants and easy to grow. They have joined bearded irises and daylilies as hobbyists' plants and new ones are being introduced faster than they can be evaluated. The newest kinds are often expensive, but if a plant proves robust the price will soon come down.

In the past, many hostas could only be propagated by division—few lily-family plants can be grown from cuttings—so those that yielded few divisions, notably *H. sieboldiana* and *H. tardiflora,* tended to remain scarce. Cloning isn't possible for people, but it is for plants. Hostas are now being raised commercially by tissue-culture propagation. This is a cloning process whereby a desirable plant can parent hundreds of identical offspring from tiny fragments of itself, grown in a laboratory environment.

Hostas are grown mainly for their foliage. Leaves may be lance-shaped, rounded or somewhere in between. Leaf sizes range from less than an inch to more than a foot across. Leaf texture may be smooth, ribbed or seersuckered, flat, wavy or twisted. Leaf colors include light green, dark green, yellow, and grayish or bluish green. Some have leaves edged or variously patterned with white, cream or yellow. Height, not including flowers, ranges from under 6 inches to over 3 feet. The flowers, shaped like small lilies, are white, mauve, violet or purple, in elegant spires as tall as 5 feet, or in chunky clusters partly buried among the leaves. Varying with variety, flowers open between early June and October. A few are fragrant.

Hostas are known to succeed from mid-Alabama to mid-Canada. They do best in moist, rich soil and light shade, but the older ones are rugged, adaptable plants, better able than most to tolerate deep shade and root competition. Some of the newer ones haven't yet been fully tested for ruggedness and adaptability.

Hostas are among the few flowering plants that do well in those dim passageways between buildings, though the flowers will be fewer and will lean toward the light. Some take full sun at 90F (32C) with surprising equanimity if the soil is moderately moist. Hostas can stand wet soil when in growth, but not when dormant.

Hostas are excellent for massing, but the large ones look better as single showpieces. Because they break dormancy late in spring, they make a good ground cover over early bulbs. Most are easily divided, but this is seldom needed. Their only serious problem is slugs and snails—the larger the leaf, the more apparent the damage. A liquid slug and snail killer sprayed on the leaves is more effective than pellets or powders scattered on the ground.

Hosta sieboldiana 'Frances Williams' was rated No. 1 in a poll of Hosta Society members.

Hosta undulata 'Albo-marginata' is an old favorite. It is shown here with *Carex morrowii* 'Aurea Variegata'.

POPULAR VARIETIES

The following list includes some good old kinds that you may already have in your garden, and some of the best new varieties, available for $10 or less, selected by Dr. Warren Pollock of the American Hosta Society. The typical flower color is mauve or pale lilac. Flowers are of secondary importance, so sizes given are for clumps not in flower.

H. albomarginata (H. sieboldii)

One-foot-tall clumps of spear-shaped leaves with a narrow white edge that disappears as the season progresses. It spreads quickly and makes a good border edging. Flowers are violet-blue. 'Louisa', found as a seedling under H. albomarginata, has white flowers and leaves with a more conspicuous white edge. 'Kabitan' has wavy, straplike yellow leaves with a narrow green edge.

'Antioch'

A medium-size, spreading plant. Leaves are green with lighter green patches and a wide, creamy-white border.

H. decorata

Blunt, 4- to 6-inch rounded leaves with a conspicuous white edge. Forms low, spreading clumps. In the United States, it is often sold as 'Thomas Hogg', which in Britain is a different plant.

H. fortunei

Large, handsome clumps of 5-inch, pale green, oval leaves, which in 'Albo-marginata' are edged white. H. crispula is similar to 'Albo-marginata' and the two are often confused. In 'Aureo-marginata', leaves are edged yellow turning to cream in summer. The young leaves of 'Albo-picta' are pale, primrose-yellow edged green, and those of 'Aurea' are translucent pale cream. In both of these, the pale coloring turns green by summer. 'Francee' is an improved version of 'Albo- marginata'. It has heart-shaped leaves with a narrow white margin. 'Gold Standard' is a new cultivar of the H. fortunei type. In early spring, the leaves are chartreuse, irregularly bordered with dark green. As the sun becomes stronger, the chartreuse color turns bright, parchment-yellow.

'Ginko Craig'

A good, small edging plant. Its lance-shaped leaves have a narrow white edge.

'Golden Tiara'

Clump height about 10 inches, spread to over 1 foot. Leaves 2 inches long, apple-green with a narrow chartreuse edge, turning golden in summer if light is good.

'Krossa Regal'

Outstanding for its 5-foot spires of flowers and blue-gray leaves held in a tall, vase-shaped clump.

H. lancifolia

Six-inch, dark green lance-shaped leaves that emerge early in spring. Clumps are medium size with abundant bloom.

H. montana

'Aureo-marginata': A medium-size plant with long, pointed green leaves with a wide gold border that turns creamy white by early summer.

H. plantaginea

Six-inch, shiny pale-green rounded leaves. Has white flowers late in the season. This species has imparted its mild fragrance to the hybrids, 'Honeybells' and 'Royal Standard'.

H. sieboldiana

Seersucker-textured, bluish leaves in clumps 2 to 3 feet tall and as much as 4 feet across. Dense heads of white flowers are partly hidden among leaves, but in 'Elegans', rise just clear of them. 'Frances Williams' has yellow-edged leaves. H. tokudama is a similar but considerably smaller species. H. t. 'Aureo-nebulosa', though still expensive, is worth seeking out for its unusual streaked variegation of cloudy gold.

H. tardiflora

One-foot clumps of narrow, dark green leaves. Flowers are darker than mauve, paler than violet. The last hosta of the season to flower. Slow to increase. H. tardiflora crossed with H. sieboldiana resulted in some beautiful, blue-leaved hostas grouped under the name, H. × tardiana. 'Halcyon' is one of the best selections of this hybrid group.

H. undulata

This species is sold by the thousands every year, even though many gardeners acquire it over the garden fence. Beautiful, undulating and twisted leaves of cream and olive-green, at their best in spring. The cultivar 'Univittata' has the creamy variegation in the form of a broad center stripe. 'Albo-marginata' is a less curly-looking plant with a broad whitish edging to the leaves. Although not always sold under this name, it is one of the most widely planted hostas. Green-leaved 'Erronema' wins no beauty prizes, but is a tough, trouble-free plant that thrives and flowers in deep shade.

H. ventricosa (H. caerulea)

A medium-size clump of pleasing, nonglossy ribbed leaves, distinguished by its brightly colored flowers—not blue, but nearer to it than any other hosta. It is easily raised from seed. 'Aureo-marginata' is a handsome, variegated cultivar.

H. venusta

The most widely distributed of the real dwarfs, H. venusta is only a few inches tall. It has lance-shaped, green leaves and 6-inch spires of mauve flowers.

Hosta decorata in a shady garden.

Hosta 'Halcyon' with *Hydrangea quercifolia*.

Bupthalmum salicifolium, (often sold as Inula 'Golden Beauty')

INULA
Family: Compositae

The best known species is probably Elecampane *(I. helenium)*, often grown in herb gardens. It is a hardy perennial, but not a particularly good one because the flowers are disproportionately small for the height of the stems. Inulas are accommodating plants, easily grown in sun or light shade and in any moderately fertile soil that does not get dry. Where summers are hot, they flower for about 2 weeks; in cool regions, much longer. Easily propagated by division.

I. ensifolia
Zone 3, 1 foot, yellow, summer ○

A useful species because of its small size, making it well suited to the front of the border. It bears 1-inch yellow daisies on 1-foot-tall mounds of well-spaced, curved leaves.

Other Species—Hardy to Zone 3, *I. orientalis (I. glandulosa)* grows to 2 feet, sometimes more, but is fairly compact and bushy. The leaves are less graceful, but the 3-inch, orange-yellow flowers are showier. A similar plant, *Bupthalmum salicifolium* or sunwheels (Zone 3), is sometimes called *Inula* 'Golden Beauty'. It is an excellent perennial, resembling *I. ensifolia* in all but its 2-foot height and slightly earlier flowering time. Plants are seldom available, but seed is, and is easy to grow.

Inula ensifolia

IRIS
Family: Iridaceae

Pictures and descriptions of irises could fill this book and still barely scratch the surface of the subject. We have included the most-popular ones, along with some others that are outstanding within stated limitations. The easiest to grow, and the best for border use, is *I. sibirica*.

The American Iris Society publishes books and pamphlets for all levels of interest including lists of recommended varieties. The society's address is on page 157. Tall bearded irises take precedence, but for those interested in other kinds, there are groups devoted to median, Siberian, spuria, Japanese, dwarf, Pacific Coast, Louisiana irises, and species. Seed of many dwarf and wild irises is available to members of the American Rock Garden Society. The address is listed on page 157.

Irises range in height from only a few inches to several feet. There are irises for wet soil, for dry soil, for acid soil and for alkaline soil. Most need sun but there are also some for shade. Fairly rich, neutral or slightly alkaline soil is recommended for tall bearded irises. Sandy, slightly acid soil of only moderate fertility suits most of the others. Irises come in all colors except true, clear red, and *I. fulva* comes close to that.

Rhizomatous irises should be planted with the rhizome showing or, in hot regions, just below soil surface, with the fan of leaves pointing the way you want the plant to grow. A few growers in hot climates mulch their plants, but most growers advise against it. If in doubt, don't use mulch.

Most species can be grown from seed. Hybrids are increased by division. Late summer is the shipping time preferred by specialist growers for most irises, but if there is a choice, early fall is better where summers are long and hot, and winter comes late.

BEARDED IRISES

Bearded irises are hardy to Zone 3. The American Iris Society divides them into six groups: *miniature dwarf, standard dwarf, intermediate, miniature tall* (table irises), *border bearded* and *tall bearded*. All but the miniature dwarf and tall beardeds are grouped under the name Median irises. Well-drained soil is an essential requirement for bearded irises.

Tall Bearded—The United States leads the world in the breeding of tall bearded irises, a complex group of mixed parentage. There are thousands of kinds with new ones being introduced each year. No other flower has such a wide range of beautiful soft colors and color combinations. They are hobbyist plants, and the comradeship of shared interest is one of gardening's greatest pleasures.

Tall bearded irises are easy to grow but not always easy to grow well. Their main shortcoming—shared with most other irises and a great many other plants—is the extremely short period of bloom. There are rebloomers for the milder regions, but this goal is as yet unrealized for the colder ones. The tawdriness of spent bloom is another flaw—conspicuous because of the size of the bloom. The leaves are handsome, but they often brown at the tips in summer. Bearded irises often need staking.

Small groups of plants in mixed borders are less likely to be afflicted with borers and other problems than those massed together. But bearded irises are not very good

Tall bearded iris 'Ermin Robe'

Tall bearded irises look their best in a formal setting.

Bearded iris 'Beverly Sills'

mixers, except with each other, and may look as out of place in a mixed border as a ball-gown at the beach. Give these sumptuous flowers the formal settings that suit them best, and choose bearded irises for the mixed border from the next group. The American Iris Society has chapters in most areas, with members able to advise about choice or varieties, sources, cultural methods and the best way of dealing with such problems as borers.

Intermediate Bearded, Miniature Tall Bearded and Border Bearded—Other than Siberian irises, the best border irises are to be found in these groups. Such rugged old "flags" as 'Albicans', 'Germanica' and 'Florentina' belong to the intermediate bearded group. Border beardeds usually have smaller flowers and more-slender stems than tall beardeds. This makes them more appealing to those concerned more with overall appearance than with flowers alone. Miniature talls are particularly fine for cutting. The color range in these groups—already wide—is rapidly being extended. It can eventually be expected to rival that of the tall bearded irises—it is hoped without sacrificing their good qualities.

Dwarfs—(Miniature Dwarf Bearded, Standard Dwarf Bearded). The chunky miniature dwarfs flower at daffodil time. They increase rapidly and look delightful as flowing sheets of color around boulders in the rock garden. Division can be postponed by top-dressing with good loam. Standard dwarfs, which include those called Lilliputs, are big enough for the front of the border but still small enough for the rock garden. Many have a thumbprint of darker spots on the falls. Both groups flower prolifically after cold winters, less so where there is no frost. The period of bloom, short at best, may be only a few days if the weather is already warm, making them scarcely worth their space where hot weather comes early.

OTHER IRISES
I.ensata (I. kaempferi in catalogs) (Japanese Iris)
Zone 5, to 4 feet, late spring or summer ○ ◑

Seeing Japanese irises growing in rice paddies that are flooded during the growing season, then drained, led to the mistaken assumption that they had to be grown this way. Japanese irises do like lots of moisture when in growth and look especially beautiful associated with water, so they are often grown in pots or boxes that are plunged in shallow water. But these exotic plants, with flowers as much as 1 foot across, can be grown in any moderately moist, humus-rich soil free of lime. Those seen growing permanently in water are usually the similar *I. laevigata,* which is lime-tolerant.

Colors include white, pale to deep blues and purples, and red-violet, often veined, marbled or speckled with a contrasting color. Flowers may be single, semidouble or peonylike. None is more beautiful than the single whites of modest size with satiny petals becoming diaphanous as they fade. Increased flower size and more elaborate form is usually achieved at the expense of easy culture and longevity. For best results, divide clumps about every third year.

If your climate is too cold for Japanese irises, try Arctic or Beachhead iris, *(I. setosa)*. It looks like a small-flowered, bluish-purple Japanese iris and thrives under the same conditions, flowering in late spring. It is Zone 2 hardy and 1 to 2 feet tall. *I. setosa canadensis,* native to coastal Maine

Bearded Iris Heights

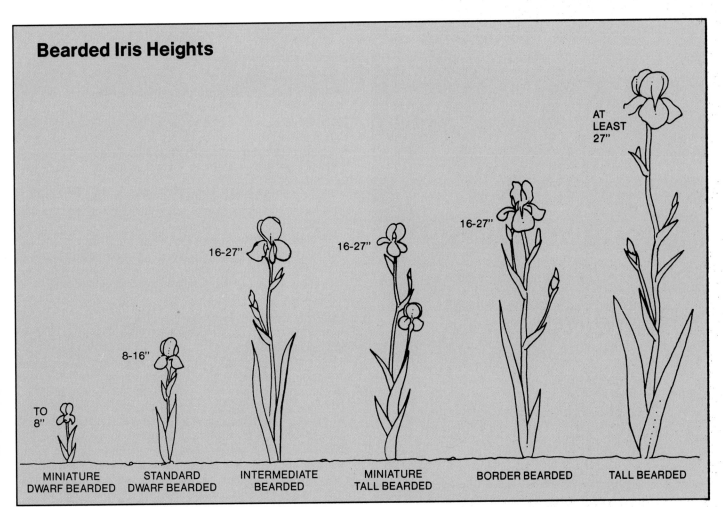

AT LEAST 27"

16-27"

16-27"

16-27"

8-16"

TO 8"

MINIATURE DWARF BEARDED

STANDARD DWARF BEARDED

INTERMEDIATE BEARDED

MINIATURE TALL BEARDED

BORDER BEARDED

TALL BEARDED

Bearded Iris Anatomy

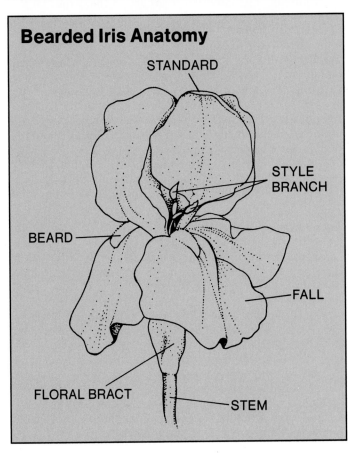

STANDARD

STYLE BRANCH

BEARD

FALL

FLORAL BRACT

STEM

Iris ensata (I. kaempferi of the trade) 'Azure'.

Iris pallida 'Aurea-variegata', sometimes sold as *I. p.* 'Zebra'.

and Labrador, is often called *I. hookeri*. It is popular with rock gardeners. *I.s. hondoensis,* 18 inches tall, is a form with particularly rich coloring.

I. pallida dalmatica
Zone 5, 3 feet, bluish purple, spring or early summer ○

This old, bearded iris can still be found fighting it out with weeds in abandoned gardens. It is still available, and though it cannot compare in glamour with modern hybrids, it is a better garden plant than most. The gray-green leaves are less apt to brown at the tips during hot weather.

This plant does not require division. If it gets borers or other pests, it seems able to survive them without the use of chemicals.

Also in this group are two outstanding foliage plants, both usually listed as 'Variegata'. One has white stripes, the other, 'Aurea-variegata', sometimes called 'Zebra', has yellow stripes. All are easy to grow in good garden soil and sun.

I. sibirica (Siberian Iris)
Zone 3, 2 to 4 feet, predominantly blue, late spring or early summer ○ ◑

Siberian irises derived from *I. sibirica* and *I. sanguinea* are among the easiest of all perennials to grow. They do best in moist, humus-rich, slightly acid soil in full sun, but they succeed in soils and sites far short of ideal.

Flowers and leaves are more graceful than those of bearded irises, and they look more at home in informal settings, mixing well with other perennials and with shrubs. Colors include blues, purples, wine-red and white. Progress is continuing toward a true yellow, 'Butter and Eggs' being the nearest so far.

Heights of most Siberian irises are in the 3-foot range. 'Little White' is exceptionally dwarf and compact, at 1-foot tall. The two mentioned, plus pale blue 'Cambridge', mid-blue 'Ego', wine-red 'Polly Dodge', near-black 'Teal-wood', miniature-flowered 'Flight of Butterflies' and 'White Swirl', would make a good starter collection. But get a specialist catalog and let yourself be tempted.

These sturdy irises are resistant to pests and diseases and seldom need dividing. If you do want divisions, first cut back the foliage, then use a sharp spade to slice the clumps of fibrous roots into sections.

The Sino-Siberians, derived from other parents, including *I. forrestii* and *I. chrysographes,* bloom slightly later than Siberians, and are less robust and adaptable. They include yellows such as 'Yellow Apricot' and 'Yellow Court'.

I. tectorum (Japanese Roof Iris)
Zone 5, 1 foot, blue or white, late spring ○ ◑

The ideal climate for this species is one with hot summers and moderately cold winters, in areas of fairly high rainfall. The ideal soil is sandy, slightly acid and of low fertility. This beardless, rhizomatous iris does especially well in the coastal regions of the upper Southeast, where it grows with weedlike ease, demanding no attention and self-sowing abundantly without being a nuisance. Cool summers inhibit flowering. Japanese roof iris will not grow in mud, nor on roofs in most regions, but almost anywhere else. It flowers most abundantly in sun or light shade. The arched fans of leaves remain evergreen down to about 20F (−29C) and are killed at lower temperatures. Propagated by seed or division.

Iris sibirica 'Super Ego' with peonies.

Iris tectorum and *I.t.* 'Album'

Crested iris, *I. cristata* (Zone 3), is much like a miniature version of Japanese roof iris. This East Coast native is at its best in moisture-retentive, humus-rich soil in light shade, where the creeping rhizomes soon form a large, free-flowering mat. Colors vary from gray-blue to dark violet, also white. All have a yellow crest. As long as it has room to spread, crested iris doesn't need dividing, but it is easily propagated by division.

I. unguicularis (I. stylosa) (Winter Iris)
Zone 8, 1 foot, violet-blue, mauve, white, November to March ○ ◑

Flowers usually open a few at a time on mild, sunny, winter days. They are raised on short, stemlike tubes among narrow, evergreen leaves that may stand erect or sprawl. Flowers picked in bud unfurl their petals within an hour or two. English growing methods—"plant in old mortar rubble against a south-facing wall" being a common recommendation—may work in the Pacific Northwest, but richer, moister soil and a modicum of shade give better results where summers are hot.

'Marginata' is the most common form—violet blue with an extremely narrow white edge to the falls. Pale lilac 'Walter Butt' is also a fine form, but those who like winter-flowering irises usually buy whatever they see offered. Slugs are the main hazard to these plants. Winter iris grows equally well in acid or alkaline soil.

Marsh and Pond Irises ○—Among the more-common irises adapted to marshy ground and shallow water are *I. laevigata, I. prismatica, I. pseudacorus, I. versicolor* and *I. virginica.* All but *I. laevigata,* which must have permanently damp soil, can be grown in ordinary border soil, preferably acid, that does not get completely dry. All flower in spring or early summer and, unless otherwise noted, flowers are blue or purple. All do best in full sun. *I. laevigata* 'Variegata' is one of the handsomest of all foliage plants, with its white-striped leaves.

Iris unguicularis 'Marginata'

Iris: Louisiana hybrid

Iris: Pacific Coast hybrid

Slender Blue Flag, *I. prismatica* (Zone 3), native from Maine to Tennessee, resembles a small form of *I. sibirica.* There is also a white form. Large Blue Flag, *I. versicolor* (Zone 3), grows wild in marshes and wet meadows from Manitoba south to Virginia, Ohio, Wisconsin and Minnesota. The Southern Blue Flag, *I. virginica,* is similar but less hardy.

Yellow Flag, *I. pseudacorus* (Zone 5), is not native but has naturalized in many parts of the United States. It may do so in your garden if seed pods are not removed. Forms vary in height from 2 to 7 feet with single or double flowers that are bright yellow, lemon or ivory. The form 'Variegata' has showy, yellow-striped leaves in spring that turn green by midsummer. Yellow Flag likes full sun if the soil is damp, light shade in drier soil and in the hottest regions.

Louisiana Irises—All the marsh and pond irises may be eclipsed by the Louisiana irises. Previously well-known only to Gulf Coast gardeners, these wild irises have been bred to produce hybrids that are likely to vie with tall bearded irises for the affection of gardeners. Species used included *I. giganticaerulea,* tall with blue flowers; *I. fulva,* the first red iris known, with flowers of yellow, copper or orange-red; *I. × nelsonii,* a larger version of *I. fulva* with flowers from yellow to crimson; and *I. brevicaulis,* a low-growing iris with blue flowers.

The hybrids were bred to achieve neater habit, more and better-formed flowers with firmer substance than other irises, neater foliage, and to overcome the tendency to produce "walking" rhizomes that need frequent controlling. In Louisiana, they bloom mid-April, later farther north, and they have been grown successfully from northern New England to the Deep South (Zones 4 to 9).

Louisiana irises make superb cut flowers. They do not need wet soil, but ideally it should be moist, humus-rich and acid. Unlike bearded irises, Louisiana hybrids should be mulched. They will grow in full sun, and in light shade if the soil is free of competing roots. Soil should be kept moist prior to and during flowering, but the plants are fairly drought resistant thereafter. The great array of colors includes near-red and the richest blue. Louisiana irises are a boon to gardens in hot, moist climates, where so many perennials fail.

Pacific Coast Natives (Pacificas, Californicas) ○ ◑—Within this group come evergreen *I. douglasiana* and *I. innominata,* deciduous *I. tenax,* other species and many hybrids. Although considered difficult to grow outside their native range, this is not entirely true. Hardiness is a limiting factor, but the hardiest, *I. tenax,* is being grown in Minnesota. Hybrids have proved long lived and easy to grow in the Zone 8 Harper garden. They are planted in the sharply drained, sandy, acid soil of the Southeastern coastal pinelands, and easily tolerate the intense, humid heat of summer. They defoliate at 5F (−15C) but renew themselves in spring. Their drought resistance is an asset, but they have also tolerated torrential summer rain, provided it drains away rapidly.

The delicate pastel colors and dainty flowers will please gardeners who prefer charm to glamour. They are easily grown from seed, so it won't be difficult or expensive to see if they will grow in your garden. They do well in full sun or light shade.

KIRENGESHOMA
Family: Hydrangeaceae

K. palmata
Zone 5, 3 feet, yellow, late summer or early fall ◑

This Japanese plant has been too rare to acquire a common name, but now it is nationally available. Most perennials used for the shaded shrub or woodland garden flower in spring. Kirengeshoma flowers late in the season. Large, smooth, maple-shaped leaves are held on sparsely branched, arching stems. The stems are tipped with satiny, nodding, creamy-yellow bells. *Hosta tardiflora,* which has mauve flowers equally late in the season, would be a good companion plant. Kirengeshoma needs light shade and plenty of peat moss mixed into the soil. Clumps build up slowly but the plant should not be crowded, so allow it 2 feet of space. Propagated by seed or careful division.

KNIPHOFIA
Red-hot-poker, Torch Lily
Family: Liliaceae

Species and Hybrids
Zone 6, 2 to 6 feet, many colors, summer or fall ○ ◑

If you don't find these listed in catalogs under *Kniphofia,* look under *Tritoma,* an earlier name. Though often called *K. uvaria*—a tall species with yellow-and-orange flowers—most of those sold are hybrids. Some grow as tall as 6 feet, the majority in the 2- to 3-1/2-foot range. Old fashioned ''pokers'' had bicolored flowers, the bottom half yellow, top half scarlet. These vibrant colors are still popular but there are also solid colors—ivory, yellows, coral, orange and scarlet. Flowering time varies with kind and climate, but bloom often coincides with daylilies and is a good contrast in form. Where they flower early, these plants often repeat bloom in fall.

Torch lilies are at their best in the warmer zones, but many are reliable in Zone 6—Zone 5 with protection. If they hold their leaves through winter, fasten the leaves together to form a canopy over the center of the plant. This provides protection through alternating periods of rain, snow, frost and thaw.

The ideal soil is deep, rich and moist, but never sodden. The ideal site is sunny or slightly shaded with protection from wind. The rhizomatous roots will rot in soils that stay wet in winter.

Clumps are best left undisturbed, so give them generous spacing—2 feet apart for groupings of smaller species, 4 feet apart for those over 4 feet tall. Gaps can be temporarily filled with annuals, or with such easily divided, shallow-rooting perennials as *Coreopsis* 'Goldfink'. Propagated by division or from basal shoots treated as cuttings.

Among those cultivars found hardy to Zone 6 are 'Earliest of All', 2-1/2 feet, coral; 'Primrose Beauty', 2-1/2 feet; 'Springtime', 2-1/2 feet, ivory and scarlet; 'White Fairy', 2 feet, cream. Under the name 'Pfitzeri' you might get a 2-foot plant with deep orange flowers, or a taller plant with yellow-and-orange flowers. Both are fairly reliable.

Kirengeshoma palmata

Kniphofia 'Prince Igor' with *Rudbeckia* 'Goldsturm' in foreground.

Liatris aspera

Liatris spicata 'Kobold' with Yucca filamentosa.

LIATRIS
Gay-feather, Blazing Star
Family: Compositae

The garden and meadow-garden potential of this North American genus has not been fully explored. There are many species—only the most readily available ones are described below. They grow from woody corms or rhizomes that can be divided, but seldom need it. They can also be raised from seed. All have spires of whiskery, rosy purple or white flowers. These bloom from crowded, purple buds. In most species, buds open in succession from the top down. In the 3-foot cultivar 'September Glory', buds open more or less simultaneously.

All liatris require full sun and deep soil, preferably sandy and not too rich. They make good cut flowers, fresh or dried. Especially handsome are the elegant, usually single spikes of *L. aspera,* shown at left. It has long, spear-shaped basal leaves, becoming smaller and rather sparse as they ascend the stem. The flowers form widely spaced, greenish-white rosettes before they open to puffs of deep, rosy-mauve.

L. pycnostachya (Kansas Gay-feather)
Zone 3, 3 to 6 feet, purple, summer ○

The slender leaves may be 1 foot long at the base, decreasing in size as they ascend the stocky stems. The rigid, rosy purple spikes are up to 1 foot long. 'Eureka' is a seed-grown selection made by the Plant Introduction Center, Manhattan, Kansas. Kansas gay-feather is native to low, moist prairies from Indiana to South Dakota, south to Florida, Louisiana and Texas. Recommended for meadow gardens. There is also a white form of this species.

L. scariosa
Zone 3, 3 to 4 feet, purple or white, summer ○

L. scariosa is native to the mountainous regions of Pennsylvania south to Georgia. Of all liatris, it is the least tolerant of wet soil, especially in winter. It is drought resistant. The cultivar 'White Spire' is the best white-flowered liatris available.

L. spicata
Zone 3, 3 feet, purple or white, summer ○

This is the most adaptable species. Native to moist fields in eastern North America but fairly drought tolerant. The forms native to mountainous areas are less tolerant of wet soil. The most widely distributed of the blazing stars, the compact, 2-foot, dark-purple 'Kobold', seems to be one of these.

Except for the white forms, the color of blazing stars may clash with those of other perennials, so it needs to be placed carefully. It goes well with pale yellows, and the pale mauve *Monarda fistulosa.*

LIGULARIA
(formerly SENECIO)
Ragwort
Family: Compositae

This genus is characterized by exceptionally handsome leaves. Many species were once in the genus *Senecio* and will be found under that name in older books and some catalogs. All need humus-rich soil and abundant moisture. Most are grown for their foliage, but the species *L. przewalskii* and *L. stenocephala,* and the cultivar 'The Rocket' are grown for their flowers. All ligularias share a common problem—the foliage wilts in hot sun, even when the roots are sufficiently moist. Propagated by division, the species also by seed.

L. dentata, L. hodgsonii
Zone 3, 3 to 4 feet, orange, summer ◑

L. hodgsonii is a smaller version of *L. dentata,* which is a bold plant with enormous leathery heart-shaped leaves. In the cultivars 'Desdemona' and 'Othello', leaves are purple underneath. Both have bright orange flowers held well above the leaves on stout, branching stems. 'Gregynog Gold' is a magnificent hybrid as much as 6 feet tall.

These plants are good for bog or streamside, but where summer temperatures are above 80F (26C), the north-facing side of the house is a better spot. If dry soil is a problem, excavate a hole 2 feet deep and line it with thick plastic sheeting punctured in a few places, or with a thick layer of newspaper, then fill the hole with rich soil. This makes it easier to keep soil moist with occasional deep waterings. These species combine pleasingly with the finer foliage of royal fern *(Osmunda regalis),* which thrives in similarly moist situations.

L. przewalskii, L. stenocephala, L. 'The Rocket'
Zone 3, 4 to 6 feet, yellow, summer ○

These three similar plants bear many 6-foot spires of bright yellow flowers on dark stems, held over mounds of delicately textured leaves. Sun is preferred, but the foliage wilts in hot afternoon sun, recovering overnight. This makes it hard to find just the right spot because in shade the flower spikes lean toward the light.

L. tussilaginea (L. kaempferi)
Zone 6, 2 feet, foliage plant, evergreen ◑ ●

The evergreen leaves of leopard plant (*L.t.* 'Aureo-maculata') are highly regarded by flower arrangers. They are kidney-shaped and leathery, randomly coin-dotted with bright yellow. The sparse flowers are dandelion-yellow. In cold-winter climates, it is grown as a houseplant. It can be bought from houseplant suppliers, who may also have the forms 'Argentea', with leaves unevenly edged in ivory, and 'Crispata' with crested-and-curled leaf edges.

Ligularia stenocephala

Ligularia tussilaginea 'Aureo-maculata'

Limonium latifolium

LIMONIUM
Sea Lavender
Family: Plumbaginaceae

The plant so widely used in dried flower arrangements, statice (*Limonium sinuatum*), is an annual. Perennial sea lavenders are more graceful in habit, but colors are limited to silvery gray or lavender.

L. latifolium
Zone 3, to 2-1/2 feet, lavender-blue, summer ○

This species is grown mainly for its cloud of pale, lavender-blue flowers on wiry stems. However, the plant is best displayed when placed where the basal rosette of large, glossy leaves is not concealed. The cultivar 'Violetta' has deeper lavender-blue flowers.

This species grows best in full sun, preferably in deep, sandy loam that stays moist. Seed-raised plants are slow to reach flowering size and need an additional 2 or 3 years to become fully effective border plants. Because of this, it would be a pity to lift the mature, deep-rooted clumps for division, should you want more plants. If done carefully, a portion can be detached without unduly disturbing the clump. Skilled propagators could try root cuttings.

Other Species—The plants listed as *Limonium dumosum* and *L. tataricum* (German statice) belong to a closely related genus, *Goniolimon*. These squat plants are not as attractive as *L. latifolium,* but are sometimes easier to grow.

L. perezii is one of the most important perennials for Southern California. Similar to *L. latifolium* but less hardy.

LINUM
Flax
Family: Linaceae

Wiry grace and extended abundance of bloom characterize the flaxes. Each batch of flowers lasts only 1 day, and in hot regions they are gone by early afternoon. But there will be another batch tomorrow. Yesterday's flowers drop their petals neatly, leaving no disfiguring dead-heads.

The flowers, an inch or more across, are among the brightest of yellows and clearest of blues. They do not open without sun. Flaxes seldom live longer than 3 or 4 years but often self-sow. They are drought resistant and tolerant of low-fertility, sandy soils—they won't grow in soggy soil. Propagated by seed or cuttings. Division is best not attempted.

L. flavum (Golden Flax)
Zone 5, 1 to 1-1/2 feet, yellow, spring or summer ○

This species has branched stems of golden yellow flowers and small green leaves on bushes slightly taller than 1 foot. The form, 'Compactum' is about 6 inches tall.

L. perenne, L. narbonense (Blue Flax)
Zone 5, 2 feet, blue, late spring and summer ○

L. perenne is the more common of these two similar species. It is a vase-shaped bush with wiry stems, branching at the top and bearing tiny leaves and hundreds of soft, sky-blue flowers nearly 2 inches across. *L.p. lewisii* is native to the West Coast, and is possibly the best for gardens there. *L.p. alpinum* is less than 1 foot tall. *L.p.* 'Album' has white flowers. Blue flax will naturalize in meadow gardens.

Linum perenne

LIRIOPE AND OPHIOPOGON
Lily-turf, Mondo-grass
Family: Liliceae

These are basic perennials for the warmer zones. They are similar, grassy-leaved evergreen plants, some with decorative flowers, some with variegated leaves, some a dense, evergreen ground cover. They can be sorted into two kinds—clump-forming and stoloniferous. Most liriopes are Zone 6 hardy, ophiopogons less hardy. The hardiest, *L. spicata* (Zone 4), is an extremely invasive, stoloniferous species. It is invaluable as a ground cover in soils too poor, sun-baked or root-filled for any other plants, and useful for preventing soil erosion. Otherwise, it is likely to be a nuisance except where so marginally hardy that it barely survives. Other stoloniferous kinds include *L. exiliflora, L. graminifolia, Ophiopogon japonicus*, the black-leaved *O. planiscapus* 'Arabicus' ('Nigrescens') and *Liriope gigantea. L. gigantea* is the tallest species at 3 feet and has the widest leaves. All these species have nondescript flowers, often hidden below the leaves.

The following clump-forming kinds have attractive flowers raised well above the leaves. They are excellent for edging paths, grouping at the front of perennial borders or filling in bays between shrubs. Though resistant to most pests and diseases, they are susceptible to slug and snail attack.

If old leaves become shabby during winter, they can be cut back hard in early spring. Plants are increased by division, most easily accomplished by levering clumps apart with two spading forks inserted back-to-back.

L. muscari (Big Blue Lily-turf)
Zone 6, 1 to 1-1/2 feet, violet, mauve, white, late summer or fall ◑ ●

The name *muscari* denotes the resemblance of the stiff spikes of flower buds to those of grape hyacinths. Leaves may be longer than 1 foot, but they arch over, limiting the height of the dense clumps. There are shorter kinds.

Among the best of the many cultivars are 'Christmas Tree', with uneven, narrowly conical, branched spikes of lilac flowers; darker, slimmer 'Lilac Beauty'; violet-blue 'Majestic', and 'Monroe White'. 'Variegata' is a favorite foliage plant, with yellow-striped leaves and violet-blue flowers. It usually needs shade. The gold stripes of 'Silvery Sunproof' turn white with age. It is sunproof only in the cooler regions. Liriopes are seldom worthwhile perennials in zones colder than Zone 6, though they may be root-hardy in those zones.

O. jaburan
Zone 7, 12 to 18 inches, white, late summer or fall ◑ ●

Though sometimes shown as a synonym in books and catalogs, this is not the same plant as *Liriope gigantea*. Plants cultivated under this name resemble liriope but have taller spikes of more widely spaced nodding white flowers. Where slugs and snails are a problem, this is a better choice than the liriopes. It usually needs some shade.

Liriope muscari 'Christmas Tree'

White form of *Liriope muscari*.

Lobelia cardinalis

LOBELIA
Family: Campanulaceae

Most lobelias come from warm regions. Blue *L. erinus* is a popular annual of trailing habit. The two East Coast natives described below are desirable for their spirelike form and clear red or blue flowers, but they are not the easiest plants to grow. There are white forms of both species. Propagated by seed or division.

L. cardinalis (Cardinal Flower)
Zone 2, 2 to 3 feet, red, summer ◐ ○
You may read in older English gardening books that this is not hardy, a misconception that arose because most of the plants being grown in England were maroon-leaved hybrids resulting from crossing *L. cardinalis* with the Mexican *L. splendens* (*L. fulgens*). The leaves of *L. cardinalis* are green, in a basal rosette, over which rises a spire of scarlet flowers. It grows in wet places and must have permanently moist soil, preferably with afternoon shade, though it tolerates sun in the cooler regions. It is short-lived but self-sows—not always where you want it. Plants can be kept alive longer by dividing and replanting the new basal rosettes each year after flowering is finished.

L. siphilitica (Blue Cardinal Flower)
Zone 4, 2 to 3 feet, blue, summer ◐ ○
Where it is hardy, this is easier to grow. It is similar to cardinal flower in all but color, which is variable but a good deep blue in the best forms. It has similar needs to cardinal flower but is not as demanding of moist soil.

HYBRIDS
As mentioned, there are hybrids, usually with reddish leaves, between *L. cardinalis* and the tender *L. splendens*. An early purple-flowered hybrid between *L. cardinalis* and *L. siphilitica* used to be called *L. × vedrariensis,* but is now *L. × gerardii.* A Canadian breeding program begun in 1940, using forms of *L. cardinalis* and *L. siphilitica,* offers hope of more adaptable plants for our gardens, with greater variation in height and color.

LUPINUS
Lupine
Family: Leguminosae

Few of the many wild lupines are adaptable to the garden. *L. perennis* can sometimes be established from seed in the acid, sandy soil it inhabits in the wild. An inexpensive handbook on the propagation of this and other wildflowers is published by the North Carolina Wild Flower Preservation Society, Totten Center 457-A, UNC-CH, Chapel Hill, NC 27514. The shrubby, 4- to 8-foot *L. arboreus* (Zone 8) from the California coast is drought resistant and gives quick results in new gardens, but it is short-lived and not adapted to hot summers or cold winters. Its flowers are usually yellow, sometimes white or bluish.

Russell lupines

The most adaptable species, *L. polyphyllus*, is native to moist soils from California to British Columbia. It is cold-hardy but not heat-tolerant, and is naturalized in parts of the Northeast. This was the main parent of the Russell hybrids raised in England early in the century.

Russell hybrids
Zone 4, 4 to 5 feet, many colors, early summer ○ ◐

Nothing else can take the place of the tall, thick, peppery-smelling spikes of these lupines. Their subtle colors, with the exception of an occasional near-orange, blend well together. Colors range from white to cream, yellow, pinks, reds, and blues to purple. Some are solid colors, other bicolors. Flowers don't last long but the palmate leaves are attractive through the growing season. Most plants are raised from seed. Color strains come fairly true from seed, but expect some variation. Most grow 3 to 4 feet tall, but there are dwarf strains such as 2-foot Minarette.

Unlike many wild kinds of lupines, the Russell hybrids will not thrive in poor, dry soil. They like a deep, moist, acid loam in sun or light shade. In all but the richest soil, a handful of 5-10-5 fertilizer sprinkled around each plant in spring and again in summer improves growth. Space plants 18 inches apart and mulch to keep the roots cool. Remove spent flower spikes. Plants can be divided but are best left alone, new plants being raised from seed or basal cuttings.

Russell hybrids are easy to grow in the Pacific Northwest and will grow in much of the Northeast and in the Southeastern mountains if given winter protection. They are unlikely to do well where summers are hot or dry, and are susceptible to aphid attack.

LYCHNIS
Family: Caryophyllaceae

Note: These plants have had their names changed several times. In catalogs, they may be listed under *Lychnis, Agrostemma, Silene* or *Viscaria*.

L. chalcedonica
Zone 3, 2 to 3 feet, scarlet, summer ○ ◐

The scarlet flowers show best in bays between spring-flowering shrubs, away from competition from other flowers. This species does best in rich, moist soil and will grow in light shade. A white form is available. Another species with scarlet flowers is *L. × arkwrightii*, 12 to 15 inches tall—the flowers are fewer in number but individually larger, combined with mahogany-colored leaves. It needs the same kind of soil and site.

L. coronaria (Rose Campion, Mullein Pink)
Zone 4, 2 to 3 feet, brilliant pink, summer ○

The brilliantly colored, rounded flowers are saved from garishness by the gray felting on the thick, upright stems and 5-inch, spear-shaped leaves, but if you still find the color too harsh, there is a white form. Worth growing for foliage alone. It does best in full sun and light soil. Cut plants back after flowering. Not easily divided but self-sows. Short-lived but seedlings reach flowering size in a year.

Lychnis chalcedonica

Lychnis coronaria. The leaves of *Begonia grandis*, which flowers 2 to 3 months later, can be seen at front.

Lysimachia clethroides

Lysimachia punctata

L. viscaria (Viscaria vulgaris) (Catchfly)
Zone 3, 12 to 15 inches, brilliant pink, late spring or summer ○

Parts of the stem are sticky, as indicated by the plant's common name. In the cultivar 'Splendens Flore-Plena', double flowers make the brilliant color even more compelling. The flowers are bunched on slender stems over easily divided tufts of grassy leaves that may rot in hot, humid weather. The flower color of 'Zulu' is nearer to red. For those preferring a restful garden, there is a white form. Plant in full sun, preferably in a porous soil that is well-drained but not overly dry.

Other Species—Red campion (Silene dioica), of which there is a pretty double form, ragged-robin (Lychnis flos-cuculi) and flower-of-Jove (L. flos-jovis) are best suited to the meadow garden. There, they could be joined by a near relative, bouncing Bet (Saponaria officinalis).

LYSIMACHIA
Loosestrife
Family: Primulaceae

The loosestrifes—a name also used for Lythrum—share two characteristics. One is a preference for moist soil, the other is widely spreading roots. Moneywort, or Creeping Jennie, L. nummularia, a prostrate ground cover, is a well-known example. The two most-popular loosestrifes are easy-to-grow, old-fashioned plants, excellent where they can run wild without overrunning less vigorous plants. Both are easily divided.

L. clethroides (Gooseneck Loosestrife)
Zone 3, 3 feet, white, summer ○ ◑

This species has graceful, arching spikes of small, tightly packed flowers. It is stunted by dry soil, and in hot regions prefers some shade. This plant could be included in a daylily bed because the flowers combine well, and the roots would fight it out on equal terms with little risk that either would overwhelm the other.

L. punctata (Yellow Loosestrife)
Zone 5, 1-1/2 to 3 feet, yellow, summer ○ ◑

This Asian species has larger, yellow flowers on upright stems. Prefers moist to wet soil but tolerates fairly dry soil if given light shade.

Other Species—Two native, yellow loosestrifes occasionally offered and well worth growing are L. ciliata (Steironema ciliatum) and L. fraseri. Both are elegant, 3- to 4-foot plants and not unduly invasive.

LYTHRUM
Purple Loosestrife
Family: Lythraceae

L. salicaria, L. virgatum
Zone 3, 1-1/2 to 5 feet, pink or purple, summer and early fall ○

The widely naturalized, European purple loosestrife (L. salicaria) is often accused of choking out native plants in the marshy meadows where it grows. We know of no instance where this has happened with named cultivars of these two species. They will grow in most moderately fertile soils, from boggy to dry and in sun or light shade. They flower profusely for many weeks and the substantial clumps of wiry stems seldom need support. The bright magenta flowers of some kinds may need toning down with nearby plantings of white-flowered or gray-foliage plants.

Others are of clearer pink. Three-foot 'Morden's Pink' has been the most popular, but the daintier, slightly shorter 'Rose Queen' is giving it a run for its money, and 18-inch 'Happy' may yet emerge the winner because of its moderate height. There are several other good cultivars, so try to see all of them before you decide. Easily propagated by division or soft stem cuttings. Pretty in a vase but the flowers soon drop their petals.

MACLEAYA
Family: Papaveraceae

These plants were once called *Bocconia*, and are still often listed as such. Two similar species are grown. *M. microcarpa* and the selected form 'Coral Plume' have running roots. Except for naturalizing, *M. cordata* is preferable because it spreads less rapidly. The two species are often confused—if in doubt, count the number of stamens. There are 24 to 30 stamens in *M. cordata* and less than half that number in *M. microcarpa*.

M. cordata (Plume Poppy)
Zone 3, 7 feet, white, summer ◑

This has branched plumes of small white flowers held well aloft, but the plant's main beauty is in its large, rounded and lobed leaves. They are well spaced along the tall stems and reveal their silvery undersides in any slight breeze. The back of the border is not the right place for this plant, despite its height. Give it specimen status, perhaps at the ell of a house, or in a bay between shrubs. *M. cordata* needs no staking. Full sun is satisfactory in cool regions, elsewhere light shade. Propagated by seed or division.

MALVA AND SIDALCEA
Mallow
Family: Malvaceae

These are closely related plants with similar flowers and cultural needs. All are fast-growing, short-lived but usually self-sowing plants. The flowers are white or various shades of pink, shaped like single hollyhocks and opening in long succession in summer or early fall. All need sun and well-drained soil but they thrive in hot climates only if the soil is deep, moderately moist, humus-enriched and free of tree roots. Light afternoon shade is beneficial unless summers are cool.

Lythrum 'Morden's Pink'

Macleaya cordata

123

Malva moschata alba with pink *M. moschata* in background.

Malva species
Zone 3 to 4, 3 to 4 feet, pink or white, summer ○ ◑

Musk-mallow, *M. moschata* (Zone 3), is a loosely bushy, 3-foot perennial with flowers of soft pink or pure white and lacy, glossy, dark green leaves. Both colors come true from seed and the easiest means of increase is to transplant the self-sown seedlings. Pink-flowered *M. alcea* 'Fastigiata' (Zone 4) is slightly taller and narrower. The leaves are matte-surfaced, rounded and shallowly lobed, otherwise similar to *M. moschata*. It is tolerant of drier soil. Easily grown from seed.

Sidalcea species
Zone 5, 2 to 4 feet, pink, summer ○ ◑

Selections and hybrids of *S. malviflora*—the name means "with mallowlike flowers"—come in shades from magenta to shell-pink. The darker shades seem more heat-resistant than the paler pinks. Four-foot 'Rose Queen' is one of the oldest cultivars still available, which is an indication of its relative robustness. The exquisite 'Elsie Heugh' has pearly pink, fringed petals. Basal leaves are glossy, green, rounded and scalloped. stem leaves are narrowly lobed. Sidalceas are at their best in cool, moist climates. Propagated by division, the species by seed but cultivars do not come true to type.

MARRUBIUM
Horehound
Family: Labiatae

M. incanum (M. candidissimum) (Silver Horehound)
Zone 4, 2 to 3 feet, white, summer ○

Look for this plant in herb-growers' catalogs. It has rondels of white, tubular flowers at intervals along the stems, and gray, suede-textured leaves. It is grown primarily for its foliage. Many silvery leaved plants turn to brown mush during hot, humid summers, but this plant won't if grown in full sun and deep, sandy soil.

Silver horehound is drought-tolerant. It will sprawl in rich, moist soil, but this tendency can be controlled by shearing back the clumps when they reach 1 foot in height—sacrificing the flowers. It is usually evergreen to Zone 8. It can be divided, but with some difficulty because the base is woody. Once established, however, it self-sows, and the seedlings can be transplanted while small.

Silver horehound *(Marrubium incanum)* is grown mainly for its silvery leaves.

MERTENSIA
Family: Boraginaceae

M. virginica (Virginia Bluebells)
Zone 3, 1 to 2 feet, blue, early spring ◑ ●

This is the only species usually found on nursery lists. It makes only a brief appearance each year. It emerges in March or April—at which time it needs moist soil—then dodges summer heat and drought by going dormant, leaving little or no top growth. Mark its location if you want to move or divide plants, because this should be done in fall. This woodland plant is most effective if used in large drifts. It looks especially good when interspersed with clumps of white daffodils between such leggily graceful, deciduous azaleas as pale pink *Rhododendron schlippenbachii.*

The loosely clustered, nodding bells—pale azure in sun—look a deeper blue in shade. Virginia bluebells combine beautifully with yellow daffodils. Hostas, which emerge later, could be interplanted to expand and fill the gaps by early summer. Both plants could be left undisturbed for many years. Chiming bells *(M. ciliata),* native to the Rockies, does not go dormant as early if the soil is kept moist.

MONARDA
Bee Balm, Oswego Tea, Wild Bergamot
Family: Labiatae

The individual flowers of bee balms emerge from a rounded head that remains attractive when the flowers fall. They are easy to grow, but reportedly short-lived in warm-winter regions. Frequent division is needed to keep plants healthy and to control the shallow, rapidly spreading roots.

M. didyma (Bee Balm, Oswego Tea)
Zone 4, 2 to 3 feet, scarlet, summer ○ ◑

Native to rich, moist woods from New York to Michigan, south to Georgia and Mississippi. Where summers are cool it does equally well in full sun if the soil is fairly rich and moist. It is not drought-tolerant. There are many selections and hybrids of this species and of *M. fistulosa,* with flower colors of white, mauve, pinks to salmon, red and dark purple. Two of the most popular cultivars are the bright red 'Cambridge Scarlet' and the soft pink 'Croftway Pink'.

M. fistulosa (Wild Bergamot)
Zone 3, 2 to 6 feet, mauve, summer ○ ◑

Native from Maine south to Texas, this species grows in dry soils as well as moist ones. It tolerates poorer, drier soil and higher summer temperatures than *M. didyma.* In the wild it is usually about 3 feet tall but the same plant moved to the garden may exceed 5 feet, bearing most of its leaves on the top half of bamboolike stems. If the plant is cut down to the base after flowering, a mound of new leaves will form and remain attractive the rest of the growing season.

Mertensia virginica

Monarda didyma 'Cambridge Scarlet'

Nepeta mussinii

NEPETA
Catnip, Catmint
Family: Labiatae

The true catnip of feline ecstasy is *N. cataria,* available from herb nurseries. It is not very ornamental. Cats are also attracted to the ornamental kinds—fortunately the plants are robust enough to survive being rolled on. They are Zone 3 hardy, doing well in sun and most nonsoggy soils. Plants flower in spring and early summer, often blooming a second time if cut back by half after the first flowering is done.

Ornamental catnips are most effective as a ribbon of blue along the front of a border. Gray-leaved, 18-inch *N. × faassenii* is sterile and does not self-sow—*N. mussinii,* raised from seed, is often supplied in its place. Selected forms and hybrids vary in height, flowers are varied shades of blue. 'Six Hills Giant' is the tallest, at about 3 feet. Propagated by division, *N. mussinii* also by seed.

Oenothera fruticosa 'Youngii'

OENOTHERA
Sundrops, Evening Primrose
Family: Onagraceae

The name "evening primrose" is best reserved for those species in which the flowers open at night and fade by morning. Day-bloomers, known as "sundrops," are obviously a better choice for all but night owls. They are carefree, undemanding plants, enjoying hot sun, drought resistant, tolerant of poor soil. Propagated by seed (species), cuttings or division.

O. missourensis (Ozark Sundrop)
Zone 4, trailing, yellow, summer ○
This species has 4-inch, saucer-shaped, upward-facing flowers of lemon-yellow that emerge at the tips of reddish, sprawling stems. This plant's trailing habit is best accommodated alongside a path or in a raised, sunny bed. Roots may rot in wet soil.

O. speciosa
Zone 5, 6 to 18 inches, white or pink, early summer ○
Attractive but extremely invasive, spreading by threadlike, running roots that are difficult to eradicate. Plant it only where it may spread at will. Flowers may be pink or white, up to 2 inches across.

O. tetragona, O. fruticosa, O. pilosella
Zone 4, 1-1/2 feet, yellow, late spring or summer ○
This is a group of similar plants with little uniformity in labeling. Because it spreads rapidly, *O. pilosella* is probably the most common in gardens. It is usually misidentified as *O. fruticosa,* and more often provided by a neighboring gardener than bought at a nursery. The dense, spreading mats of flat-leaved rosettes are evergreen in moderate climates, turning purple in winter. In May or June, the stiff, hairy stems bear at their tips several 2-inch, bright yellow, saucer-shaped flowers. This plant does not repeat bloom. It is easy to grow in moist or dry soil. Rapid spread

does not make it a nuisance because it roots so shallowly that it can easily be pulled out by hand.

Of the other, less rapidly spreading kinds, one of the best is 'Fyrverkeri' ('Fireworks', 'Illumination'). This has yellow flowers that emerge from waxy, red buds on wiry, branched stems. It flowers over a longer period and may repeat bloom in fall.

Oenothera speciosa

OMPHALODES
Navelwort
Family: Boraginaceae

O. cappadocica
Zone 5 (see note below), 8 inches, blue, spring ● ◐

The borage family abounds in flowers of clear, bright blue, and this plant is no exception. Sprays of flowers resembling forget-me-nots, but larger and of deeper blue, rise over neat clumps of oval, hairy leaves. This is a plant for filtered shade, even dry shade, or the front of a north- or east-facing shrub border. A nurseryman in northern California puts it among his six best perennials. *O. cappadocica* is propagated by seed or division. *O. verna* (blue-eyed Mary) is similar, but spreads rapidly and makes good ground cover for the woodland or shrub garden.

Note: Reliable information as to hardiness in colder zones could not be obtained.

Omphalodes cappadocica

OPUNTIA
Prickly Pear
Family: Cactaceae

O. humifusa (O. compressa)
Zone 6, 6 inches, yellow, early summer ○

If you can forgive the fierce spines and tiny, barbed bristles—as hard to see as they are to extract from your fingers—there are several moderately hardy opuntias suitable for the border. *O. humifusa* would be a good choice for the front of sunny, sandy borders.

The satiny flowers come at the same time as those of butterfly weed *(Asclepias tuberosa)* and combine well with this and such other sun-and-sand plants as gaillardia and chrysopsis. If natural increase is not fast enough, the fleshy, oval pads will quickly root if broken off and planted. The rosy purple fruits that follow the flowers are decorative for several months. The shallow, wide-spreading roots of drought-tolerant opuntias enable them to benefit from the lightest showers.

Opuntias and other cacti are important landscape plants for the arid Southwest, where numerous species are readily available. For more information, see HPBooks' *Plants for Dry Climates, How to Select, Grow and Enjoy,* by Mary Rose Duffield and Warren Jones.

Opuntia humifusa

Paeonia officinalis 'Rubra Plena'

PAEONIA
Peony
Family: Paeoniaceae

There's nothing quite like peonies—they form a genus shared with no other plant. There are two kinds of peony: *Tree peonies* are not trees but shrubs. They grow to about 4 feet tall, with a gaunt, woody framework that must not be cut down in winter. *Herbaceous peonies,* described here, die to the ground in winter.

Most cultivated herbaceous peonies are hybrids. Two distinct species remain in demand: *P. mlokosewitschii* (Zone 5) grows 2 feet tall and has single, yellow flowers. *P. tenuifolia* (Zone 4) is the daintiest peony, a 1-foot cloud of finely dissected leaves with small, single flowers of a brilliant crimson. *P.t.* 'Plena' has double flowers.

That old clump of peonies in grandmother's garden was probably a Memorial Day peony (*P. officinalis),* with pink or red double flowers.

Hybrids
Zone 2 (with some exceptions), 2 to 4 feet, many colors, spring ○ ◑

Peony hybrids come in a wide range of colors, occasionally two-tone. As yet, there are no blue peonies, and yellows are pale and creamy. Brighter yellows are found in the tree peonies. Flowers are usually 4 to 6 inches across but can be smaller or larger. They take five forms:
- Single, with conspicuous central tufts of yellow stamens.
- Japanese, with a carnationlike center within a flattish petal collar.
- Anemone, often grouped with Japanese, but of shaggier, less-distinctly zoned appearance.
- Semidouble, with stamens apparent.
- Double, with stamens missing or not apparent.

By choosing a mixture of early, mid-season and late-blooming kinds, you can have peonies in bloom for about 6 weeks. No one kind flowers for much more than a week, a shortcoming partly offset by foliage that is attractive throughout the growing season. Most grow 2 to 4 feet tall. Tall doubles may need staking—the best supports are the metal rings on legs, usually called peony rings, available from garden suppliers. Some peonies are fragrant; others are not. Peonies make excellent cut flowers. Leave at least three complete leaves below each cut stem or the plants will be weakened and grow poorly.

Peonies are cold-hardy but they benefit from winter protection in areas without snow cover where temperatures fall below −20F (−29C). They can stand considerable summer heat but require a winter chilling, and cannot be grown in subtropical sections of the southern states. Late-flowering, double peonies do poorly where hot weather starts early.

Planting Tips—September is the best planting time for peonies in the North, October in the South. The soil should be deep, well drained and rich in organic matter. In excessively acid soils, add 1 cup of lime per plant. If manure has been used or if fertilizer is needed, keep these away from the roots as shown in the planting diagram on the facing page. Each plant needs 3 feet of space. In hot regions, light shade will prolong the all-too-brief flowering period. Elsewhere, peonies do best in full sun. They can be left undisturbed for many years. Mulch is helpful in hot

Planting Diagram

Fertilizer should not be in direct contact with newly planted roots. In the South, eyes should be only 1 inch below the ground.

Peony Adaptability Zone Map

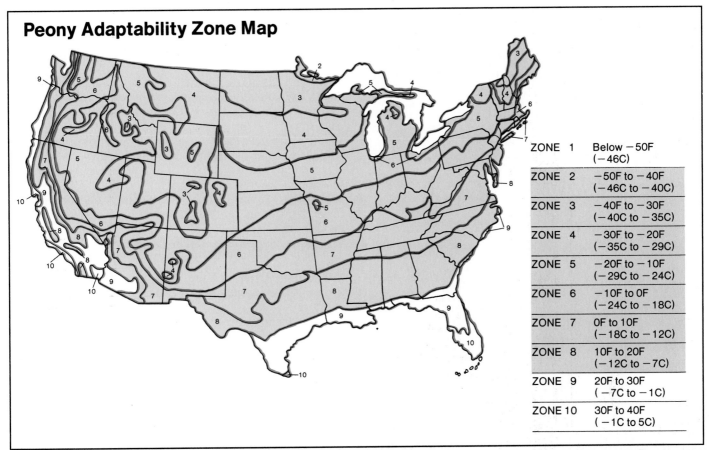

ZONE 1	Below −50F (−46C)	
ZONE 2	−50F to −40F (−46C to −40C)	
ZONE 3	−40F to −30F (−40C to −35C)	
ZONE 4	−30F to −20F (−35C to −29C)	
ZONE 5	−20F to −10F (−29C to −24C)	
ZONE 6	−10F to 0F (−24C to −18C)	
ZONE 7	0F to 10F (−18C to −12C)	
ZONE 8	10F to 20F (−12C to −7C)	
ZONE 9	20F to 30F (−7C to −1C)	
ZONE 10	30F to 40F (−1C to 5C)	

Peonies can be grown in zone 2-8 with following exceptions: *California*—Water thoroughly every 2 or 3 days if there is no rain. Peonies may succeed as far south as San Diego in the higher altitudes. South of Sacramento, tree peonies do better than herbaceous peonies at lower altitudes. *Texas, New Mexico, Arizona*—In the Texas panhandle and similar climates, peonies do well if given abundant water. In sections with only occasional frost, peonies do well at higher altitudes as far south as the Mexican border. To force dormancy in the warmer areas, withhold water from September 1 to October 15 and cut herbaceous peonies to the ground. *Alabama, Georgia, Mississippi, Louisiana*—Water when necessary. Plant peonies with the *eyes* (growing points) not more than 1 inch below the soil surface. Success is doubtful south of Montgomery, Alabama. Tree peonies may succeed farther south. In southern climates, it is best to use early blooming varieties as high temperatures usually prevent the opening of late double varieties. Map courtesy of Charles Klehn & Son Nursery.

regions, but the eyes should never be more than 2 inches below the surface, so allow for the mulch when planting. Specialist nurseries sell both small and large divisions—both are satisfactory. If a friend gives you a large clump, divide it into sections with three to five eyes each before replanting. To do this, wash the roots so the eyes are visible and use a sharp knife to divide the clump. Make sure each division has at least one strong root.

If the young foliage of peonies wilts, then turns black and dies, or withered flower buds have a mildewed look, the plant is probably infected with *botrytis blight*. To prevent this and other diseases, cut down and remove all stems and leaves in fall. You may grow peonies for many years and encounter no such problem. If it does occur, cut out diseased stems and foliage at once, putting them in a plastic bag before disposal. Badly diseased plants and the soil in which they grew should be similarly disposed of. Sterilize tools in a strong solution of household bleach. Then spray all remaining peonies with a fungicide such as Benomyl when growth begins each spring. Repeat applications every 2 to 3 weeks until flowering is done and all spent flowers have been removed.

The American Peony Society publishes a handbook con-taining useful information on the choice and care of peonies. It is available to nonmembers for $3.50 (at time of publication). See page 157 for the society's address. Included in the handbook are the following tips:

Reasons why peonies do not bloom:
- Plants too young.
- Planted too deep. Eyes should be no more than 2 inches below soil surface.
- Large clumps planted without first being divided.
- Buds killed by late frost or waterlogged from constant rain.
- Buds killed by disease or attacked by thrips. Use an appropriate spray.
- Roots diseased. Destroy plants.
- Plants undernourished. Use a high-phosphate fertilizer such as 5-10-5.
- Ground too dry. Water thoroughly.
- Excessive hot weather. Late-blooming full doubles are especially susceptible.
- Planted too close to trees and shrubs, or crowded by other plants.
- Too much shade, making plants tall and leafy.
- Plants undermined by gophers or moles.

Papaver orientale 'Glowing Embers'

PAPAVER
Poppy
Family: Papaveraceae

Many plants of other genera are also called poppies. Blue poppy *(Meconopsis* species) is difficult to grow and not available. California poppy *(Eschscholzia californica)* is usually grown as an annual. Celandine or wood poppy *(Stylophorum diphyllum)* is a yellow, spring-flowering woodland plant, available from some from wildflower nurseries. Horned poppy or sea poppy *(Glaucium flavum),* with silvery foliage and yellow flowers, is a short-lived plant. Welsh poppy *(Meconopsis cambrica),* with dainty yellow or orange flowers, grows in light shade and can be invasive. Matilija or California tree poppy is the shrubby *Romneya coulteri.* For plume poppy, see *Macleaya.* Iceland poppy, *Papaver nudicaule,* is short-lived and usually grown as an annual.

P. orientale (Oriental Poppy)
Zone 3, 1 to 4 feet, many colors, late spring or early summer ○

Oriental poppies are hardy, long-lived plants, thriving in well-drained, light or heavy soil. Division is needed only about every fifth year. Hybrids come in brilliant colors and pastels, most in shades of red, pink and orange. In cool climates, poppies thrive in full sun; in hot ones, they benefit from light afternoon shade. In warm-winter regions, the related orange-flowered *P. pilosum* usually does better.

Established clumps occupy about 1 square yard when in flower, then go dormant, leaving gaps. Many gardeners grow gypsophila alongside it to spread out and fill the bare spaces. Growth starts again in late summer or early fall, which is the best time for planting and dividing. When clumps are moved, new plants often spring up from pieces of root left behind. This trait can be a nuisance at times, but it also allows propagation from 3- to 4-inch sections of root, taken in later summer. Poppies are exotic flowers that need subtler companion plantings or green foliage to set them off. Grouped together, they vie with each other for attention.

Oriental poppies have several undesirable characteristics. They are poorly adapted to warm-winter climates. Stems have a tendency to sprawl. The brilliant flowers appear only briefly, with few to follow when they are damaged by wind or rain. The 'Minicap' range is the result of 12 years of hybridizing by James DeWelt of Mohn's in California, aimed at eliminating these shortcomings. *P. californicum* was used, among other species. Because these new perennial poppies are sterile, they bloom for a much longer time. Plants in Mohn's trial beds have borne between 25 and 100 flowers over a period of 2 to 4 months. Unlike traditional poppies, all of which have a prominent seed capsule, in the new range it is small and hidden among the stamens, hence the name 'Minicap'. Most grow 2 to 4 feet tall. Orange-flowered 'Lil Darling' and 'Downtown' make compact, 1- to 2-foot mounds. 'Uptown' (orange), 'Tara' (pink) and 'Maya' (salmon) may attain a majestic 6 feet. 'Brittany' has delicate, unmarked orange flowers. The others all have the typical dark purple central cross or spoked wheel.

PENSTEMON
Family: Scrophulariaceae

About 250 species of penstemon, or beard-tongue, are native to North America, most to the West Coast, which is where they do best. No one kind does well in all climates. The majority are ill-adapted to intense heat or severe cold, and are usually short-lived.

Penstemon flowers are shaped like gape-mouthed, obese goldfish with silky whiskers inside the upper lip. They are plentifully borne along numerous slender stems. Colors include red, scarlet, orange, pink, blue, lavender, deep purple and white. Yellow is rare. The foliage is neat, often glossy, and usually evergreen. They flower in late spring and summer.

Because penstemons rot in soggy soil, a slope or raised bed is a good place for them. The soil need not—and for most, should not—be rich.

P. barbatus
Zone 3, 1-1/2 to 3 feet, scarlet-pink, summer ○

The penstemons best combining bright color with hardiness (Zone 3) are *P. barbatus* and its selections and hybrids. The national best-seller is probably 'Rose Elf', 18 inches, with flowers of rosy sunrise color. Scarlet 'Prairie Fire', 2 feet, is also popular. Salmon-colored, 12-inch 'Bashful' seems to belong to this group. None of these live long in warm-winter climates.

Penstemon 'Garnet'

Phlox divaricata

P. × gloxinoides
Zone 9, some parts of Zone 8, 2 to 3 feet, many colors, summer ○

The showiest penstemons are the tender kinds usually grouped as *P. × gloxinoides*. These are perennials in parts of the West Coast. Elsewhere they're usually renewed annually from cuttings. Scarlet 'Firebird' ('Schoen-holzeri') and port-wine-red 'Garnet' are among the most reliable, both about 2 feet.

Other Species—'Blue Bedder' *(P. heterophyllus purdyi)* is a bushy, 18-inch plant with bright blue flowers that does well in West Coast gardens.

The following penstemons are hardier, but less brightly colored. *P. hirsutus* (Zone 4) makes dense clumps of shiny leaf rosettes, over which rise slender, 15-inch stems of mauve flowers given a misty haze by the glistening stem hairs. Eight-inch *P.h.* 'Pygmaeus' is a compact form for the front of the border. Both build up fast into congested clumps and are short-lived unless divided annually. Division is easy. Native from Missouri to Texas, *P. cobaea* has large flowers, varying from white to purple, held on sturdy, 2-foot stems. It is usually reliable to Zone 5. *P. smallii,* introduced by the North Carolina Botanical Garden, is fairly new to gardens but proving hardy and adaptable. It forms substantial, glossy-leaved 2-foot clumps. The flowers come in shades of pinkish purple, striped with white inside.

It is only possible to skim lightly over this immense genus. Enthusiasts are advised to join the Penstemon Society, whose stated aims include providing advice on culture, making regional recommendations, identifying species and putting enthusiasts in touch with one another. The society's address is on page 157.

PHLOX
Family: Polemoniaceae

P. divaricata (Wild Sweet William, Blue Phlox)
Zone 3, 12 to 15 inches, blue, spring ◐ ●

Excellent and easy to grow in the wildflower garden or a shaded border. In moist, rich soil, it makes large clumps if not devoured by rabbits, for whom it is a favorite food. Flowers are usually pale blue to lilac, but variable in color. Selected forms include periwinkle-blue *P.d. laphamii*, and 'Fuller's White' with slightly creamy flowers with notched petals. When you have these two in the same border, seedlings appear in a range of intermediate colors. Easily propagated by seed, cuttings or division. *P.d. laphamii* is thought to be one parent of the 9-inch, floriferous 'Chattahoochee' with blue, maroon-eyed flowers. 'Chattahoochee' likes sandy soil and full sun, where it flowers non-stop for many weeks in spring or early summer.

P. paniculata, (P. decussata) (Border Phlox)
Zone 4 (Zone 3 with protection), 3 to 4 feet (with a few exceptions), many colors, summer and early fall ○ ◐

Cared-for border phlox are a delight, neglected plants a sorry-looking sight. They need deep, rich, porous soil in sun or light shade, protection from wind, a period of winter dormancy and, most important of all, abundant water during summer.

In cool-summer regions, border phloxes flower all

Phlox paniculata 'Starfire' with *Echinops ritro.*

summer. In hot ones, they bloom for a much shorter time. Nowhere are they labor-free plants. They are particularly susceptible to powdery mildew, especially toward the end of the season. Powdery mildew is not caused by damp conditions, and is much more prevalent during hot, dry weather. To control powdery mildew, spray with a fungicide every 2 weeks. If insects or mites disfigure the leaves, switch to an all-purpose spray.

Space phlox 18 inches apart. Divide them every third year, replanting sections from the outside of the clump and discarding the center. To encourage flowering side shoots and discourage self-sowing, remove the main flower truss when it fades. "Why have my phloxes reverted?" is a frequent question. They haven't—the inferior, magenta-flowered plants are seedlings that have crowded out the original plant.

Border phlox flowers, often mildly fragrant, are massed in large pyramidal heads. Colors include white, pink, rose, almost red ('Starfire'), salmon ('Prince of Orange' or 'Orange Perfection'), lavender, lilac or purple. Mix them together and you have the makings of a fine color clash! There is no pure blue and no yellow. In one or two kinds, the dark green, lance-shaped leaves are variegated. Heights run from 18 inches—occasionally less—to over 3 feet. Recommended selections include pale pink, red-eyed 'Bright Eyes' and salmon-pink 'Sir John Falstaff'.

For the longest possible period of bloom, include also the white, 'Miss Lingard', which belongs to a different species. Most nursery catalogs include it with the other border phloxes, but you might find it listed under *P. carolina* or *P. maculata*. This plant flowers a month before the *P. paniculata* hybrids. It grows 2 to 3 feet tall and has white flowers with small, yellow eyes, in cylindrical rather than pyramidal clusters. Leaves are a glossier, brighter green. Basal leaves are narrow, those higher up spear-shaped. It is sterile and does not self-sow. Amaranth-pink 'Rosalinde' is another phlox that starts flowering early and finishes late. *P. maculata* 'Alpha' (lilac-pink) and *P. maculata* 'Omega' (white with a lilac eye) are excellent recent additions to this range.

Commercially, border phlox are increased by root cuttings, using short sections of the slender roots, usually laid horizontally 3/4 inch below the surface. If done in fall and wintered in a frame, they will start to grow in spring and usually bloom the same year. For the home gardener division will usually suffice.

P. subulata (Moss Pink)
Zone 2 to 3, prostrate, many colors, spring ○

Selections and hybrids of moss pink make outstanding evergreen ground-cover plants or border edgings. They do best in sun and sandy soil, and are fairly drought-resistant in deep soil. Don't let the overuse of the screaming-pink form discourage you from growing the many other kinds, both in bright colors and pastels. Some of the best were raised—often "bee raised"—in the garden of Linc and Timmy Foster, "Millstream," in Connecticut. These include 'Millstream Coraleye', white with a crimson eye; 'Millstream Laura', a delicate pink; 'Millstream Daphne', bright rose pink; and 'Jupiter', the darkest blue.

P. nivalis is similar to *P. subulata*, but less hardy. All are easily divided. If clumps get ragged, cut them back after flowering.

Phlox maculata 'Alpha' (pink) and *P. m.* 'Omega' (white with lilac eye).

Phlox subulata cultivar with *Marrubium incanum*.

Physostegia virginiana

Other Species—North America is rich in native phloxes. Wildflower nurseries often sell locally adapted species. These may be easier to care for than border phlox, requiring less water and being more resistant to pests and diseases.

Creeping phlox *(P. stolonifera)* resembles *P. divaricata* but makes dense, creeping mats of foliage and bears its blue, pink, mauve, violet or white flowers on shorter stems.

PHYSOSTEGIA
Obedient Plant, False Dragonhead
Family: Labiatae

P. virginiana
Zone 3, 2 to 5 feet, pink, late summer or fall ○ ◑

Nicknamed *obedient plant* because each snapdragon-shaped flower is on a hinged stalk and holds its new position if pushed to right or left. It has stiff, square stems, usually firmly upright, and neat, spear-shaped leaves. Its big attraction is that it flowers late in the season.

Obedient plant will grow in wet soils and, reduced in height, in dry ones. The typical flower color is a harsh pink, which may or may not be pleasing to you. The plant is invasive, particularly in moist, light soil. This tendency can be controlled by pulling up the plant and replanting it every second year to restrain the running roots.

'Vivid', little more than 2 feet tall, goes on blooming well into fall. The 3-foot, white-flowered 'Summer Snow' flowers earlier and spreads less rapidly. 'Variegata', 3-feet tall, is an excellent foliage plant, each leaf evenly edged in white. Many gardeners think it would be even more desirable if the flowers were white instead of pink. Physostegia doesn't need staking, but in shaded sites and rich, moist soil, it benefits from tip-pinching early in the season to control lankiness.

PLATYCODON
Balloon Flower
Family: Campanulaceae

P. grandiflorus
Zone 3, 1-1/2 to 3 feet, blue, white, pink, summer ○ ◑

A beautiful, adaptable perennial that grows best in a sunny location with light, acid, moderately fertile soil. Under ideal conditions, plants naturalize by both seed and root spread. In heavier soil and cooler climates, clumps take several years to show at their best. Though full sun is appreciated, those with delicate, shell-pink flowers keep their color best in light shade.

Inflated buds open to star-shaped flowers, deep blue in the species, with cultivars in white and pale pink. They vary in height and there are double-flowered kinds in all three colors—not the shaggy, pompon doubles, but flat, neat semidoubles that are as graceful as the single-flowered kinds. The 18-inch, single-flowered, blue 'Mariesii' is the most popular. 'Apoyama' is a 6-inch dwarf if true to name, which often it is not.

Platycodon grandiflorus, single and double forms.

Balloon flower is reputedly difficult to transplant, but our experience refutes this, provided you dig deep enough not to sever the carrotlike roots. Where winters are long and cold, transplanting should be done in spring. Plant with the crown barely below the soil surface, spacing plants 18 inches apart to allow room for expansion. Division is seldom needed for the health of the plant. Balloon flower is slow to start growing in spring, therefore vulnerable to damage during that burst of digging and planting fever than comes to gardeners with the first warm days. It is easily grown from seed, flowering the second year. Seed of doubles yields a mixture of single and double flowers. A good cut flower if the milky stem is singed or held in boiling water.

Polemonium reptans

POLEMONIUM
Jacob's-ladder
Family: Polemoniaceae

Species
Zone 3, 1 to 2-1/2 feet, blue, spring or summer ◑

These are dainty plants for moist, humus-rich soil in light shade. The leaflets are in horizontal pairs, resembling the rungs of a ladder. First to flower is the spreading Greek-Valerian *(P. reptans)*, native from New York south to Alabama. It has white-stamened, pale violet-blue, bell-shaped flowers held in loose sprays. The orange-stamened, European *P. caeruleum* flowers later and for a longer period—into July in cool climates. It forms a more upright plant with as many as 13 pairs of leaflets. The nodding flowers are usually blue but there is a white-flowered form. European gardeners consider *P. foliosissimum* (to 2-1/2 feet) from the Rockies the best species, but few nurseries here sell it. The plant sold as 'Blue Pearl', to be found in catalogs under all three species names above, usually turns out to be *P. reptans*. Polemoniums are easy to divide. Handle the fragile foliage carefully.

POLYGONATUM
Solomon's-seal
Family: Liliaceae

Most of the Solomon's-seals of Europe, North America and Asia are similar, but vary in size. Typically, they have strong, flexible, arching stems of thick egg-shaped leaves. They are pest-free and attractive all season. In spring, small, narrow, creamy bells dangle along the underside of the stem. Solomon's-seals are woodland plants, associating well with such shrubs as rhododendrons and with such perennials as primroses, hostas and ferns. Deep, moist soil is ideal but those recommended here will—if given a fair start—compete with tree roots in dry shade. The stout, spearlike shoots will emerge in steadily increasing circles each spring without ever becoming a nuisance. Available kinds vary in height from 6 inches to over 4 feet. Plant names are often muddled, so if you're buying by mail, read the description carefully. Solomon's-seals will not root from cuttings but are easily divided.

Polygonatum odoratum thunbergii 'Variegatum'

135

The 16th century herbalist John Gerard recommended the crushed roots of Solomon's-seal as a cure for bruises "gotten by falls or women's willfulness, in stumbling upon their hasty husband's fists . . .". There are better remedies for battered wives, so grow these described only for their ornamental qualities.

P. commutatum
Zone 3, 4 feet, white, spring ◑ ●

Sold by some nurseries under the name, *P. canaliculatum,* this is the tallest available species, reputedly growing to over 6 feet under ideal conditions, but we have not seen plants this tall. The flowers are also proportionately large.

P. odoratum thunbergii 'Variegatum'
Zone 4, 2 to 3 feet, white, spring ◑ ●

This—the only variegated Solomon's-seal generally available from nurseries—might also be found listed as *P. japonicum* 'Variegatum', or *P. falcatum* 'Variegatum'. Under whatever name it's sold, this plant is highly recommended. It is one of the loveliest and easiest to grow of all foliage plants. The tip and edges of each leaf are lightly brushed with white—the leaves make superb cut foliage. It flowers at the same time as the evergreen Japanese azaleas and would add lightness and grace to the brilliance of such popular red azaleas as 'Hinodegiri', 'Hershey Red' and 'Ward's Ruby'.

POLYGONUM
Smartweed, Knotweed, Fleece Flower
Family: Polygonaceae

So many species of polygonum are native to or naturalized in the United States that many of us are familiar with the deep, pink spikes or small pompons. Mat-forming *P. capitatum,* and the tall annual Prince's-feather, *P. orientale,* are regionally well known.

P. bistorta 'Superbum'
Zone 3, 2 to 3 feet, pale lilac, early summer ○ ◑

The pokers of flower are among the showiest in the genus. Best in cool summer climates and moist-to-wet soil. Where summers are hot, give shade to compensate. Known to become weedy, but not usually a nuisance.

P. cuspidatum (Chinese Bamboo, Mexican Bamboo)
Zone 3, 6 to 8 feet, white to pink, late summer or fall ○ ◑

Impressive in size, with handsome heart-shaped leaves, it looks like a shrub but the canelike stems die with winter. In its favor is the ability to grow in impoverished soil, but the fleecy greenish-white flowers are not sufficiently ornamental to compensate for extreme invasiveness. *P. sachalinense* is even bigger and more rampageous. We recommend avoiding both.

P. cuspidatum 'Compactum' is less invasive but keep an eye on it. It stays under 4 feet, with widely arching habit. As the seeds form in fall, it becomes a bright pink cloud. We hear of a non-invasive form but always, like the Yeti, seen by the friend of a friend, never directly encountered.

A scene at Sissinghurst, England. *Polygonum bistorta* 'Superbum' with *Symphytum* × *uplandicum,* an easily grown perennial but not readily available.

The plant widely distributed in the U.S. as *P. reynoutria* is now considered a form of *P. cuspidatum* 'Compactum'. This is of low, reclining habit, under 18 inches, with branched flower spikes aging to bright pink. An excellent deciduous ground cover for banks and other sizeable sunny sites, but not to be trusted in the border.

Other Species—Many more kinds of polygonums are grown in England, including 'Painter's Palette' (formerly called *Tovara*) with variegated foliage. *P. affine* (Zone 3, 9 inches) is a tufted plant for the front of the border and grows best in sun and moist soil. It has massed spikes of flowers in late summer or fall, which are pink in 'Donald Lowndes' and deeper pink in 'Darjeeling Red'. A new one, 'Superba', has proved better than either in England. At present, these selections are on trial at several major nurseries here, and should be readily available in the near future.

POTENTILLA
Cinquefoil
Family: Rosaceae

The genus includes such vigorous ground-cover plants as *P. verna (P. tabernaemontani)* and *P. tridentata,* and some fine ones for the rock garden, notably *P.×tonguei* with trailing stems of apricot-colored flowers. *P. rupestris,* 1 to 1-1/2 feet, is a dainty white-flowered species that might be mistaken for an anemone. It is a delightful spring-bloomer for such informal settings as the sunny fringes of a woodland garden and is easily grown from seed.

P. arbuscula, P. davurica and *P. fruticosa* are shrubs, but their rounded, twiggy habit and modest size make them good candidates for the perennial border. They are extremely hardy (Zone 2), but less well-adapted to long, hot summers. They flower for a long time in white, pale and bright yellow, apricot, orange, red and several shades of pink. These shrubs may be more satisfying in the border than the perennial potentillas.

P. nepalensis, P. atrosanguinea
Zone 5, 18 inches, red, yellow, orange, late spring or summer ○

These species have brilliantly colored flowers, but their adaptability is limited and their sprawling habit is hard to display properly. Like the geums they resemble, they do best in climates without extremes of heat or cold. The stems often splay out sideways, so those of a single plant can be effective when spread over a large rock. In the border, they look better grouped, planted close for mutual support. Rosy crimson 'Miss Willmott' comes true from seed. 'Gibson's Scarlet' has red, single flowers of exceptional brilliance. 'William Rollison' has semidouble flowers of gleaming, deep orange and yellow. 'Fire Dance' is a frilly, scarlet-centered yellow. There are many more.

P. recta (Sulphur Cinquefoil)
Zone 3, 2 feet, yellow, summer ○

This pale yellow, naturalized European species is pictured in many wildflower books. *P. hirta* is similar. These are best left to beautify hot, dry wasteland. A form suitable for the garden is the larger-flowered, bright-yellow 'Warrenii', usually sold as 'Warrensii'. It is a neatly bushy,

Potentilla 'William Rollison'

Potentilla recta 'Warrenii'

Candelabra primulas growing in a boggy area with ostrich fern (*Matteucia struthiopteris*) and *Rodgersia podophylla*.

Primula × tomasinii (P. vulgaris × P. veris) is the botanical name for the cowslip primrose.

self-supporting plant that self-sows, but not invasively. Seedlings produce plants with flowers the same color as the parent plant. Peak bloom is usually summer but in short-winter, cool-summer climates it is seldom without a few flowers from late spring to fall.

PRIMULA
Primrose, Polyanthus
Family: Primulaceae

There are hundreds of primroses. They come from such varied habitats as mountains, meadows, woodlands and bogs. Many are collector's plants, such as *P. auricula,* with thick, smooth, evergreen leaves, often gray-dusted. Enthusiasts can join the American Primrose Society, the best source for seed of rarer kinds. Most garden centers sell only those called polyanthus, but other kinds can be bought from mail-order nurseries.

The climate of the Pacific Northwest is ideal for most primroses. Unfortunately, it also suits their biggest enemy—the slug. Japanese species such as the silver-haired, stoloniferous *P. kisoana,* and the dainty *P. sieboldii,* do exceptionally well in the Northeast. Primroses need moisture-retentive soil and light shade. Cold, wet winters are less a problem than hot, dry summers. The primroses described below are hardy at least to Zone 5. Most flower in early spring, the candelabra kinds slightly later. All primroses look best in large drifts. All can be divided, the species grown from seed.

English Primrose, Cowslip, Oxlip ◑ —The English woodland primrose, *P. vulgaris (P. acaulis),* has short-stalked, creamy-yellow, lightly fragrant flowers. These are held over dense, 6-inch-tall clumps of wrinkled, paddle-shaped leaves. Cowslip *(P. veris)* has smaller flowers, usually deep yellow, held in nodding, one-sided clusters on sturdy, 8-inch stalks. In the wild it grows in moister, sunnier places than the English primrose.

A primrose usually known as "cowslip primrose" *(P. × tommasinii)* is a hybrid between the above two species. Grown in Southeastern gardens, probably since colonial days, it has primrose color and cowslip habit. It sets little if any seed, and is not commercially available. But in areas where it is established in gardens, a start can usually be begged from friends or neighbors.

The oxlip *(P. elatior)* is rare, but an old form or hybrid with hose-in-hose flowers (one flower inside another) can be seen in many New England gardens. *P. juliae* from the Caucasus is not an easy plant to grow, but hybrids such as purple-flowered 'Wanda' are robust plants. They are similar in habit to the clump-forming English primrose, and more tolerant of dry soil than most primroses.

The Barnhaven acaulis strain of English primroses are outstandingly beautiful and robust plants. They retain the charm and light fragrance of *P. vulgaris,* but with slightly larger flowers in a wide range of predominantly pastel shades. These include white, cream, yellow, pink, mauve, blue and orange. Old-fashioned double primroses are hard-to-grow collector's items, but the Barnhaven range includes sturdy, long-lived doubles. Barnhaven primroses grow quickly into substantial clumps that will deteriorate if not divided at least every third year. They are extremely hardy, succeeding in some parts of Zone 2. They are evergreen to about 15F (−10C), but may go dormant in summer drought.

Polyanthus *(P. × polyantha)* ◑—Polyanthus have taller stalks than primroses, each with several flowers. The vividly colored 'Pacific Giants' are the largest among them, with flowers over 2 inches across. Colors coming true from seed include blue, carmine, crimson, pink, scarlet, lemon, yellow and white. Pots of the Dwarf Jewel strain can be seen in florists' greenhouses early in the year. Thousands of these polyanthus are bought each spring but they are seldom long-lived and often treated as annuals. Barnhaven polyanthus, available in a wide range of colors, are longer-lived plants.

Primulas For Moist or Boggy Soil ○ ◑—Many of these are of the candelabra type, with whorls of flowers spaced along 1- to 4-foot stems. All are hardy to Zone 5. Species include *P. beesiana, P. bulleyana, P. florindae, P. helodoxa, P. japonica, P. pulverulenta.* Colors include rosy pinks, crimson, yellow, orange and purple. They need abundant moisture and are often grown along the margins of streams and bogs. They flower in late spring or early summer. *P. japonica* is the best known, to 2 feet tall, white, rose, crimson or purple. 'Miller's Crimson' and 'Postford White' are excellent selected forms. Drumstick primula *(P. denticulata),* often sold as *P. cashmeriana,* likes the same deep, rich, even muddy soil, but will also grow in soil only moderately moist. It is quite distinct with 1-foot stems topped in spring with knobs of pale lilac, purple or white flowers.

P. sieboldii (Japanese Star Primrose)
Zone 4, 9 to 15 inches, many colors, late spring ◑

Considered by many the best primrose for the Northeast. It has beautiful, scalloped-and-crinkled, bright green leaves. The dainty, deckle-edged flowers are typically rosy purple, but a white variety is available. The Barnhaven hybrids include pale and deep pinks, purples and wisteria blue, some with the backs of the petals a different color from the fronts. All do best in light shade and moist, but not soggy, soil. They protect themselves from summer heat and drought by going dormant.

PRUNELLA
Self-heal
Family: Labiatae

P. grandiflora
Zone 4, 1 foot, white, pink, pale-violet, summer ○ ◑

P. grandiflora bears short, thick spikes of hooded, violet-blue flowers over low, broad clumps of oval leaves. The 'Loveliness' hybrids have flowers of white, pink or pale violet-blue. In cool climates, they need only ordinary garden soil and can be grown in full sun. In warmer climates they require moist, rich soil and light shade. Propagated by division, the species from seed. Self-sown seedlings of the hybrids are seldom as good as the parents, so remove spent flower spikes before they set seed.

Primula sieboldii: Barnhaven hybrids

Prunella 'Pink Loveliness'

Pulmonaria 'Mrs. Moon', flowers.

Pulmonaria 'Mrs. Moon', leaves.

PULMONARIA
Lungwort
Family: Boraginaceae

Lungwort's early flowers like sun, but fully developed leaves wilt during hot weather, even if soil is moist. This suggests a site shaded by deciduous trees. Species with gray-dappled leaves make a delightful edging for a shaded path. Lungworts tolerate deeper shade than most perennials, doing best in moist, rich soil. If summer drought seems to have killed them, wait until the cool season before removing the plants—rain often brings them back.

Flower colors include blue, pink and white—the favorites have flowers that open pink and fade to blue. Divide lungworts in fall because they'll be in bloom during spring.

P. angustifolia (Blue Lungwort)
Zone 3, 9 inches, blue, early spring ◑ ●

This species has bright blue flowers, held over low, gappy clumps of green leaves, smaller than those in other species. They are lovely with such early, yellow flowers as daffodils and forsythia.

P. officinalis, P. rubra, P. saccharata (Lungwort, Soldiers-and-sailors, Bethlehem Sage)
Zone 3, 1 foot, many colors, early spring ◑ ●

These species are similar in size and habit. *P. rubra* has rosy pink flowers, rarely white and usually plain green leaves. *P. officinalis* and *P. saccharata* have leaves blotched with silvery gray. *Pulmonaria* got its name because early physicians saw in the spotted leaves a resemblance to diseased lungs. 'Mrs. Moon' is the prettiest available cultivar and one of the best foliage plants. The flowers are pink, fading to blue as they mature. They are narrowly cup-shaped with frilly edges, each held in a vase-shaped flower cup (calyx) with an incised rim.

Stems, leaves and flower cups glisten with silky hairs. Stem leaves are fairly small, but the silver-dappled, olive-green basal leaves that develop later are almost 1 foot in length, spreading horizontally into dense circular clumps. Clumps remain ornamental until hard frost, are evergreen in mild climates. The leaves of the cultivar, 'Margery Fish', have larger areas of dappling.

Other Species—*P. longifolia* has narrow, spotted leaves and blue flowers. It is a scarce, but desirable species. Many more kinds await introduction from Europe.

The plant sold as yellow lungwort or "Pulmonaria lutea" is really *Symphytum grandiflorum,* one of the best plants for dry shade.

RANUNCULUS
Buttercup
Family: Ranunculaceae

Waxy, bright yellow petals are common in the buttercup family, which includes winter aconite *(Eranthis),* globeflower *(Trollius)* and marsh marigold *(Caltha).* Most species need moisture-retentive soil, and some grow in bogs, but the brilliantly colored Persian ranunculus *(R. asiaticus)* must have well-drained soil. It is a tender, tuberous plant, usually treated as an annual.

A refined buttercup well worth seeking out is Fairmaids-of-France *(R. aconitifolius* 'Flore Pleno'), 2 feet tall with small, white, button flowers on branched stems. It is hardy to Zone 5.

R. repens 'Flore Pleno' (Creeping Buttercup)
Zone 3, 18 inches, yellow, spring ○ ◑

This is a double form of a colonizing European buttercup that has naturalized in many parts of the United States. It will colonize your garden if the soil is moist—and if you let it—but it can be controlled with occasional attention.

Creeping buttercup has 3/4-inch, green-centered, waxy yellow flowers that resemble turbans. Flowers are held on sparingly branched, 18-inch stems. The three-lobed leaves are triangular and 3 to 4 inches across. Each lobe is cut halfway to the base into three wavy-edged sections. Creeping buttercup spreads by stolons that root at the nodes—if these are kept pinched off, the plant will not get out of control. It does best in a moist, sunny site. *R. acris* 'Flore Pleno' has similar flowers, grows twice as tall (to 3 feet), and is not invasive. However, plants sold under this name are often *R. repens* 'Flore Pleno'—you can tell by checking the height description.

RODGERSIA
Family: Saxifragaceae

The rodgersias are splendid plants for the marshy waterside, or for moist, lightly shaded beds and borders. Unless the soil is permanently moist, the leaves scorch and turn brown at the edges and become unattractive. Rodgersias do extremely well in boggy ground. They bear handsome flower plumes of pink, cream or white, but they are grown primarily for their impressive foliage. If you like—and can grow—one kind, you will probably want them all. Usually propagated by division, some by root cuttings. Those described are the only ones for which we know a source at the time of writing.

R. aesculifolia
Zone 4*, 4 feet, cream, summer ◑ ○

The name tells us that the leaves resemble those of a horse-chestnut tree *(Aesculus).* They are held on long stalks and are usually bronze tinted. The flower color varies from cream to pinkish.

R. podophylla
Zone 4*, 3 feet, cream, summer ◑ ○

This species will slowly colonize in moist soil. The leaves are similar to those of *R. aesculifolia* except that the leaflets have lobed tips—in shape they resemble a duck's foot, which is what *podophylla* means. Sometimes, the leaves are bronze throughout the growing season. More often they change from bronze to green as leaves mature, then back to bronze as fall approaches.

Other Species—The plant *Peltiphyllum peltatum* is not a species of *Rodgersia,* but is closely related. It is included here because it thrives in similar conditions. This native of the western states is also grown primarily for its leaves, which are umbrellalike and as much as 18 inches across when the plant is grown in moist soil. Dome-shaped clusters of pink, starry flowers rise up on tall stalks from the bare earth in very early spring.

*Hardiness not established for colder zones.

Ranunculus repens 'Flore Pleno'

Rodgersia podophylla

Rudbeckia fulgida with *Miscanthus sinensis* 'Variegatus'.

Rudbeckia nitida 'Goldquelle' with striped leaves of *Phalaris arundinacea* 'Picta'.

RUDBECKIA
Coneflower, Black-eyed Susan
Family: Compositae

The black-eyed Susans of Eastern fields and roadsides are among the best of flowers for meadow gardens. So are two other plants once called *Rudbeckia* and still found under this name in some catalogs. They are purple coneflower, described under its correct name of *Echinacea purpurea,* and Prairie Coneflower, *Ratibida columnifera,* with drooping petals that give the flowers the shape of shuttlecocks. Some rudbeckias, including the colorful gloriosa daisies, are annuals or short-lived perennials. 'Golden Glow' is a double-flowered form of the 6-foot *R. laciniata.* It is a showy plant, but too vigorous a colonizer for the border.

The following long-lived, easily grown perennials prefer moist soil but tolerate any moderately fertile soil that gets neither soggy nor extremely dry. In heavy soil and in cool climates, plants usually need dividing once every 4 years. In warm, light, moist soil, they spread fast and need more frequent division to keep them in check.

R. fulgida
Zone 3, 2 to 3 feet, yellow, late summer and fall ○

R. fulgida is one of the best perennials. It is blanketed for several weeks with golden-yellow, black-eyed daisies on branching, upright stems. The black, central cone remains attractive after the flowers are dead, but by then the stems have usually started to topple. It is a variable plant, especially the leaves, which may be dark green, smooth, pointed ovals, or gray-green and narrow.

'Goldsturm' is a compact selection of *R. fulgida,* with slightly larger flowers. It does not come true to type from seed, and must be propagated by division. Plants labeled 'Goldsturm' in nurseries are often a different form of *R. fulgida,* but we have yet to see a bad one.

R. nitida
Zone 3, 4 to 7 feet, yellow, late summer ○

The flowers are a bright, lemony yellow and they lack the dark eyes of *R. fulgida.* Seven-foot, single-flowered 'Herbstsonne' ('Autumn Sun') has its petals reflexed around a green cone. This tall plant needs to be staked. 'Goldquelle', under 4 feet tall, has slightly tousled double flowers. It needs no support, except in rich, moist soil.

SALVIA
Sage
Family: Labiatae

Many sages have aromatic, rabbit-deterring foliage that is characteristic of plants that grow in dry, sunny places. Few sages will survive soil that stays wet. Most are drought-tolerant and live longest in light, sandy soil that is only moderately fertile. They are propagated by division, seed or cuttings, depending on the species.

Some of the semishrubby sages mix well with perennials, especially culinary sage *(S. officinalis).* Its attractive foliage forms include 'Icterina' with variegated yellow and green foliage, 'Purpurascens' with purple foliage and 'Tricolor' with variegated pink, gray and green foliage. The annual, red-flowered scarlet sage *(S. splendens)* is the best known of all sages.

All things considered, we think the following are the most useful perennial sages:

S. azurea grandiflora (S. pitcheri)
Zone 5, 3 to 5 feet, blue, late summer and fall ○ ◐

Although this species is listed as hardy to Zone 5, factors other than cold affect its longevity. This plant has been found hardy in Ottawa but not in Vermont.

Slender, branched stems clad in narrow, gray-green leaves form graceful, open bushes. A tendency to laxness can be lessened by cutting the plant back by half when it reaches 1 foot in height. Azure flowers open randomly along gradually elongating spikes. They fall from the plant intact, leaving behind rondels of small, gray-green, vase-like calyces, so each day begins with a scattering of blue on the ground and pristine, newly opened flowers on the plant. Grow it from seed, divide it carefully, or feel around the base in spring for rooted pieces than can be detached and replanted.

S. farinacea (Mealycup Sage)
Zone 8, 1-1/2 to 4 feet, blue, late spring to fall ○ ◐

One of the best long-flowering, evergreen perennials for warm zones, and one of the best annuals for colder ones. It does well in sun or light shade and makes an excellent cut flower. 'Blue Bedder' is a popular cultivar, excelled by the slightly hardier, 18-inch 'Victoria'. The species itself is attractive—tall but self-supporting. White-flowered forms look as if flowers were laundered in "the other brand." Propagated by seed, cuttings or division.

S. × superba
Zone 5, 1-1/2 to 3 feet, purple or dark violet, summer ○ ◐

The present trend is to group under this name several similar cultivars formerly listed under *S. nemorosa, S. pratensis* or *S.* × *sylvestris*. All have abundant spikes of purple or violet-blue flowers. The most readily available are 'East Friesland', purple, and 'Mainacht' ('May Night'), a dark violet-blue. Both are 1-1/2 to 2 feet tall. From this group come the best perennial sages for Northern gardens. All do best in sun but will tolerate light shade. Propagated by division.

Other Species—Most sages with red flowers are tender and grow best in the warmer parts of the country. Best known is pineapple sage, *S. elegans (S. rutilans),* Zone 9.

Other tender species include *S. patens* (Zone 9), with fleeting flowers of gentian blue, and fall-flowering *S. leucantha,* with slender leaves that are white-felted underneath, and plentiful 4-foot spikes of white flowers extruded from velvety, royal-purple calyces. The latter is a die-back perennial in Zone 8, shrubby in warmer zones. Both are available from herb growers.

Hardy perennial sages include: *S. jurisicii,* under 1 foot tall, with outspread spikes of violet-blue, resupinate flowers. *Resupinate* is the botanical term for "upside-down." *S. argentea* has flower spikes reminiscent of the biennial Clary sage *(S. sclarea)* and beautiful, large basal leaves covered with silky down. It is a short-lived perennial that can be grown as an annual. The European *S. haematodes* has massed spikes of pale lavender-blue in late spring or early summer. It has a tendency to be biennial.

Salvia argenta with *Lobularia maritima* and (bottom left) *Artemisia splendens.*

Salvia × *superba* (front) with *Achillea filipendulina.*

Creamy flower spikes of *Sanguisorba canadensis* with *Sedum* 'Autumn Joy' in front.

SANGUISORBA
Burnet
Family: Rosaceae

Although they belong to the rose family, the burnets are nothing like a rose. Only the pinnate leaves bear some slight resemblance. Even when seen through a magnifying glass, the tiny individual flowers don't conform, having four petals (sepals) instead of the usual five found in rose-type flowers. Salad burnet *(S. officinalis)* is probably the best known of the genus. The two below are more ornamental. Propagated by division or seed.

S. canadensis (Great Burnet, American Burnet)
Zone 3, 3 to 6 feet, cream, later summer or fall ○ ◑

In the Northeast this is valued as.one of the last flowers of the season. Bugbane *(Cimicifuga simplex)* flowers later, but two years out of three, bugbane is spoiled by frost.

As flower spikes of great burnet start to open, from the bottom up, they resemble common plantain on a grand scale. Fully open, they become creamy brooms of upright bottlebrushes. Great burnet is native to marshy ground from Labrador to the mountains of Georgia. It does well in neutral or slightly acid garden soil with plenty of peat mixed in to keep it moderately moist. Light afternoon shade is helpful in hot regions, but too much shade will cause it to lean. It may grow as tall as 6 feet in boggy soil, a self-supporting 3 feet in the border. *S. sitchensis,* native to northwest North America, is similar.

S. obtusa (Poterium obtusum) (Japanese Burnet)
Zone 4, 3 feet, pink, summer ○ ◑

Similar pinnate leaves, grayish instead of bright green and similar, fuzzy inflorescences of rosy pink that, in this species, arch like a cat's tail.

Saxifraga × urbium (S. umbrosa)

SAXIFRAGA
Family: Saxifragaceae

The name saxifrage, meaning rock-breaker, is appropriate because most species are small plants best suited to the rock garden. Those described here are evergreen, carpeting plants for moist shade. Bloom may be inhibited in areas where winters are too warm.

S. stolonifera (S. sarmentosa) (Strawberry Geranium)
Zone 6, 1 foot, white, spring ◑ ●

The white-veined rounded leaves, and the way it forms new plantlets at the end of long, slender runners, have made strawberry geranium a popular houseplant, especially for hanging baskets. Outdoors it makes a dense, evergreen ground cover in moist, shady sites, becoming a cloud of starry, white flowers for 1 or 2 weeks in spring. The variegated pink-and-cream 'Tricolor' is appealing but less hardy. Easily propagated by division.

S. × urbium, S. umbrosa (London Pride)
Zone 6, 1 foot, pink, spring ◑ ●

In England, London Pride is a commonplace, grow-anywhere plant, often used as border edging. It should do equally well in the similar climate of the Pacific Northwest. Where summers are hot or dry, it needs moist, rich shade. The leaf rosettes are massed into dense, evergreen carpets, over which rise stiff red stems bearing small, pink flowers in graceful, airy profusion. London Pride is less well adapted to hot climates than *S. stolonifera*. Easily divided.

SCABIOSA
Scabious
Family: Dipsacaceae

S. caucasica is the only plant of the teasel family (Dipsacaceae) featured in this book, and a very distinct one. *S. atropurpurea* and *S. stellata* are annuals. Several uncommon perennials once called *Scabiosa* are now called *Cephalaria, Knautia, Pterocephalus* or *Succisa*. Giant Scabious *(Cephalaria gigantea)* grows 6 feet tall, has pale yellow flowers.

S. caucasica (Pincushion Flower)
Zone 3, 1-1/2 to 2-1/2 feet, blue or white, summer ○

The frilly petalled flowers are up to 3 inches across and delicate in form and color. They're usually a powdery blue or lavender, occasionally white or deeper blue. Held on long, pickable stalks, the flowers don't come in quantity, but if clumps are dead-headed and if the temperature stays under 80F, bloom will continue for several weeks. The few stem leaves are jagged, those in the basal clump are not.

S. caucasica prefers a climate without extremes of heat or cold, and a light loam soil, either alkaline or neutral. The plant rots in wet, heavy soil, and where summers are hot and humid. Mixing chicken grit or coarse sand into heavy soil will improve texture and drainage—use a bucketful for each plant. Plants need light shade in hot regions, otherwise they prefer full sun. Several plants will be needed for a worthwhile effect. Plant them shallowly, 1 foot apart, and do not divide them until obvious deterioration signals a need for it. Division is best done in spring. Purchased seed germinates erratically, fresh seed sown in fall gives better results. *S. caucasica* can be rooted from heel cuttings, but they often rot.

Named forms are propagated by division in spring. Pale lavender-blue 'Clive Greaves' is one of the best. 'Miss Willmott' is a creamy white. Seed of the large-flowered hybrids bred by nurseryman Isaac House—sold as the ''House seed strain''—produces large, shapely flowers in a range of mostly pale blues. Other, deeper blues seem to come and go.

Other Species—*S. columbaria* has light pink or mauve flowers that are smaller than flowers of *S. caucasica*. It is a less effective plant for the border, but in Southern California it flowers all year if kept dead-headed. *S. graminifolia* makes mats of grassy, silvery leaves, has lilac flowers on 1-foot stems. Neither species is grown extensively.

Scabiosa caucasia

Scabiosa caucasia 'Clive Greaves'

Sedum 'Autumn Joy' in late summer.

Sedum 'Autumn Joy' in winter.

Sedum maximum 'Atropurpureum'. With it is *Convolvulus mauritanicus,* a beautiful trailing perennial suitable only for mild-winter regions.

SEDUM
Stonecrop
Family: Crassulaceae

Sedums vary in height, habit and hardiness. All have succulent-type leaves. Many are evergreen. The starry flowers are individually small but often massed in showy heads. The genus includes annuals such as *S. caeruleum,* unusual for its blue flowers. It also includes tender perennials usually grown as houseplants, such as burro's-tail *(S. morganianum),* and a great many midget perennials that got the name *stonecrop* because they are often found growing on rocks. Those described here do best in moderately fertile, well-drained but moisture-retentive soil. Most sedums are easily increased by cuttings—even a leaf will often root. They're also easily increased by division, sometimes *too* easily. For example, every scattered fragment of *S. acre* and *S. album* will grow into a new plant.

There are few sedums over 1 foot in height, but among them are some of the best perennials. All go dormant in winter, but comparatively briefly. The best selections are listed here.

S. aizoon
Zone 3, 15 inches, yellow, spring ○ ◑

This is a a tough, adaptable plant, more often obtained from a neighboring gardener than bought at a nursery. It is recommended for the purple-thumbed. Leathery stems of bright green leaves form sturdy clumps, topped in spring with flat clusters of yellow, starry flowers. *S.a.* 'Aurantiacum' is an especially good cultivar, with flowers of a darker, less harsh yellow, darker green leaves and red-tinted stems and seedheads.

S. × albo-roseum, S. maximum, S. telephium, S. telephioides
Zone 3, 1 to 2 feet, pink, late summer or early fall ○ ◑

Under these names, much intermingled, will be found several similar border sedums with fleshy leaves. If gently massaged, the upper and lower membranes of the leaf can be loosened and the leaf blown up—one folk name is *pudding-bag plant.* It is also called *pig squeak,* because the leaves can be made to emit a piercing whistle. Flowers come in various shades of pink and occasionally white. The leaves are green, gray-green, purple or variegated. All flower in late summer or fall.

The important quality of *S. maximum* 'Atropurpureum' *(S. telephium maximum* 'Atropurpureum') is its maroon foliage, which is unusual among perennials. The small heads of dusky pink flowers match the leaves nicely. The only undesirable feature is its sprawling, 2-foot stems. Tucking the plant among stockier ones will help to corset it. *S. maximum* is thought to be one parent of two dark-leaved, chance seedlings, 'Vera Jameson' and 'Sunset Cloud'. These are only half the height of *S. maximum.*

'Autumn Joy' ('Herbstfreude')
Zone 3, 2 feet, pink, fall ○ ◑

'Autumn Joy', also called 'Indian Chief,' is thought to be a hybrid between *S. spectabile* and *S. telephium.* Most experienced gardeners consider it to be the best of the sedums, and many rank it among the top-ten perennials grown in the U.S. today. It's easy to see why. Unless beaten down by snow, it is attractive all year long. Early in spring, gray-green buds emerge through the soil. By mid-summer it is a sturdy clump of pest-free foliage with heads of incipient flowers resembling broccoli. Gradually these turn pale pink, at this stage attracting hoards of butterflies and bees. A deepening of color indicates that the flowers are dying. Flowers turn to a rosy-red color, then coppery, finally—dead now but still attractive—rust. In the garden, the dead-heads remain attractive through winter. They're also excellent for dried-flower arrangements.

'Autumn Joy' is among the most carefree and rewarding of perennials, needing no staking and only infrequent division. For a succulent, it is surprisingly tolerant of wet soil and it does well in light shade as well as full sun.

The 18-inch *S. spectabile* cultivars 'Brilliant' and 'Meteor' are similar to 'Autumn Joy'. They have large, inverted saucers of brilliant carmine flowers, and are also excellent, easy-to-grow plants.

Other Species—The following are good, low-growing sedums for small patches of ground cover that will not be walked on: *S. lineare* 'Variegatum' (Zone 7) has slender, white-edged leaves and soft, yellow flowers in spring. It is usually evergreen to Zone 8. Evergreen *S. reflexum* is hardier. A good form of this is 'Oxbow Hybrid', with trailing stems of needlelike leaves that turn bronze in winter and yellow flowers that bloom in spring. *S. rubrotinctum* (Zone 9) is grown for its glossy, red-and-green leaves that look like jelly beans. *S. spurium* is one of the toughest and most adaptable species, hardy to Zone 3. This has wiry interlacing prostrate stems tipped in summer with flattish heads of white, pink or dark red flowers. There are many forms of this species.

The next group contains the best of the clump-forming, low-growing sedums for rock garden use or border edging: *S. kamtschaticum* and its variegated form (Zone 3), have yellow flowers in spring. *S. rosea (Rhodiola)* is grown less for its greenish-yellow flowers than for its whorled gray-green leaves. *S.* × 'Ruby Glow' ('Rosy Glow') has butterfly-attracting, bright pink flowers at the end of the season, and grayish leaves. *S. sieboldii* (Zone 3) is outstanding where the fall season is long and mild, bearing showy heads of bright pink flowers at the tips of low-arching stems clad in blue-gray leaves. There is also a variegated form. Because this sedum flowers late in the season, it's not recommended in climates where frosts come early. A better choice for fall color in cold climates would be *S. cauticola,* which blooms 2 to 3 weeks earlier.

There is a family resemblance to sedums in the related plant, *Crassula falcata*. It has similar bee-attracting heads, but of brilliant scarlet. It is recommended only for those who garden in mild, coastal climates (Zone 9).

Sedum spectabile 'Brilliant'

Related to sedums, *Crassula falcata* has similar bee-attracting flower heads, but of bright scarlet.

Senecio cineraria

Smilacina racemosa with hosta and azaleas in front.

Solidago 'Peter Pan'

SENECIO
Ragwort, Groundsel
Family: Compositae

The genus includes several rather weedy wildflowers with ragged, dark-yellow, daisy-type flowers. It also includes such frost-tender plants as string-of-beads (*S. rowleyanus*), German-ivy (*S. mikanioides*), and the florists' cinerarias (*S. cruentus*). Some attractive hardy ragworts once called *Senecio* will now be found under *Ligularia*.

S. cineraria (Cineraria maritima) (Dusty Miller)
Zone 8, 2 feet, silver-gray, summer ○

The common name "dusty miller" is applied not only to this plant, but to many others with gray leaves, including *Centaurea cineraria* and the frost-tender *Chrysanthemum ptarmicaeflorum*.

The many selections of *S. cineraria* vary in hardiness. Winter wet and snow take their toll as often as do low temperatures, so these plants are reliable, woody-based evergray perennials only in Zone 8 and up. Elsewhere, they are popular as annuals. Like almost all plants with felted, silvery leaves, *S. cineraria* needs well-drained soil, preferably sandy, and plenty of sun. Propagated by seed, selected forms from cuttings.

Other Species—In the warmer coastal regions of California, velvet groundsel (*S. petasites*) can be seen as a burly evergreen bush, 8 feet tall and as much across. It has large, velvety leaves on red stalks and ragged yellow flowers massed in large heads. Velvet groundsel flowers during winter or early spring. It is not hard to grow in frost-free regions, but needs summer watering.

S. adonidifolius, available but scarce, has 1-foot-tall stalks of yellow daisies in early summer, but is grown mainly for the cut-and-curly green leaves, pleasing all season. It is an excellent foreground plant.

SMILACINA
False Solomon's-seal
Family: Liliaceae

S. racemosa
Zone 3, 3 feet, cream, spring ◑ ●

This woodlander is the showiest of several North American species. It has bright green, spear-shaped, ribbed leaves, alternating along slightly zig-zagged, arching stems tipped with short, fluffy plumes of creamy flowers. Freed from root competition from trees, it luxuriates in the moisture-retentive soil of lightly shaded borders. The flowers are followed by translucent red berries. Add acid peat if the soil is not already slightly acid. Propagated by seed or division. Except for propagation purposes, it needs no dividing.

SOLIDAGO AND × SOLIDASTER
Goldenrod
Family: Compositae

Goldenrods are so numerous and so readily interbred, that even experts have difficulty identifying many of them. Experts do agree that goldenrod pollen is heavy, not wind-borne, and does not cause hay fever. The real culprit is the less-showy ragweed that flowers at the same time.

Although many gardeners consider them weeds, there are beauties among the goldenrods growing by the roadside. If you choose to grow one in your garden, be aware that they are likely to grow taller and spread more rapidly in rich soil. Some wild goldenrods also self-sow weedily.

Although most goldenrod species are native to North America, most commercially available hybrids have been parented by a compact form of a European species, *S. virgaurea* 'Brachystachys' (Zone 4). Available selections include 30-inch 'Golden Mosa', 18-inch 'Cloth of Gold', 1-foot 'Golden Thumb' and 2-foot 'Peter Pan'.

× *Solidaster hybridus,* also called *Aster hybridus luteus,* is believed to be a cross between an aster and a goldenrod. It bears sheaves of small, curved-petal daisies in late summer. Flowers are lemon yellow fading to cream, held on 1-1/2- to 2-foot stems that are inclined to sprawl. The leaves are narrow and roughly hairy.

All these thrive in sun or light shade, in moist, moderately fertile soil. Easily increased by division.

SPIGELIA
Indian Pink
Family: Loganiaceae

S. marilandica
Zone 5 (probably colder than that), 9 to 18 inches, scarlet and yellow, late spring or early summer ◑

This Southeastern woodland native has remained obscure because the selection of perennials available in this country has largely been influenced by what does well in England—and this does not.

Scarlet is an uncommon flower color among hardy perennials, which alone would commend this plant. The trumpet-shaped flowers face upward, displaying yellow stars on the inner side of the lobed rim. The leaves are neat and glossy green, the stems self-supporting except in deep shade, where the plant becomes leggy.

Indian pink has not been tested in most parts of the country but has proven hardy as far north as Boston. It prefers slightly acid soil and, in warm climates, light shade. In cooler regions, it can take full sun if the soil is moist and humus-rich. Indian pink cannot compete with surface-rooting trees. The rhizomatous clumps divide easily, and stem cuttings taken in early summer will root in 2 to 3 weeks.

STACHYS
Betony
Family: Labiatae

Betony prefers well-drained soil, not too rich, and sun during most of the day. Betonies can be increased by division, or from seed.

S. byzantina (S. lanata, S. olympica) (Lamb's-ears, Woolly Betony)
Zone 4, 18 inches, gray, summer ○ ◑

Lamb's-ears is at its best where the dense mats of felted, silvery leaves can overflow onto a path. It grows best in full

× *Solidaster hybridus* (× *Solidaster luteus*)

Spigelia marilandica

149

Stachys macrantha

sun and poor, dry soil, especially in regions where humid heat causes gray-leaved plants to rot. The woolly spikes of small, purplish flowers are not particularly appealing. With the non-flowering form, 'Silver Carpet', the gardener is saved the trouble of dead-heading them.

S. grandiflora (S. macrantha, Betonica grandiflora)
Zone 3, 18 inches, violet-purple, summer ○

Showy whorls of nettlelike flowers are held on stiff stems over basal tufts of heart-shaped, hairy green leaves with scalloped edges. *S. macrantha* does not object to light shade, and in hot regions prefers it. The form 'Robusta' has the richest flower color.

Other Species—Scarlet-flowered, 18-inch *S. coccinea* from Mexico (Zone 9) can only be grown in the mildest climates. *S. officinalis (Betonica officinalis)* (Zone 4), historically a medicinal herb, is attractive enough for the border but less showy than the similar *S. macrantha*.

STOKESIA
Family: Compositae

S. laevis (S. cyanea)
Zone 5, 1 to 2 feet, blue, summer ○ ◑

Named for the English botanical author, Dr. Stokes, and pronounced *Stoke-si-a*. Stokesia resembles a refined China aster. Flower color is usually a soft wisteria blue, hard to capture on film. Flowers are 2 to 5 inches across, borne singly on branched stems 1 to 2 feet tall. 'Blue Danube', 15 inches tall, has large flowers of a clear, soft blue, 'Blue Moon' has a hint of mauve, 'Silver Moon' has flowers of a good, but not pure, white. Pink and yellow forms are known. The name *laevis* means smooth, describing the spear-shaped, usually evergreen leaves that make up the basal clump.

Stokesia, native from South Carolina to Florida and Louisiana, is a good-to-outstanding perennial, depending where you live. In the Southeast it flowers mainly in June with a smattering of blooms in fall. In the Northeast it blooms through much of summer; in Florida most of winter; and in Southern California intermittently all year if dead-headed.

In the milder regions, stokesia soon makes a mound 2 feet across. Elsewhere, plant it closer and in groups for a more immediate effect. It needs sun but tolerates light shade, and is reliably long-lived in sandy soil or light loam that is only moderately fertile. Soil should never be so wet that water can be squeezed from it. Wet soil in winter is the main cause of death. Winter protection is needed where alternating frost and thaw heave roots out of the ground.

Named forms are propagated by division. Seed, easily raised, produces plants with flowers of varying soft blues. Stokesia is a long-lasting cut flower.

Stokesia laevis

THALICTRUM
Meadow Rue
Family: Ranunculaceae

The airy sprays of single-flowered meadow rues are reflected in the common name, lavender-mist. In the double forms, myriad, thready little powderpuffs are close-packed and cloudlike. Elegantly single or fluffily double—the choice is yours.

Meadow rues are moisture-loving plants. One of the handsomest native species, the white-flowered tall meadow rue *(T. polygamum)* grows in swampy meadows, thickets and ditches from Ontario south to Tennessee. Varying in height from 3 to 10 feet, it is unmanageably tall for most gardens, but worth trying in spots too boggy for other kinds. At the other extreme comes 3- to 5-inch, mauve-flowered *T. kiusianum* from Japan, a slowly spreading, stoloniferous gem for moist and shaded parts of the rock garden.

The following plants are among the best of available border kinds. If the soil is moist, but not soggy, they can take full sun where summers are cool, otherwise light shade. At 2- to 3-foot spacing, plants will not need division for about 4 years. Propagated by division, the species also from seed. All are good for cutting.

T. aquilegifolium
Zone 5, 2 to 3 feet, mauve, late spring or early summer
◑○

The name *aquilegifolium* means *columbine leaf,* which adequately describes the foliage of this and other *Thalictrum* species. Tufted flowers are borne in profusion at the same time tulips bloom, and for about as long. Those with single flowers are more elegant, but if all the meadow rues were placed side-by-side at garden centers while in full bloom, *T. aquilegifolium* would probably outsell the others. There are white and pink selections as well as mauve. No staking is needed.

T. delavayi (T. dipterocarpum of gardens)
Zone 4, 5 to 7 feet, summer ◑○

This is the only species that does well in all parts of California. A white-flowered form is uncommon, and because it divides less easily than others, 'Hewitt's Double', with fully double flowers, is hard to find. The flowers of *T. dipterocarpum* and *T. rochebrunianum* are almost identical—see photo at right. May need staking.

T. speciosissimum (T. glaucum, T. flavum glaucum)
Zone 5, 5 feet, yellow, summer ◑○

Massed fluffy flowers of soft, creamy yellow combine nicely with the blue-green foliage. It will need staking.

T. rochebrunianum
Zone 5, 5 feet, mauve, late summer ◑○

This has more refined foliage than *T. dipterocarpum,* and flowers later and for longer. Otherwise it is similar. It will need staking unless put behind a low wall or bushy plants against which it can lean.

Thalictrum aquilegifolium

Thalictrum rochebrunianum

Thermopsis villosa (T. caroliniana)

THERMOPSIS
Aaron's-rod, False Lupine
Family: Leguminosae

T. villosa (T. caroliniana) (Carolina lupine)
Zone 3, 3 to 5 feet, yellow, late spring or early summer ○

This Southeastern species is found growing wild in dry woodland clearings and by roadsides from North Carolina south to Georgia but is hardy much farther north. If planted in deep, light, well-drained soil, thermopsis is drought resistant. It has the usual pea-family ability to grow in soil of low fertility. In full sun it is usually self-supporting, but in rich soil or shade it may lean. Dividing it—seldom necessary—is a tough task, so give plants 2 to 3 feet of space.

The flowers last for only a week or two, often less in hot weather, so it hardly earns its place in small gardens. In larger ones it is worthwhile because tall, yellow flower spires are not common among perennials. Fresh seed sown in fall and exposed to frost germinates freely in spring. Old seed germinates slowly, if at all. Placing seeds in the freezer for 1 or 2 weeks, or soaking them in warm water, sometimes speeds germination. When used for flower arrangements, the flower spikes should be cut when only the bottom flowers are open.

T. montana from the West Coast is a shorter, earlier-flowering species with looser clusters of flowers. It spreads into large patches.

TRADESCANTIA
Spiderwort
Family: Commelinaceae

The genus includes such almost unkillable houseplants as wandering Jew. The hardy kinds are just as easy to grow and can often be seen thriving on neglect in abandoned gardens. Most of those long called *T. virginiana* are now called *T. × andersoniana*, as described below.

T. × andersoniana (T. virginiana of gardens)
Zone 4, 2 feet, colors vary, late spring or summer ○ ◑

It used to be thought that these plants were forms of *T. virginiana*, a species native from Connecticut to Georgia, west to Missouri. But they were recently found to be hybrids with other species, so the name was changed to *T. × andersonia*. However, plants sold in wildflower nurseries as *T. virginiana* usually *are* that species. *T. virginiana* is variable in form, but the flowers are usually blue, and smaller than those of hybrids.

The three-petalled flowers of the hybrids measure 1 inch or more across, and come in sky blue ('J.C. Weguelin'), deeper blue ('Blue Stone'), mauve, ('Pauline'), purple ('Purple Dome'), almost red ('Red Cloud'), white-flushed pale violet ('Iris Pritchard'), and a satiny white of exceptional purity ('Snowcap'). They grow best—sometimes too well—in moist or even boggy soil, and light shade. However, they are adaptable, disliking only prolonged drought. The top of each zig-zag stem holds numerous clustered buds that open a few each morning over a period of many weeks. The flowers are gone by early afternoon, the petals dissolving neatly away, leaving no untidy deadheads. The foliage is not as neat—by midsummer it

White-flowered cultivar of *Tradescantia × andersonia*

sprawls, but if cut to the ground, it will re-emerge later and plants may flower again in fall.

Other Species—A similar species, *T. hirsuticaulis,* has not yet been evaluated in all areas but is hardy at least to Zone 5. It is shown on page 34. It is a neater plant at 1 foot tall, and earlier to bloom, after which the leaves die back, then re-emerge in fall to last through winter, if the weather isn't too severe. Because it is native to dry, rocky outcrops and sandy woods of the southern United States and goes dormant in summer, *T. hirsuticaulis* should prove better adapted than other spiderworts to hot, sunny sites and summer drought. Flower color varies but commercially available plants have brilliant, purple-blue flowers.

Tradescantias are easily—if brutally—divided by slicing clumps into sections with a sharp spade.

TRICYRTIS
Toad lily
Family: Liliaceae

The name toad lily doesn't have much sales appeal, but don't let it put you off. Every species you can find is recommended if you want something different.

T. hirta
Zone 5, 2 to 3 feet, mauve, early fall ◑

This is the only species available nationally. Fuzzy, ear-shaped leaves alternate along hairy, unbranched, upright stems. In the leaf axils and clustered at the tip of each stem are flowers so intriguing that few pass them by without stopping for a closer look. Flowers make no great impact at a distance, so locate plants near a path. In sites with light shade and rich, moist, preferably acid soil, clumps attain a height of 3 feet. In drier soil they grow to about 2 feet in height. The flowers last 2 to 3 weeks. If the stems are not cut down or killed by frost before seed is ripe, a crop of young plants as dense as crabgrass will appear at the base of the clump in spring. However, it does not self-sow weedily all over the garden. Division is seldom needed. There is a form with variegated leaves, and one with white flowers.

TROLLIUS
Globeflower
Family: Ranunculaceae

Globeflowers are hardy and are at their best in the cooler parts of the country. In rich, moist soil—even boggy ones—they make handsome clumps of deeply fingered, glossy green leaves. In dry soil, if they survive, they merely shame the gardener.

The globular flowers, varying from pale primrose to deep orange, have the same waxy texture as their relatives, the buttercups. Fresh seed, sown as soon as it's ripe, germinates quickly, but old seed may take 2 years. If using old seed, plant it in pots, cover the pots with plastic wrap, and put them in the freezer for a few days before moving them to a warm place. This may speed germination.

Clumps build up slowly but can be divided when big enough, preferably in late summer or fall.

The curious flowers of the toad lily *(Tricytris hirta)* always attract attention. Flowers open late in the season.

Trollis × cultorum 'Orange Globe'

Veronica 'Blue Charm' with *Coreopsis verticillata*.

Veronica teucrium with Japanese painted fern (*Athyrium goeringia-num* 'Pictum').

VERONICA
Family: Scrophulariaceae

If during a spring drive you see a lawn turned to a lake of pale blue, it is probably a creeping speedwell, *Veronica filiformis*—a beautiful sight if it isn't your garden. But don't worry, none of those described here is invasive. All have similar flowers, individually small, but usually packed into dense spikes. The shrubby, evergreen veronicas, now put in the genus *Hebe,* are important plants for mild climates but are neither heat nor cold resistant.

Veronicas do well in sun or light shade, and in any moderately fertile soil that gets neither soggy nor very dry. They are easily increased by cuttings or division. Cultivars of uncertain origin have been placed under the species they most resemble.

V. gentianoides
Zone 4, 2 feet, blue, early summer ○ ◑

This is the first of the veronicas to bloom. Not gentian-blue as the name implies, but a delicate, pale blue that is ideal for toning down brighter colors. The name marks a similarity between the dark green basal leaves and those of some gentians.

V. grandis holophylla
Zone 4, 2 to 3 feet, blue, summer ○ ◑

This is the best of the taller kinds, with glossy, dark green leaves on a bushy plant. It has abundant, long-lasting spikes of deep blue flowers. Plants sold as 'Blue Charm' seem to belong in this category.

V. incana
Zone 3, 1 foot, blue, summer ○ ◑

This plant is grown more for its foliage than for its blue flowers. Mats of silvery, 3-inch, lance-shaped leaves are evergreen in the warmer zones and dense enough to make a good ground cover. 'Saraband' is similar, with more abundant, bright blue flowers. The hybrid 'Minuet' has pink flowers and gray-green leaves. These have the same dense, spreading habit but more abundant bloom. Their gray-green leaves are less silvery in color.

V. longifolia, V. spicata
Zone 3 or 4, 1-1/2 to 2 feet, blue, summer ○ ◑

V. spicata (Zone 3, 1-1/2 feet) resembles *V. incana*, except it is taller and has matte-green leaves. *V. longifolia* (Zone 4) is taller yet, and likely to need support, but the bushy form discussed here, *V. longifolia subsessilis,* is 2 feet tall and self-supporting. Selections and hybrids of 2 feet or less include 'Blue Spires', the slightly more compact 'Sunny Border Blue', white 'Icicle', the newer 'Blue Fox', 'Red Fox'—not red, but a deep rosy pink—and 'Snow White'. Some of these are inclined to sprawl if soil is rich.

V. teucrium (V. austriaca teucrium, V. latifolia)
Zone 3, 18 inches, blue, late spring or summer ○ ◑

If you don't object to its tumbling habit, or are willing to provide brushwood support, this species earns its place with a brilliant display of bright blue flowers early in the season, often repeating later if cut back. Flowers are less spikelike than most veronicas. 'Crater Lake Blue' is the most compact form, with flowers of the brightest blue. The golden foliage of 'Trehane' combines beautifully with its blue flowers.

V. virginica (Veronicastrum virginicum)
Zone 3, 2 to 6 feet, white, late summer ○ ◑

An elegant plant with slender, multiple spires, native from Massachusettes south to Florida, usually in rich, moist woods or meadows. Flowers are sometimes pale lavender. Height varies, but plants sold are usually about 4 feet tall with white flowers. The leaves are lance-shaped, in whorls around the stem.

Other Species—Among several trailing or matlike perennial veronicas, *V. prostrata (rupestris),* with 6-inch stems of bright blue flowers, could be used at the front of the border. Some more suitable for the rock garden are *V. pectinata* with woolly, gray leaves and blue or pink flowers; *V. satureioides* with bright blue flowers; and the almost mossy *V. repens,* usually pale blue but sometimes white or pink. Being shallow-rooting, *V. repens* makes a good ground cover for small bulbs.

YUCCA
Family: Agavaceae

For such tropical looking, evergreen plants, some yuccas are surprisingly hardy. Neat and firm in form, they combine well with sand, boulders or paving, where they are not crowded by other plants.

Yuccas are really shrubs, many growing tall with trunk-like stems, but those described—chosen as the hardiest and most readily available—*look* like perennials, with leaves that spring from ground level. Though stiff and pointed, those named below pose less threat to the eyes of playing children—and the behinds of weeding gardeners—than such fiercely impaling kinds as Spanish bayonet (*Y. aloifolia*).

Yuccas are plants for full sun, well adapted to high temperatures and tolerant of both wet and dry summers. Flowering time varies with the amount of sun and heat plants receive—from early summer to early fall. Patient gardeners may want to try growing yuccas from seed, but most will prefer to buy their first plant. Offsets (sometimes called "pups") can be removed from established plants without disturbing the main clump.

Y. filamentosa, Y. smalliana (Adam's-needle)
Zone 5, 4 to 5 feet, cream, summer ○

The similar plants sold under these names have a white, pencil-fine "thread" edging the leaves and peeling back at intervals into flaxen curls. This greatly enhances the ornamental quality of the 2- to 3-foot clumps. Large, creamy waxen bells are carried in branched spikes that may tower to 10 feet, but in the following selections, spikes are 4 to 5 feet tall. 'Bright Edge' has leaves with a creamy edge, and 'Golden Sword' has yellow-striped leaves. 'Sunburst', slightly less hardy than the other two, has shorter, broader leaves, with ivory streaks and edges that turn pink in winter. This is an outstanding foliage plant, shaped like a giant waterlily.

Y. glauca (Soapweed)
Zone 3, 3 feet, greenish-white, summer ○

The hardiest of all yuccas, this is a good foliage plant to carry interest through the winter months. The leaves are gray, rapier-slender, about 3 feet long with thready margins. The flowers are carried in slender spikes.

Yucca filamentosa

Yucca 'Golden Sword' with Asclepias tuberosa in front.

NURSERY SOURCE LIST

Each of these nurseries has a list or catalog. Catalog prices vary. Please inquire, enclosing a stamped, self-addressed envelope. Space does not permit inclusion of many nurseries that sell wildflowers, herbs or alpine plants, or nurseries specializing in one kind of plant. Most of the nurseries listed have extensive plant lists. Some offer fewer plants but of a kind not widely available.

Applewood Seed Co.
5380 Vivian St.
Arvada, CO 80002
Seed for meadow gardens. Separate mixtures formulated for eight regions.

Bluebird Nursery Inc.
515 Linden St.
Clarkson, NE 68629
Specializes in supplying landscapers. Minimum order $100.00

Kurt Bluemel Inc.
2543 Hess Road
Fallston, MD 21047
Perennials and extensive list of ornamental grasses.

Bluestone Perennials Inc.
7211 Middle Ridge Road
Madison, OH 44057
Inexpensive, six-pack perennials.

Borbeleta Gardens
10078 154th Ave.
Elk River, MN 55330
Lilies, daylilies, irises, daffodils.

Burpee Company
300 Park Avenue
Warminster, PA 18974
Perennials, bulbs, herbs, wildflowers and seed.

Busse Gardens
635 E. 7th St.
Route 2, Box 13
Cokato, MN 55321
Siberian irises, hostas, daylilies, other perennials.

Caprice Farm Nursery
15425 S.W. Pleasant Hill Road
Sherwood, OR 97140
Peonies, daylilies, hostas, Japanese irises.

Carman's Nursery
18201 Mozart Ave.
Los Gatos, CA 95030

Carroll Gardens
P. O. Box 310
444 East Main St.
Westminster, MD 21157

Clifford's Perennial & Vine
Route 2, Box 320
East Troy, WI 53120

Clyde Robin Seed Co. Inc.
P. O. Box 2366
Castro Valley, CA 94546
Wildflower seed, ornamental grasses.

Cooper's Garden
212 W. Co. Road C.
Roseville, MN 55113
Extensive iris list, including spuria, Louisiana, special kinds. Also daylilies, other perennials.

Country Hills Greenhouse
Route 2
Corning, OH 43730
Houseplants, including choice perennials such as variegated *Aspidistra*.

Crownsville Nursery
1241 Generals Highway
Crownsville, MD 21032

C.A. Cruickshank Ltd.
1015 Mount Pleasant Road
Toronto, Ontario
Canada, M4P 2M1
Bulb-type perennials: *Allium, Clivia, Eremurus, Fritillaria,* lilies, *Lycoris, Montbretia, Trillium.* Also Stewart propagators from England.

Daystar
R.F.D. 2
Litchfield, ME 04350
Small plants of perennials suitable for the rock garden.

DeGiorgi Co. Inc.
P. O. Box 413
Council Bluffs, IA 51502
Extensive seed list.

Dooley Gardens
Hutchinson, MN 55350
Mums selected for hardiness.

Dunford Farms
P. O. Box 238
Sumner, WA 98390
Headbourne hybrid *Agapanthus. Alstroemeria.*

Far North Gardens
16785 Harrison
Livonia, MI 48154
Barnhaven primroses, seed and plants. Also rare flower seed.

Fleming's Flower Fields
P. O. Box 4617
Lincoln, NE 68504
Address for visitors: 3100 Leighton Ave.

Forestfarm
990 Tetherow Road
Williams, OR 97544
Some uncommon perennials but mostly trees and shrubs.

The Fragrant Path
P. O. Box 328
Fort Calhoun, NE 68023
Seed only. Perennials and other fragrant plants.

Garden in the Woods
(New England Wildflower Society)
Hemenway Road
Framingham, MA 01701
Wide range of native perennials. Do not ship.

Garden Place
6780 Heisley Road
P. O. Box 388
Mentor, OH 44061

Gilson Gardens
3059 U. S. Route 20
P. O. Box 277
Perry, OH 44081
Emphasis on ground-cover plants.

Hauser's Superior View Farm
Route 1 Box 199
Bayfield, WI 54814
Inexpensive quantity rates. Not less than six of a kind supplied.

Holbrook Farm & Nursery
Route 2, Box 223B, 5025
Fletcher, NC 28732

Chas. Klehm & Son Nursery
2E Algonquin Road
Arlington Heights, IL 60005
Hostas, peonies, daylilies, irises.

Lamb Nurseries
E. 101 Sharp Ave.
Spokane, WA 99202
Many less common kinds.

Laurie's Garden
41886 McKenzie Highway
Springfield, OR 97478
Exceptionally wide range of species irises.

A. M. Leonard Inc.
6665 Spiker Road
Pique, OH 45356
Horticultural tools and supplies.

Lilypons Water Gardens
6800 Lilypons Road
P. O. Box 10
Lilypons, MD 21717
Waterlilies, water plants, some bog plants, including irises. Garden pools.

Maver Rare Plant Nursery
P.O. Box 18754
Seattle, WA 98118
Perennials suitable for the rock garden.

Milaeger's Gardens
4848 Douglas Ave.
Racine, WI 53402

Mohn's Inc.
P. O. Box 2301
Atascadera, CA 93423
"Minicap" strain of oriental-type poppies bred for extended flowering period, warm winter tolerance.

Nature's Garden
Route 1, Box 488
Beaverton, OR 97007

Walter F. Nicke
Box 667G
Hudson, NY 12534
Smaller gardening tools and accessories, including Stewart propagators from England and peony rings.

Park Seed Co. Inc.
Greenwood, SC 29647
Seed of many perennials.

Plants of the Southwest
1570 Pacheco St.
Santa Fe, NM 87501
Wildflower meadows a specialty. Many penstemons. Plants at nursery only but seed shipped.

Powell's Gardens
Route 2, Box 86 Highway 70
Princeton, NC 27569

Prairie Nursery
P. O. Box 365
Westfield, WI 53964
Prairie perennials for wet or dry soils, many of which are unobtainable elsewhere.

Rakestraw's Perennials Gardens
3094 S. Term St.
Burton, MI 48529
Smaller perennials suitable for rock gardens, dwarf conifers.

Rice Creek Gardens
1315 66th Ave. N.E.
Minneapolis, MN 55432
Rock-garden plants, woodland flowers.

Rocknoll Nursery
9210 U.S. 50
Hillsboro, OH 45133
Perennials for the rock garden.

Russell Graham
4030 Eagle Crest Road N.W.
Salem, OR 97304
Perennials, bulbs, ferns, grasses, hardy
cyclomen, native plants.

Sandy Mush Herb Nursery
Route 2 Surrett Cove HPB
Leicester, NC 28748

Shady Oaks Nursery
700 19th Ave. N.E.
Waseca, MN 56093
Plants for shady places.

Siskiyou Rare Plant Nursery
2825 Cummings Road
Medford, OR 97501
Alpine plants, Pacific Northwest natives, ferns
and perennials for woodland and rock gardens.

Smith & Hawken Fine Gardening Tools
25 Corte Madera
Mill Valley, CA 94941

Sunnyslope Gardens
8638 Huntington Drive
San Gabriel, CA 91775
Chrysanthemums, including exhibition and
cascade types.

Sweet Springs Perennial Growers
2065 Ferndale Road
Arroyo Grande, CA 93420
Some less common perennials such a *Gaura
lindheimeri* and *Francoa ramosa*.

Thon's Garden Mums
4811 Oak St.
Crystal Lake, IL 60014
"Mums" selected for hardiness.

Tranquil Lake Nursery
45 River St.
Rehoboth, MA 02769
Large selection Siberian irises. *Iris pseudacorus*
form, Japanese irises, daylilies.

Ty-Ty Plantation
Box 159
Tyty, GA 31795
Warm-zone perennials, mostly bulbous or
tuberous rooted: *Belamcanda, Canna, Crinum,
Hibiscus, Hymenocallis, Ismene, Zingiber.*

Andre Viette Farm & Nursery
Route 1, Box 16
Fisherville, VA 22939
Long-established, experienced perennials
nursery. Cultivars true to name, not grown
from seed.

Wayside Gardens
Hodges, SC 29695

We-Du Nurseries
Route 5, Box 724
Marion, NC 28752
Unusual plants, especially Southeastern natives
and Japanese plants.

Well-Sweep Herb Farm
317 Mt. Bethel Road
Port Murray, NJ 09685
Herb-type perennials.

Western Native Plants
Box 1
Midpines, CA 95355
Penstemons, Santa Ana heucheras.

White Flower Farm
Litchfield, CT 06759
Very informative catalog.

Weston Nurseries
Route 135, P.O. Box 186
Hopkinton, MA 01748
New England's largest variety of landscape-size
plants. Pickup or local deliveries only.

Gilbert H. Wild & Son Inc.
HPB-84
1112 Joplin St.
Sarcoxie, MO 64862
Peonies, irises, daylilies.

Woodlanders Inc.
1128 Colleton Ave.
Aiken, SC 29801
Plants of Southern Piedmont and coastal plain.

PLANT SOCIETIES

American Horticultural Society
Box 0105
Mount Vernon, VA 22121

American Dahlia Society Inc.
Michael L. Martinolich
159 Pine St.
New Hyde Park, NY 11040

American Fern Society
Department of Botany
University of Tennessee
Knoxville, TN 37996-1100

American Hemerocallis Society
Mr. B.F. Ater
3803 Greystone Drive
Austin, TX 78731

American Hibiscus Society
Sue J. Schloss
Executive Secretary
P. O. Drawer 5430
Pompano Beach, FL 33064

American Penstemon Society
Orville M. Steward
P. O. Box 33
Plymouth, VT 05056-0033

American Peony Society
Greta M. Kessenich
250 Interlachen Road
Hopkins, MN 55343

American Primrose Society
Brian Skidmore
6730 W. Mercer Way
Mercer Island, WA 98040

American Rock Garden Society
Norman Singer
Norfolk Road
S. Sandisfield, MA 01255

Hardy Plant Society
124 N. 181st St.
Seattle, WA 98133
Joint membership in the English parent society
and the Pacific Northwest group arranged.

National Chrysanthemum Society Inc.
B.L. Markham
2612 Beverly Blvd.
Roanoke, VA 24015

New England Wild Flower Society Inc.
Garden in the Woods
Hemenway Road
Framingham, MA 01701

North American Lily Society Inc.
Dorothy B. Schaefer
Executive Secretary
Box 476
Waukee, IA 50263

The American Hosta Society
Mrs. Joe M. Langdon
5605 11th Ave. South
Birmingham, AL 35222

The Cactus & Succulent Society of America
Miss Virginia F. Martin
2631 Fairgreen Ave.
Arcadia, CA 91006

The Delphinium Society
1630 Midwest Plaza Building
Minneapolis, MN 55402

The Herb Society of America
2 Independence Court
Concord, MA 01742

The American Iris Society
Mrs. Larry D. Stayer
Secretary
7414 E. 60th St.
Tulsa, OK 74145

The Perennial Plant Association
Secretary, Steven M. Still
Department of Horticulture
Ohio State University
2001 Fyffe Court
Columbus, OH 43210
Membership limited to nurserymen and
professional horticulturists.

The Royal Horticultural Society
Vincent Square
London SW1P 2PE
England

Index

158